Joseph Anderson

Scotland in pagan times

The iron age

Joseph Anderson

Scotland in pagan times
The iron age

ISBN/EAN: 9783743347502

Manufactured in Europe, USA, Canada, Australia, Japa

Cover: Foto ©ninafisch / pixelio.de

Manufactured and distributed by brebook publishing software (www.brebook.com)

Joseph Anderson

Scotland in pagan times

SCOTLAND IN PAGAN TIMES

Printed by R. & R. Clark

FOR

DAVID DOUGLAS, EDINBURGH

LONDON	. . .	HAMILTON, ADAMS, AND CO.
CAMBRIDGE	. .	MACMILLAN AND BOWES.
GLASGOW	. .	JAMES MACLEHOSE AND SONS.
ABERDEEN	. .	LEWIS SMITH AND SON.

SCOTLAND

IN

PAGAN TIMES

The Iron Age

THE RHIND LECTURES IN ARCHÆOLOGY
FOR 1881

By JOSEPH ANDERSON, LL.D.

KEEPER OF THE NATIONAL MUSEUM OF THE
ANTIQUARIES OF SCOTLAND

Ornament of Bronze Mirror.

EDINBURGH: DAVID DOUGLAS

1883

PREFATORY NOTE.

On the conclusion of my second series of Lectures on *Scotland in Early Christian Times*, the Council of the Society of Antiquaries of Scotland having done me the honour of again appointing me to the Rhind Lectureship for a term of two years, that I might deal with the antiquities of the Pagan Period in Scotland, I have devoted the present series of Lectures to the investigation of the remains of the Iron Age, leaving those of the Bronze and Stone Ages to be dealt with in the succeeding series.

I have to thank the Council for their permission to use such of the Society's woodcuts as might be suitable for the illustration of the Lectures, and my thanks are also due to Mr. J. Romilly Allen for the use of some of his drawings and measurements of Brochs, to Messrs. Chambers for the view of the Broch of Mousa, and to Mr. Thomas S. Muir for the use of his etching of the Broch of Clickamin, which forms the frontispiece to the present volume.

J. A.

14 GILLESPIE CRESCENT, EDINBURGH,
15th *March* 1883.

CONTENTS.

LECTURE I.

CHRISTIAN AND PAGAN BURIAL—VIKING BURIALS.

LECTURE II.

NORTHERN BURIALS AND HOARDS.

LECTURE III.

THE CELTIC ART OF THE PAGAN PERIOD.

LECTURE IV.

THE ARCHITECTURE OF THE BROCHS.

LECTURE V.

THE BROCHS AND THEIR CONTENTS.

LECTURE VI.

LAKE-DWELLINGS, HILL-FORTS, AND EARTH-HOUSES.

LIST OF ILLUSTRATIONS.

LECTURE I.

(17TH OCTOBER 1881.)

CHRISTIAN AND PAGAN BURIAL—VIKING BURIALS.

AT the outset of my first series of Lectures I stated that the necessity of abandoning the historical method of inquiry was involved in the very nature of the investigation which I contemplated, because the relations which the materials to be investigated bear to each other, and to special phases of human culture and civilisation, are neither disclosed by historical record nor discoverable by historical methods of research. I therefore proposed that, for the purposes of this inquiry, we should consider ourselves engaged in the exploration of an unknown region; and that, starting from the borderland where the historic and the non-historic meet, and ascending the stream of time, we should proceed to make such observations of the facts and phenomena encountered in our progress as would enable us to determine their relations by comparison with facts and phenomena already familiar to us, and to deduce conclusions which, so far as they are sound and relevant, would serve as materials for the construction of a logical history of culture and civilisation within the area investigated.

Having thus traversed the region characterised by the phenomena of the Early Christianity of Scotland, all that is distinctively Christian is now left behind. Before us lies the whole extent of the Pagan period, resolvable into three great

B

divisions, characterised as the Ages of Iron, of Bronze, and of Stone. In each of these we shall meet with distinctive manifestations of culture, disclosing their peculiar characteristics by their special products. These products are the materials of our investigation, and they fall to be dealt with by the same methods that have been employed in the disclosure of the nature and quality of the culture and civilisation of the Early Christian Time in Scotland.

I have adopted this division of the general subject into " Christian Times " and " Pagan Times," because the phenomena with which I am dealing do themselves exhibit a clearly defined distinction, and are separable from each other by their characteristics according as they are products of Christian or of Pagan forms of culture and civilisation.

For instance, while Paganism existed, there were two customs which gave a distinctly typical character to the archæological deposits of the heathen period. These were (1) the burning of the bodies of the dead; and (2) the deposit with the dead (whether burnt or unburnt) of grave-goods— urns, weapons, clothing, personal ornaments, and implements and utensils of domestic life. Previous to the introduction of Christianity, the burials are characterised by cremation or by the association of urns, arms, implements, and ornaments. After the introduction of Christianity these characteristics cease. The substitution of Christianity for Paganism thus produced an alteration in the character of the archæological deposits exactly comparable to that which was produced by the substitution of bronze for stone, or of iron for bronze; and the difference between the Christianity and the Paganism of a people or an area, as thus manifested, is therefore a true archæological distinction.

But no archæological boundary is of the nature of a hard and fast line. The deposits which constitute the periodic divisions of archæology (like those of the geological series)

are always to a greater or less extent products of a re-forma-
tive process, by which portions of pre-existing systems are
imbedded in the new formation, in whose constitution the
disintegrated elements of the older system are often quite
clearly visible. There is therefore necessarily a series of
transitional phenomena along the whole line of contact, and
though the new system may have been characterised by a
gradually increasing number of new types, the older types are
often continued with altered characteristics, caused by an
increasing conformity to the new conditions. It thus becomes of importance that the character of these transitional
phenomena should at least be indicated before we finally pass
from the region of Christianity into that of Paganism. Their
investigation is essentially an examination of the disintegrated
elements and altered fragments of the Pagan systems that
have entered into the composition of later Christian forma-
tions ; and no branch of this inquiry is more instructive than
that which takes cognisance of the survival of Pagan customs
in the usages connected with Christian burial.

" The first Christians," says Aringhi, " did not follow the
heathen custom of placing deposits of gold, silver, and other
precious articles in their sepulchres." But it is plain from
his further statement that they followed it partly, or, in other
words, that the older custom was continued in a modified
form ;[1] for he goes on to say that " they permitted gold, inter-

[1] The body was swathed in linen, sometimes with the insignia of office, or
with ornaments of gold, or gems placed in the coffin or sarcophagus.—Euseb.
Vit. Const. iv. 66; Ambros. *Orat. in obit. Theodos; August. Conf.* ix. 12,
cited in Smith's *Dict. of Christ. Antiq.*, *sub voce* " Burial of the Dead." The
insignia of office, if the deceased had held any such position—gold and silver
ornaments in the case of private persons—were often flung into the open
grave, and the waste and ostentation to which this led had to be checked by
an imperial edict.—*Cod. Theodos.* xi. tit. 7, 1, 14. *Ibid.* So common was
the burial of weapons and ornaments in Early Christian times among the
Franks, that enactments against the violation of graves in search of treasure
form a special feature in the Salic Laws. Gregory of Tours tells of the

woven with the cloth used in the preparation of the body for burial, and such things as gold rings on the fingers; with young girls, too, they often buried their ornaments and such things as they most delighted in."

Although the Pagan form of burial in which the dead were placed in their tombs, apparelled in their richest robes, and with their arms, ornaments, and insignia, is clearly opposed to the doctrine taught in all ages of the church, that the dead are for ever done with the things of this life,[1] we find it strangely surviving as a Christian ceremonial in the burial of kings and clergy. Childeric, the last of the Pagan kings of France, was buried seated on a throne, in his kingly robes, and with the arms, ornaments, and insignia of royalty. Charlemagne, the establisher of Christianity (who meted out the punishment of death to the Saxons who dared to burn their dead after the old manner),[2] was also buried seated on a throne, with his royal robes, his arms and ornaments, and the

robbery of the grave of the wife of Gonthram, who was buried in the Church of Metz, "cum auro multo rebusque preciosis;" and Montfaucon adds that from this we see that it was not the kings only, but the great of the land also, who were at that time buried with things of price.

[1] There are records of occasional cases in which the converts rebelled and went back to their old customs in spite of the efforts of the clergy to restrain them. Thus we find in A.D. 1249, that in Livonia, where heathenism lingered longer than in almost any other part of Europe, there is a solemn deed of contract entered into between the converts and the brethren of the Holy Cross, by which the converts become bound, for themselves and their heirs, never again to burn their dead or to bury with them horses or slaves, or arms or vestments, or any other things of value, but to bury their dead in the cemeteries attached to the churches. — Dreger, *Codex Diplomaticus Pomeraniæ*. Again we find that the Esthonian converts rebelled in 1225, took back the wives they had given up, exhumed the dead they had buried in the Christian cemeteries, and burned them, after the fashion of the old Pagan times.—Gruber, *Origines Livoniæ*, cited by Wyllie in *Archæologia*, vol. xxxvii. p. 46.

[2] Si quis corpus defuncti hominis secundum ritum paganorum flamma consumi fecerit, et ossa ejus ad cinerem redigerit, capite punietur.—*Capitulary*, A.D. 785.

book of the Gospels on his knee. The Scandinavian Viking was buried with his arms because his Valhalla was a fighting place; but the Christian kings of Denmark continued to be buried with their arms although there was no Valhalla prepared for them.[1] Giraldus Cambrensis, describing the miserable death of Henry II. of England, laments that when the body was being prepared for burial " scarcely was a decent ring to be found for his finger or a sceptre for his hand, or a crown for his head, except such a thing as was made from an old head-dress." When the custom was disused for kings, it was retained for the clergy.[2] Archbishops and bishops have always been buried with their insignia and robes of office.[3] Their graves, containing the crosier or staff, the chalice and paten, the robes and ring, although necessarily of Christian time and Christian character, are directly related in the line of archæological succession to those of the earlier Paganism. The custom also survives in the pompous acces-

[1] When the grave of King Olaf at Sore was opened, a long sword was found over the body from the head to the feet. In the coffin of King Erik Glipping, in the Church of Viborg, his sword lay at his side. Kornerup, *Aarboger for Nordisk Oldkyndighed*, 1873, p. 251.

[2] In the *Capitularia Regum Francorum* we are told that the custom which had grown obsolete among the common people was retained for the clergy :—Mos ille in vulgo obsoletus in funeribus episcoporum et presbyterum retinetur.

[3] Durandus says, "Clerici vero, si sint ordinati, illis indumentis induti sint, quae requirunt ordines, quos habent; si vero non habent ordines sacros more laicorum sepeliantur. Verumtamen licet in aliis ordinibus propter paupertatem hoc saepius omittatur, in sacerdotibus tamen et Episcopis nullo modo praetermittendum est."—*De Div. Off.* lib. 7. Kornerup, describing the practice in Denmark, says of the burials of the higher orders of the clergy in the Middle Ages—"On their heads they bore the mitre, on their shoulders the cloak of gold brocade, on the finger the Episcopal ring, and the crosier lay by the side of the corpse. Their feet were shod, and the chalice and paten were placed in their hands." These particulars have been verified in many instances, among which it is only necessary to mention the graves of Bishop Absalon at Sore, and Bishop Suneson at Lund.—Kornerup, *Aarboger for Nordisk Oldkyndighed*, 1873, p. 251.

sories of a military funeral. When we see the sword laid
over the coffin, and the horse led in procession to the grave,
we witness the survival of one of the oldest ceremonies ever
performed among men—the difference being, that of old the
weapon was laid in the grave beside the hand that had wielded
it, and the horse was slaughtered to accompany his master to
the unseen world.[1] Some forms of this survival gradually
passed into distinctively Christian usages[2] with a definitely
Christian significance, and others became actually incorpor-
ated in the ritual of the Church. One of the most striking of
the sepulchral customs of the Pagan Northmen was that of
binding the "hell-shoes" on the feet of the dead. It is
stated in the Saga of Gisli the Outlaw that when they were
laying Vestein in his grave-mound, Thorgrim the priest went
up to the mound and said, " 'Tis the custom to bind the hell-
shoes on men so that they may walk on them to Valhalla,
and I will now do that by Vestein;" and when he had done
it he said, "I know nothing about binding on hell-shoon, if

---

[1] In a tumulus opened near Picton Castle, there were found, along with
the skeleton of a man, a sword, a breastplate, four horse-shoes, and a gold
ring, on the bezel of which were engraved the arms of Sir Aaron ap Rhys,
a knight of the Holy Sepulchre. The latest instance of this custom carried
out in its integrity occurred at the interment of Frederick Casimir, a knight
of the Teutonic Order, who was buried with his horse and his arms at Treves
in February 1781.

[2] A variety of the custom of burial clothed took the form of burial in a
monkish habit. It was not uncommon in the twelfth century for laymen to
be thus buried, under the notion that the sanctity of the dress preserved the
body from molestation by demons. Thus Erik Ploupenning sets forth in a
deed dated 1241, "Votum fecimus ut in habitu fratrum minorum mori
deberemus et in ipso habitu apud fratres minores Roeskildenses sepiliri."—
Pontoppidan, *Annales Eccl. Dan.* 1669. The idea of sanctity connected with
the monastic orders led people to seek for burial, not only in the consecrated
ground about the monastery, but in the habit of the monks. The right was
in early times purchased by the great men of Brittany by the gift of lands
and other offerings, as we have seen to be the case in Ireland.—Stuart's
Sculptured Stones of Scotland, vol. ii. p. 63.

these loosen." This custom is often found in Christian as well as in pre-Christian graves in Central Europe. It was well known to the liturgical writers of the Middle Ages. Durandus says : " The dead must also have shoes on their feet by which they may show that they are ready for the judgment." Members of religious orders were usually thus buried, but the custom was not confined to them alone.[1] The idea of providing for a journey which was implied in the Northern custom of the " hell-shoon," is curiously illustrated by the statement of Weinhold, that in some remote districts of Sweden, up to a very recent period, the tobacco-pipe, the pocket-knife, and the filled brandy-flask, were placed with the dead in the grave.

Broadly stated, the archæological effect of the establishment of Christianity was to cut off the presence of grave-goods from the burials of the area. But these examples show that while this was the general and final result, it was neither obtained absolutely nor at once. The burial usages of a people are among the most unalterable of all their institutions. Other observances may change with the convictions of individuals, but the prevailing sentiment which leads to the disposal of the dead—" gathered to their fathers "—in the same manner as the fathers themselves were disposed, resists innovation longer and more stubbornly than any other. In

---

[1] Bernard, grandson of Charlemagne, who died in 818, was found with shoes on his feet when his coffin was opened in 1638. William Lyndewode, Bishop of St. David's, who died in 1446, was buried in St. Stephen's. When his grave was recently disturbed during repairs, the body was found unclothed, but with shoes on the feet.—*Archæologia*, vol. xxxiv. p. 403. In the cathedral of Worcester a skeleton was found in 1861 having shoes or sandals on its feet, the soles of which were quite entire.—*Gent. Mag.*, Oct. 1861. The Abbé Cochet mentions a large number of instances in France, proving the existence of the custom there from the twelfth century to the seventeenth. In an account of the funeral expenses of Roger Belot, who died in 1603, there is a charge of twelve sous six deniers for a pair of shoes to place on the feet of the defunct.—*Revue Archæol.*, vol. xxv. (1873) p. 12.

point of fact we find that from the beginning there have been but two great typical forms of burial—viz. burial with grave-goods, which is the universally Pagan type, and burial without them, which is the universally Christian type.

These typical forms of burial are respectively products of the opposing doctrines of Paganism and Christianity as touching the future life. I cannot tell what may have been the precise attitude of mind which induced my Pagan an-cestor to provide his dead with grave-goods. In view of the general prevalence of the custom, I cannot doubt that it was an attitude which regarded their provision as a sacred duty, universally binding and almost universally performed. But the Christian belief in a resurrection to newness of life recognised no such duty to the dead, and steadily opposed the practice as amounting to a denial of the faith. On this account it is plain that when we find the dead in Christian graves provided with grave-goods we have a form of burial which cannot be accounted for by anything in the essential elements of Christianity itself, and therefore it must be re-garded as a survival of the older custom, which logically ought to have died with the death of the Pagan system,—of which it was a distinctive usage.

The Christian fathers appear to have drawn the line of demarcation between Pagan and Christian burial so as to prevent the continuance of cremation. Yet the practice of strewing charcoal and ashes ritually in the open grave, and laying the unburnt body upon them, was a wide-spread Christian custom of the early Middle Ages.[1] I cannot con-

---

[1] The Christian liturgists account for this custom on other grounds than as a simulation of the effect of cremation, or a survival by symbol; but we should not expect them to recognise it as a survival of the Pagan custom. Durandus says :—" Carbones ponantur in testimonium quod terra illa in com-munes usus, ampling redigi non potest; plus enim durat Carbo sub terra quam aliud." Is not the "ashes to ashes" of the burial service a lingering echo of this ritual ?

ceive the process by which a custom like this could have
been evolved from any of the distinctive usages of Christianity,
if the custom of cremation had not preceded it. Again the
practice of placing vessels of clay in the cist with the unburnt body, which was one of the most widely diffused and
most distinctively Pagan customs connected with the interment of the dead, was continued with certain modifications
of form and significance as a Christian usage.[1] In Pagan
times these vessels contained food and drink; in Christian
times they held holy water and charcoal and incense. The
holy water vessel was shallow and basin-like, and was placed
usually at the feet of the corpse. Johannes Belethus, in the
twelfth century, notices this custom, and after him Durandus,
Bishop of Mende,[2] who says that the holy water is used "that
the demons who are greatly afraid of it may not come near
the body;" and that incense is used "to indicate that the

[1] Vases of glass and of clay were buried with the early Christians in the
catacombs. The glass vessels were drinking cups, the clay vessels are in all
probability such as were in domestic use. Garrucci gives a list of 340 of these
glass vessels, many of which have the Christian monogram, or scenes from
Scripture, depicted on them. There are others, however, ornamented with
scenes from domestic and civil life, and even with subjects from the Pagan
mythology.

[2] Mabillon also notices this custom:—"L'on trouvent assez souvent dans
l'anciens tombeaux des Chretiens des petits vases de terre pleins de charbons."
—*Dissertation sur le culte des Saints inconnus*, p. 25. "Aquam benedictam
et prunas cum thure apponerent." — Beleth, *De Divinis Officiis*, c. 161.
"Deinde ponitur in spelunca in qua ponitur aqua benedicta et prunae cum
thure. Aqua benedicta ne demones qui multum cam timent ad corpus
accedant; solent namque desaevire in corpora mortuorum, ut quod nequiverunt
in vita, saltem post mortem egant. Thus propter factorem corporis removen-
dum, seu ut defunctus creatori suo acceptabilem bonorum operum odorem in-
telligatur obtulisse, seu ad ostendendum quod defunctis prosit auxilium
orationis."—Durandus, *De Off. Mortuorum, In Rationale Div. Off.* lib. vii. c.
35. "Vascula cum aqua lustrali in sepulchris apponebantur."—Aringhi,
Roma Subterranea, vol. i. p. 94. "Statutum etiam fuit ut in sepulchris crux,
et aqua lustralis seu benedicta apponeretur."—Durantes, *Ex Antiq. Ritual.
Sacr. Libris.* apud Aringhi, *loc. cit.*

dead person has entered his Creator's presence with the
acceptable odour of good works, and has obtained the benefit
of the Church's prayers." That the latter usage was widely
extended throughout Christendom is proved by the frequent discoveries of vases pierced with holes, and containing the remains of charcoal, which have occurred in Italy,
Switzerland, France, and Denmark.[1] It was not unknown
in Scotland, as the following examples will show. On the
demolition of the old town steeple of Montrose in 1833, in

[1] The following are a few of the localities in which these vases have
occurred most abundantly :—Braquemont, Martin Eglise, Bouteilles, where
over 100 vases occurred, Roux Mesnil, Neuchatel, etc. It may be interesting
to indicate the range in time of the custom, by a few instances, with well-
defined dates. In the coffin of Urson, Abbot of Jumieges, who died in 1127,
two pierced vases were found. At Leure, near Havre, among many interments
with similar vases, there was one with an inscribed slab identifying it as that
of Pierre Berenguier (1270-1290). In the stone coffin there were six of these
pierced vases. The stone coffin of Simon de Goucans, Bishop of Amiens, who
died in 1325, contained three vases, two being placed at the shoulders and one
at the feet, all pierced with holes and partly filled with charcoal. In the
coffin of John Count Dunois, who died in 1468, seven vases occurred. In
that of Francis Longueville, who died in 1491, twelve pierced vases with
charcoal were ranged along the sides of the coffin. On the right side of the
wooden coffin of the Abbé François d'Orignai, who died in 1483, two pierced
vases were found. In the leaden coffin of Agnes of Savoy, Duchess of Dunois,
who died in 1508, there were four vases of common red unglazed ware containing charcoal. The latest precise date is furnished by an interment in the
graveyard of the Benedictine monastery at Mans. The coffin, on which the
inscription was still legible, CHARLOTTE LE NORMANT DE BEAUMONT, DECEDE
LE 12 AVRIL 1688, contained a vase with charcoal. This curious and little
known custom is fully illustrated in the Abbé Cochet's works, *La Normandie
Souterraine*, 2d edition, Paris 1855, and its sequel *Sepultures Gauloises,
Romaines, Franques et Normandes*, Paris 1857. See also *Bulletin Monumental*, vol. xxii. pp. 329-364, 425-447 ; vol. xxv. pp. 103-132, 273-311 ;
Mémoires de la Société des Antiquaires de Normandie, vol. xxii. pp. 11, 12,
294-298, vol. xxiv. p. 5-8 ; *Archæologia*, vol. xxxv. p. 233, vol. xxxvii. p.
399, vol. xxxviii. p. 66, vol. xxxix. p. 117 ; *Proceedings of the Society of Antiquaries of London*, 1855, pp. 206, 290 ; *Revue de l'art Chretien*, vol. ii. (1858),
p. 420 ; De Caumont, *Cours d'Antiquites Monumentales*, vol. vi. p. 316 ; A.
Murcier, *La Sepulture Chretienne en France*, p. 159-164.

removing the soil under the base of the structure, a rude stone cist was discovered at a depth of three feet. The cist contained a skeleton disposed at full length, and beside the skeleton were four vessels of clay placed two at the head and two at the feet. One of these vessels (Fig. 1) is still preserved in the Montrose museum. It is of reddish clay, 4 inches in height, 5 inches in diameter at the widest part, and 3 inches across the mouth. Its form is shown in the accompanying woodcut, from which it is also observable that it is pierced with holes which exhibit irregular outlines. There are five of these holes in the

Fig. 1.—Clay Vase, one of four found in a mediæval stone coffin at Montrose.

circumference of the widest part of the vase, and it is evident from their appearance that they have been pierced by driving a sharp-pointed instrument through it, not when the clay was soft but after it was fired.[1] All the characteristics of the interment—the stone-lined grave, the full-length burial, the vases placed two at the head and two at the feet[2]—are those of the commonest form of Christian burial with incense vases, as manifested in continental examples later than twelfth century.

The form of the vase figured is not that of any known variety of urn found with interments of Pagan type. But it closely corresponds with the form of the incense vases represented in an illumination from a manuscript of the

---

[1] This is a frequently-occurring characteristic of the vessels partially filled with charcoal found in graves of the Carlovingian period and down to the seventeenth century in France. They are usually pierced with holes irregularly placed. In some cases the holes have been made when the clay was soft. In others the vessels have been pierced by holes driven through their sides after they were fired, as if by a nail or other pointed instrument.

[2] At Bernay, where 150 of these incense vases were found, the most common arrangement was four in one coffin, two at the head and two at the feet.

fourteenth century (Fig. 2), as placed alternately with candles on the floor round the coffin during the funeral service, and

which, as we learn from contemporary documents, were afterwards placed in the grave.[1] In the illumination the red colour of the fire within the vases appears through the holes pierced in their sides. (This cannot be shown in the woodcut here given, but the escaping smoke indicates the position of the apertures). There is

Fig. 2.—Illumination from a fourteenth century MS., representing incense vases, placed, alternately with candles, round the coffin during the funeral service.

in the National Museum another pierced vase, in which the holes have been made when the clay was soft. It was found in 1829, with two others, under a flat stone at the Castle Hill of Rattray in Aberdeenshire. It is here figured (Fig. 3) along with one of the two others found with it, of which the Society possesses a drawing (Fig. 4). From a note attached to the drawing

[1] Two instances are cited by the Abbé Cochet. Claud d'Escarbotte left orders in his will that the young lads, orphans, who were to follow him to the grave should carry each a torch and a pot with incense. Jehan Thelinige described the custom more particularly, for he prescribes in his will that the small pots with the fire and the incense shall be thrown into the grave. In the district of Morvan, says M. Jules Chevrier, the peasants even in our own days continue the custom of using funeral vases. They throw upon the coffin, when it is lowered into the grave, a porringer or some such dish of earthenware which had been ordinarily used by the defunct ; and in certain parts of La Bresse they still throw into the grave the holy water vessel which had stood at the feet of the defunct previous to the ceremony of inhumation.

we learn that the three vessels were filled with ashes when they were first discovered. No other record of the phenomena of this interesting deposit exists; but, from the character of the

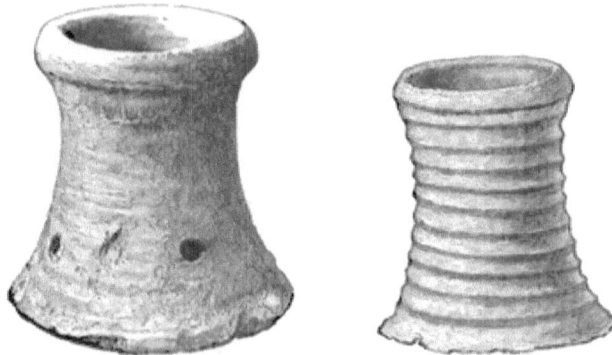

Figs. 3, 4.—Clay Vases found at Castle Hill of Rattray, Aberdeenshire (5 inches high).

vessels themselves, which is totally distinct from that of all known types of vessels deposited with Pagan interments in this country, they may be assigned to the class of vessels deposited in Christian graves of twelfth to fifteenth and sixteenth centuries with charcoal and incense.

In the special features of such survivals as these we read the story of the transition from the older to the newer forms of burial resulting from the change of faith. We see the custom of burial with grave-goods retained as a ceremonial observance in Christian sepulture, and the practice of cremation succeeded by the symbolic act of strewing charcoal in the open grave, and by a ritual which still regards the act of burial as a consigning of "ashes to ashes;" and by these and similar links of connection we pass gradually from the Christian system to the system of Paganism that preceded it.

But when we advance beyond the Christian boundary in Scotland we enter on a region singularly destitute of materials by which the burial customs of the people may be correlated with those which offer indications of their culture and civilisation. The general phenomena of the burials of the Celtic Paganism of the Iron Age in Scotland are not disclosed by any recorded observations known to me. If they exist, they exist either as phenomena of unrecognised character or as phenomena which are still unobserved. I therefore proceed to the examination of a group of phenomena disclosing the existence within the Celtic area of a system of Paganism which was not of Celtic origin; and I turn to these phenomena as the only materials available for the demonstration of the character of Pagan burial—premising that they belong to a time when, owing to the intrusion of a foreign element, the Christian form and the Pagan form were closely contiguous and contemporary in Scotland.

In the autumn of 1878 the late Mr. William Campbell of Ballinaby, on the west coast of the island of Islay, passing through the sandy links there, had his attention arrested by the unusual appearance of a patch of iron-rust in a hollow from which the sand had drifted. Examining the spot more closely, he found that there was a deposit of iron implements in the sand. Digging out the deposit, he discovered that it had been disposed in two contiguous graves, each containing a skeleton laid at full length, with the head to the east and the feet to the west, the boundary of each grave being marked by an enclosure formed of stones set on edge in the sand.

In grave No. 1 he found the following objects deposited with the skeleton :—

An iron sword in its sheath (Fig. 5).

The iron boss of a shield, with its handle of bronze or brass still attached. (The boss and handle are shown in Fig. 6, and the handle separately in Fig. 7.)

An iron spear-head with wide blade and long socket (Fig. 8).

An iron object, having a wide socket at one end of a long shank (Fig. 9).

A conical iron object with the remains of wood adhering to the interior surface (Fig. 10).

A number of fragments of corrugated iron (Fig. 11).

A hollow cylindrical object of bronze with a globular end, probably the mounting of the end of a small sheath (Fig. 13).

An iron axe-head, not differing greatly from the modern form, the eye broken (Fig. 14).

An iron axe-head of similar form, but longer in the shank, the eye entire (also shown in Fig. 14).

The iron head of a small adze, nearly entire (Fig. 15).

The iron head of a hammer, entire (Fig. 16).

A pair of forge-tongs, partially broken (Fig. 17).

The broken fragments of a large iron pot, and its bow-handle, broken (Fig. 18).

In grave No. 2 he found the following objects deposited with the skeleton :—

A pair of oval bowl-shaped brooches of bronze, ornamented with pierced and chased work and with plaited bands of silver wire and studs, of which the pins only remain (Fig. 20).

The brass spring-pins of the two brooches (Fig. 19).

Portions of three pairs of discs of thin bronze, plated with silver, each pair connected by a narrow band, the discs ornamented with bosses arranged in circles, and the bands with borders all in *repoussé* work (Fig. 21).

A silver hair-pin with a globular head, ornamented with filigree work, and furnished with a ring of wire fastened by a peculiar twisting of one end round the other (Fig. 22).

A silver chain-like ornament, formed of fine silver wire knitted as a hollow tube, knotted at the two ends, and furnished at one end with a ring fastened by a peculiar twisting of the ends round each other (Fig. 23).

Seven beads of coloured glass, enamelled on the surface with patterns in different colours (Fig. 24).

A saucepan of thin bronze, with a long flat handle (Fig. 25).

A hemispherical lump of black glass, in shape nearly resembling the bottom of a bottle, and having its convex side rubbed and striated by use (Fig. 26).

A small object like a needle-case, of silver, broken, and containing what seems to be a portion of a broken needle of bronze.

It is apparent, from the nature of the groups of objects severally associated with the two burials, that No. 1 was the

grave of a man, and No. 2 was the grave of a woman. The
man was buried with his arms and implements, the woman
with her personal ornaments and housewife's gear. It is equally
apparent, from an examination of the whole phenomena of the
burials, that there is an obvious absence of all indications of
Christianity. They are not destitute of characteristics possessing a special significance, but they are destitute of characteristics possessing such significance as could be attributed
to the faith and hope of the Christian creed, or explained by
reference to any recognised customs of Christian burial.
They suggest, for instance, a condition of life considerably
removed from absolute poverty; they present indications of
culture and taste, of skill and industry, of manly vigour and
womanly grace. But the position of the graves, with the
head to the east and the feet to the west, is the opposite of
that referred to by the liturgical writers of early Christian
times as the proper position of the Christian dead, who
should be placed with their feet to the east, so that in rising
they may face their Lord as He comes from the east. And
there is no feature which can be more surely relied on as an
indication of early Christian burial than this orientation of
the grave which is here so plainly disregarded.

If the absence of all indications of Christianity be thus
obvious, there is no less obviously a complete absence of all
the characteristics of art and art-workmanship with which
we have become familiar in the progress of our investigation.
There is no Celticism apparent in the art of the decorated
objects placed in these graves. The characteristics which we
have found to be constantly present in the decorative metal-
work of the Celtic school of art are notably absent, and
those that are present are mostly new and strange to us. If
the phenomena of the burials are clearly not Christian, the
characteristics of the art are as clearly not Celtic.

To find such weapons of bronze or stone as are commonly

styled prehistoric deposited with the dead excites no feeling
of surprise, because we know, in a general way, that this was
the common custom of prehistoric Paganism. But when we
find in a grave, along with the ordinary weapons of war, a
collection of implements like this—a group of actual tools of
iron—scarcely differing in shape, and not differing in material
from those now in use in our workshops, we instantly realise
the presence of a phenomenon at once unusual and suggestive.
It is unusual in this country because our forefathers received
Christianity early, and Christianity abolished the custom of
placing implements in graves. It is suggestive
because it enables us to perceive how closely
the characteristic customs of the man we call
primeval may be linked with the arts and
culture of modern times. It is therefore a
phenomenon which it is desirable to investigate
as fully as possible.

For this purpose it will be necessary to
examine in detail the principal objects found
in the graves, with the view of determining
their typical characteristics and relations.

First, I take the sword (Fig. 5) as the most
important, and therefore the most likely to
disclose its typical relationship by comparison
with others. It is a long, broad-bladed, double-
edged weapon, tapering slightly and evenly from
hilt to point. Its whole length is 36½ inches.
The blade is 2¾ inches wide at the junction
with the guard of the hilt, 2½ inches in the
middle of its length, and 1½ where it begins to
be rounded off at the point. The grip of the
hilt, which is covered with leather, is 3¾ inches
in length. The guard, which forms a straight collar to the
blade, flattened on the upper and under surfaces, and convex

Fig. 5.—Sword found in the grave at Ballinaby, Islay (36½ inches in length).

on both sides, is 4½ inches in length. The pommel, which is triangular in outline and convex from the apex to the base, is 2½ inches high, 4 inches from side to side, and 1½ inches thick. Portions of the wooden lining of the scabbard still adhere to the blade.[1]

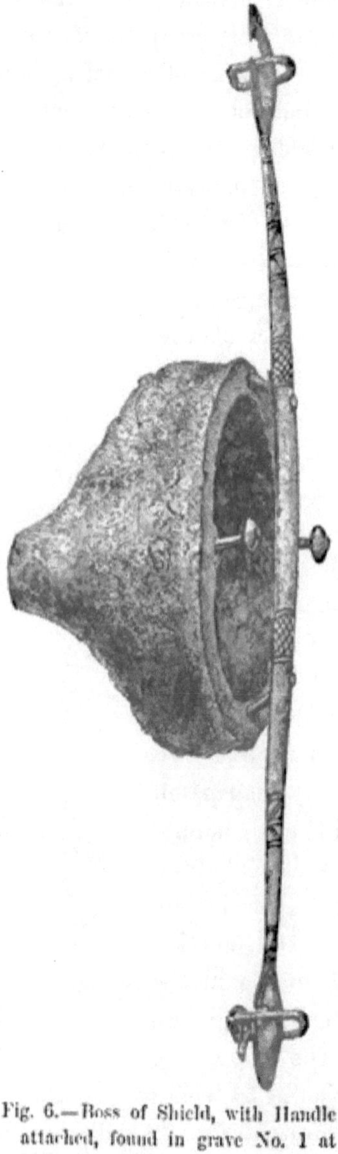

The shield boss (Fig. 6) is a round piece of hammered iron, like a hollow truncated cone, the outlines being those of an ogee curve instead of rectilinear. It measures 3¼ inches diameter and 3½ inches high, the flattened top being half an inch across. The base of the cone impinged upon the wood of the shield, to which it was securely fastened by two rivets passing through the flange of the boss and through the wood. Other two rivets, placed in the circumference of the flange midway between these two, also passed through the wood of the shield and were riveted into the handle. The handle is of brass or bronze, 7¼ inches in length, convex on the exterior

Fig. 6.—Boss of Shield, with Handle attached, found in grave No. 1 at Ballinaby, Islay.

[1] Pennant figures an iron sword of this type in the second volume of his *Tour in Scotland*, plate xliv., but dismisses it with the remark that it is "part of an iron sword found in Islay."

surface, and concave internally in the direction of its breadth, and slightly convex also in outline in the direction of its

Fig. 7.—Handle of Shield, front view (7¼ inches in length).

length. It is ornamented (as shown in Fig. 7) by bands of engraved lines forming reticulated patterns, and terminates at both ends in slightly raised circular discs, furnished with loops in front and back. The front loops apparently passed through the wood of the shield, those on the backs of the discs must have stood free on the inside of the shield, and were probably used for its suspension by a strap slung across the shoulder. Portions of the wood of the shield still adhere to the edges of the boss. This specimen shows what has never before been seen in this country, viz. the method of attachment of the boss and handle through the wood of the shield.

The spear-head (Fig. 8)

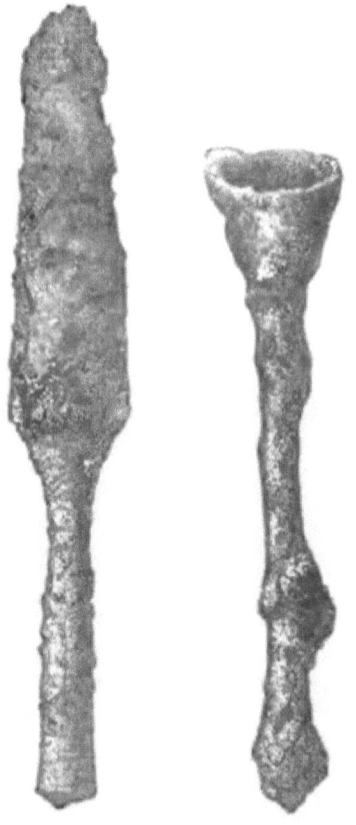

Fig. 8.—Spear-head found in grave No. 1, at Ballinaby, Islay (7 inches in length).

Fig. 9.—Ferrule found in grave No. 1 (6 inches in length).

is a long and stout-bladed weapon, straight-edged, and tapering equally from the butt of the blade, which is unbarbed,
the short neck of the blade passing gradually into the rounded
socket. The blade is now only 7 inches in length, but was
probably about 10 inches long and 2 inches wide at the butt.
The socket still contains a portion of the wood of the shaft.

With these weapons there are other relics to which it is
less easy to assign a definite purpose, such as the iron object
(Fig. 9), 6 inches in length, which may have been the ferrule
of a shaft, if not the heel of the spear-shaft itself, which was
often mounted with an iron prong for convenience of thrust-
ing it into the ground.

Akin to this object is the broken portion of a conical
ferrule (shown in Fig. 10), and there are a number of frag-

 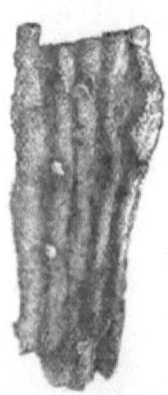 

Fig. 10.—Iron Ferrule   Fig. 11.—Fragment of   Fig. 12.—Bronze Plaque,
found in grave No. 1   Iron from grave No.   from Oland (actual size).
at Ballinaby.   1 at Ballinaby.

ments of an iron object with a corrugated surface, as if
formed of thick wires laid side by side (Fig. 11). None of the
fragments suggest the probable size or form of the object
when entire, or reveal its purpose. But in the figure of a
warrior represented on a small bronze plaque (Fig. 12), dug
up in the island of Oland, we see a helmet formed of bands of

somewhat similar appearance, and the sword he bears in his hand is a sword of the peculiar type associated with these peculiar relics.

A small and elegantly-formed and ornamented object of bronze (Fig. 13), with a cylindrical socket, terminating in a globose and lobated expansion, with a rope-like moulding round the upper part of the terminal expansion, appears to have been the mounting of the end of a small sheath. A similar object, nearly of the same size, having its globose termination ornamented with a grotesque face was found in a grave in the island of Westray, in Orkney, and will be hereafter referred to. (See Fig. 50.)

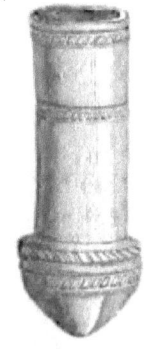

Fig. 13.—Sheath Mounting of Bronze from grave No. 1 at Ballinaby (actual size).

The implements associated with these weapons and accoutrements in the man's grave are equally worthy of special examination, because, when regarded as a representative group, it

Fig. 14.—Axe-heads of Iron (⅓), from grave No. 1 at Ballinaby.

will be seen that they point with equal definiteness to the

same conclusion as to the typical character and relations of
the special form of burial with which we are dealing.

The iron axe-heads (Fig. 14) found in the grave were two
in number, nearly alike in form and dimensions, though
somewhat mutilated. They do not differ greatly from the
modern form of the implement, and are good serviceable
tools.

The small adze-head (Fig. 15) and the hammer-head (Fig. 16)

Figs. 15 and 16.—Adze and Hammer (½), from grave No. 1 at Ballinaby.

of iron are also good serviceable tools, not differing greatly
from forms that are still in use, but possessing, in common
with the axes, sufficient individuality of form and character
to establish their typical relationship as members of a special
group.

The forge-tongs (Fig. 17), in the same manner, present
features of individuality which are capable of being correlated
with a special variety of this type of tool confined to a special
area, and usually occurring in certain special associations
of a similar character to those in which this example occurs.

The broken fragments of the large iron pot present no features of character that can be recognised as distinctive.

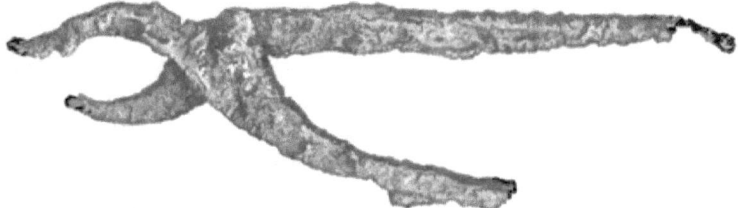

Fig. 17.—Forge-Tongs (⅓), from grave No. 1 at Ballinaby.

They are simple fragments of a large culinary pot, the diameter of which is indicated by the span of the iron bow-handle (Fig. 18), of which about half remains entire. But

Fig. 18.—Bow-Handle of Iron Pot, one end broken (⅓), from grave No. 1 at Ballinaby.

though the pot itself is not a specially remarkable object, the occurrence of an iron culinary pot in such associations is a fact of sufficiently remarkable character to be of importance in the determination of the special relations of a burial distinguished by such a group of unusual phenomena.

Let us now examine in detail the special characteristics of the ornaments and other articles found in the grave of the woman.

The most peculiar and striking objects among these ornaments are the two brooches. They are determined to be brooches by the fact that they are each furnished with a pin on the under side. These pins, which are of brass, are of very peculiar construction.[1] The head of the pin (Fig. 19) is bent

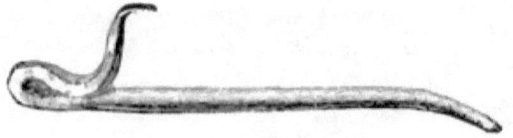

Fig. 19.—Brass Spring-Pin of Brooch, from grave No. 2 at Ballinaby.

back to form a loop, by which the pin is secured in a socket formed by two projections from the inner surface of the brooch, in which a small rod is riveted passing through the loop of the pin. On this rod, the pin plays as on a hinge. The free end of the loop of the pin, doubled back and recurved, impinges on the inner and concave surface of the brooch, and acts as a spring when the point of the pin is pressed back to be slipped under a projecting catch on the opposite end of the brooch. When in its place it lies under the concavity in a line with the longest diameter of the brooch, which is oval and bowl-shaped, convex externally and

Fig. 20.—Oval Bowl-shaped Brooch found in grave No. 2 at Ballinaby, Islay.

concave internally. The body of the brooch (Fig. 20), which is 4¾ inches in length, 3 inches in width, and 1½ inch in height,

---

[1] The pins of all the other specimens of this type of brooch that are preserved in the Museum have been of iron, and have consequently disappeared by oxidation. Without the Ballinaby brooches we should not have known the construction of the pin.

is double,[1] consisting of an outer and highly ornamented shell of pierced open work, placed over an inner shell which is smooth and highly gilt on the upper surface, so that the gilding may appear through the open work above it. This open work consists of a series of patterns which are similar as to the general effect, though they vary in their details. They are arranged in equal segmental divisions of the convexity of the brooch, and separated by continuous bands of unpierced metal. These bands are traversed longitudinally by furrows, in which plaited strands of fine silver wire are laid and carried through perforations at the junctions where they cross each other. At these junctions are circular spaces, each of which has borne a knob or stud, probably of coloured paste or enamelled glass. These are all gone, but the pins that fastened them remain. The patterns themselves are zoomorphic in character, but their zoomorphism is radically different from that of the Celtic school. It is zoomorphism in which the details are sacrificed to the general effect, as if in the mind of the artist the idea of the ornament was dominant, and the idea of the form of its parts subordinate. No two styles of ornament could be more widely dissimilar. The artist of the Celtic school produced his effects by simple variation of the arrangements of his stereotyped forms. In all the intricate interlacements of his zoomorphic patterns, the typical forms employed to produce the most bewilderingly beautiful combinations are substantially the same, and their parts are the same. His zoomorphism was consistent throughout. If the conventional beast was there at all, his tail was there, and his crest, and his limbs—he was there in unvarying completeness of form and conventionality of feature. But this zoomorphism renders nothing distinctly. There is a suggestion of heads here and wings there, but

[1] See the figure of the Tiree brooch, which is engraved with the upper shell removed from its place, and each shown separately (Fig. 31).

there may be no bodies and no limbs, or there may be a suggestion of limbs to which no bodies effeir. The Celtic artist built up his patterns with the forms of his conventional beasts laboriously expressed. This artist simply blocks out his pattern and covers it with suggestions of animal forms.

But if the art of these brooches is not Celtic, the form differs no less widely from that of the Celtic brooches, which is penannular, with flattened and expanded ends. No brooch of this oval bowl-shaped form occurs within the Celtic area, either ornamented with Celtic art, or associated with objects of exclusively Celtic origin.

Equally characteristic, and as widely different from anything that we have seen of Celtic forms or Celtic art, are the forms and the art of the double discs of plated metal (Fig. 21), of which three were found in the same grave with the brooches. They are so thin and so sorely wasted that they could only have been recovered from a sandy soil, and even then, if they had been subjected to less careful handling, we should have been unable to establish their original form. They are all imperfect, the most entire being $7\frac{1}{2}$ inches in length, consisting of a pair of buckler-like discs, ornamented with bosses and concentric circles, and connected by a band ornamented with zigzags and pellets, all in *repoussé* work. It is difficult even to conjecture what may have been their use. They are of silvered bronze, and if they had occurred in the man's grave, they might have been supposed to have been ornamental mountings of the shield. But Mr. Campbell's testimony as to their occurrence in the grave of the woman is distinct, and it is equally clear from their form and character, that they are objects of ornament, but neither the form nor the character of the objects gives any clue to the manner in which they were worn.

The silver hair-pin (Fig. 22), with globular head and ring attached by a loop, is 5 inches in length. The globular head is

Fig. 21.—Double Disc of thin Bronze, from grave
No. 2 at Ballinaby (7½ inches in length).

Fig. 22.—Silver Hair-Pin,
from grave No. 2 at
Ballinaby (actual size).

ornamented with double reversing spiral scrolls of filigree
work of notched wire, finely executed. The ring of wire
which hangs in the loop on the summit of the globular head
of the pin, is also notched, and the ends twisted round each
other in a fashion which is characteristic of many similarly
joined rings of this type; as, for instance, the ring attached to
the end of the chain of knitted wire to be next described.

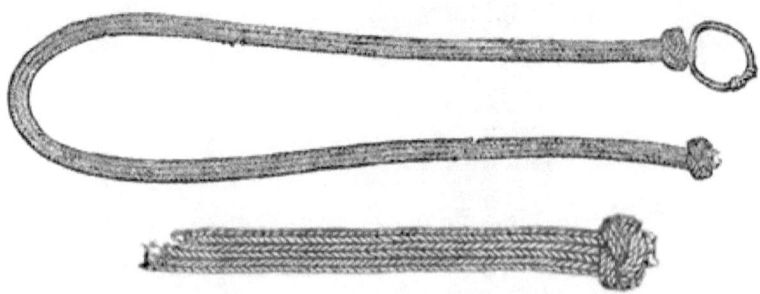

Fig. 23.—Chain of Knitted Silver Wire, 15 inches in length, and end portion
of the Chain of the actual size, from grave No. 2 at Ballinaby.

The chain of knitted silver wire (Fig. 23) is an object of
very peculiar character, but its relations are not difficult to

Fig. 24.—Beads found in grave No. 2 at Ballinaby (actual size).

establish.[1] Its total length is 16 inches, and its width $\frac{1}{4}$ inch.
It is formed of silver wire of the fineness of sewing thread,

---

[1] A portion of a similar chain occurred in the Croy find (*Scotland in Early
Christian Times*, Second Series, p. 23) ; also in the Skaill hoard, to be subsequently described ; in the hoard at Cuerdale ; and in a small hoard found in
the Isle of Inchkenneth.

knitted as a hollow tube, with the common knitting-stitch used in knitting stockings. The knots at the ends of the tube are produced separately, and fastened on. The ring at the end of the chain has its ends twisted together in the same manner as the ring attached to the hair-pin.

The beads of coloured glass found in the graves (of which the different varieties are shown in Fig. 24), were seven in number. In all probability, only a part of them were recovered. They present the peculiarity of being formed of glass of different colours fused together so as to present a variegated surface, sometimes in regular patterns of different colours.

The saucepan of thin bronze (Fig. 25) is extremely light,

Fig. 25.—Saucepan of thin Bronze, from grave No. 2 at Ballinaby (17½ inches in length).

of good shape and excellent workmanship. Its whole length is 17½ inches,—the handle being 12 inches in length, the bowl 5½ inches wide and 3½ inches deep. It is formed of extremely thin beaten bronze, not much thicker than writing paper. A T-shaped fillet surrounds the rim, giving strength and rigidity to the upper part of the bowl. Below the rim are three slight mouldings in *repoussé* work. The handle is strengthened by a T-shaped fillet on either edge, and the circular expansion at the end is ornamented with a disc hammered up from the under side.

The hemispherical implement of black glass (which is here shown in Fig. 26), is the most peculiar object found in this

grave. In shape it nearly resembles the bottom of a common
black bottle, though flatter in the concavity and scarcely so
large, being 3 inches in diameter and $1\frac{1}{2}$ inches in thickness.
It has been made by "throwing" a lump of glass in fusion,
and has evidently been "thrown". in this special form for
a special purpose. That purpose, as we shall see hereafter, is
indicated by the marks of use on its convex side,—which is

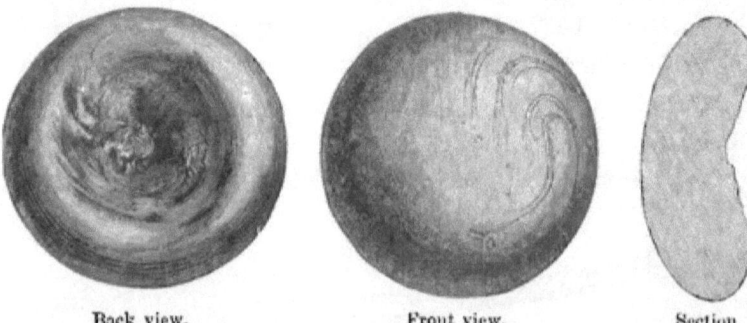

Back view.   Front view.   Section.

Fig. 26.—Implement of Black Glass, from grave No. 2 at Ballinaby (3 inches
in diameter).

considerably rubbed and striated, chiefly towards the centre
where the surface is most prominent.

Lastly, a little cylinder of bronze plated with silver, about
2 inches in length and scarcely so thick as a common pencil-
case, contains in its interior, adhering to one of its sides, what
seems to be the point end of a needle of bronze.

From this detailed examination of the objects associated
with these interments, we perceive that they are for the most
part objects presenting a strongly marked individuality of
character. The weapons form a peculiar group, consisting of
a long, broad-bladed, double-edged sword, with short, straight
guard and triangular pommel ; a light wooden shield with a
truncated boss of iron, and a long, stout-bladed, and unbarbed
spear. The ornaments also form a peculiar group, the brooches
being large, oval, and bowl-shaped, and covered with patterns

of zoomorphic decoration, imperfectly expressed. Reverting to the remarks made on the essential qualities of this peculiar style of decoration, it will be remembered that it differs widely in character and spirit from the decoration of the Celtic school with which we have now become familiar; and if the general teaching of these Lectures, in regard to the value of decoration as an index to the archæological relations of the objects on which it is found, has been successfully applied, it must be obvious that there is no Celticism apparent in these objects. We are unable to compare the forms of the weapons and implements with forms obtained from Celtic burials, because no iron sword, no iron spear, or wooden shield has ever been found in Scotland in association with any burial demonstrably of Celtic character. And no such group of implements as axes and smithy-tools of iron has ever been found in association with any interment on the mainland of Scotland. The obvious inference is that these two burials, with their associated groups of weapons, implements, and ornaments possessing such strongly marked and unusual characteristics, may be outlying examples of a form of burial and associated types of objects, whose special area is not Celtic, and therefore probably not in Scotland.

I have already explained that since it is difficult, if not impossible, to point to any given area which has remained unaffected by movements of populations, invasions, colonisations, and other changes not dependent on purely physical conditions, we must be prepared for the occurrence, among the products that are indigenous to the soil, of other products archæologically characteristic of other areas; and I have endeavoured to show how these are separable from the purely indigenous types by their difference in character and decoration, and how they are assignable to their parent area by their identity with the types native to the region from which they are derived. This is the problem we have now to deal with.

The most prominent features of the form of burial exhibited by these Islay graves are that it is burial unburnt, and with grave-goods. I have already shown that these are features that are common to almost all forms of Paganism. But there seems to be a special suggestiveness in the character of the group of objects deposited in the man's grave. Since he took with him his sword and spear, his axe and shield, and took also with him his smithy-tools to keep them in repair, it seems a fair inference that his form of faith must have taught him to look for a continuance of warfare in the life beyond the grave. We know that such a faith existed, and that the Northern and Western Isles of Scotland were overrun by men who held it at a time when such implements and weapons of iron were in common use. The special feature which distinguished the wild creed of the Northmen from most other forms of heathenism was that it promised a place in Odin's Hall to all men wounded by arms or slain in battle. Spears supported the ceiling of this Valhalla; it was roofed with shields, and coats of mail adorned its benches. It was the perpetual pastime of its inmates to fight and slay each other every day, to be revived again before evening, and then to ride back to the feast of boar's flesh and mead. If, therefore, it can be shown that the forms of the weapons, implements, and ornaments thus found in these Islay graves are the forms of the Norwegian area, and that, when they occur in Scotland, they are found in those portions of Scottish territory that were possessed and colonised by the Norwegians—and found only there—the demonstration of the character, period, and relations of these burials will be complete.

The materials for forming an estimate of the typical character of the burials of the Viking time in Norway are ample, and they have been very fully described by the Norwegian archæologists. Upwards of a thousand graves of this period are known. The form of burial which they exhibit is burial with grave-goods. The burial is usually covered by a mound, either round or oblong in shape. The mounds vary greatly in size, but they differ from those of the early Iron Age, and of all previous ages, in being usually unfurnished with either cist or chamber. Stones are often found set round the burial, which, when the body was unburnt, was simply laid on the natural surface, and the mound heaped over it. In Norway the custom of burning the body exceeds in frequency the custom of burying unburnt by about four to one. Where the body has been burnt it is usually found that the grave-goods have also passed through the fire, but this is not always the case. The burnt remains are either found spread over the area of the base of the mound or gathered together in a heap in the centre. Very frequently they are found placed in an urn. The urns of the Viking time are very rarely made of clay, but are either hollowed out of some soft stone, such as steatite, or they are caldrons made of thin plates of iron riveted together, or beaten out in bronze. The grave-goods buried with these interments include the clothing, weapons, implements, or ornaments used or possessed by the deceased, and the furnishings of the grave are thus rich in proportion to the wealth and station of the individual.

The sword which is characteristic of these interments in Norway is a peculiar weapon. It is long, broad-bladed, often double-edged, and usually furnished with a short, straight guard and a triangular pommel. One which was ploughed up from a grave-mound at Vik, in Flaa Sogn in Norway, in 1837, is shown in Fig. 27 for comparison with those of the same type found in Scotland. I have said

Fig. 27.—Sword found at Vik, in Norway.

that we have no Celtic sword of this type. It is the type which prevailed in Scandinavia during the last three centuries of their heathen period. It differs from the types that preceded and succeeded it in Norway, and it differs also from the types of swords of the later Iron Age in other countries of Europe. It is specially the sword of the Norwegian Viking.

As the sword is the most characteristic object among the grave-goods of the man, the brooch is also the most characteristic object among the grave-goods of the woman. The brooch, which is constantly found in these interments in Norway, is a most peculiar ornament. It is always of brass, massive, oval, and bowl-shaped in form, and is distinguished from all other brooches that are known, not only of this, but of every other area and every other time, by the fact that it is an article of personal adornment which (though as capable of being used singly as any other form of fibula might be), is almost never found singly, but constantly occurs in pairs— the one being usually an almost exact duplicate of the other. This singular type of brooch is the special ornament of the female dress which prevailed in Norway during the last three centuries of their heathen period.[1] It differs entirely from the types that preceded and succeeded it ; and it differs as completely from the types of the later Iron Age in all other European countries.

We therefore see that if the sword thus found in Islay

[1] For this reason the geographical distribution of these brooches marks the range of the Scandinavian conquests of the ninth and tenth centuries. In Iceland, in Russian Livonia, in Normandy, in England, in Ireland, and on our own shores in Shetland, Orkney, Caithness, and Sutherland, and in the Hebrides, including even the remote St. Kilda, their presence attests the historical fact of the Viking settlements from Norway. But the area in which they are specially abundant, of course, is in Scandinavia itself. I find on comparing the different records that there are now upwards of five hundred of them known in Norway. When we add the number known in Sweden, which exceeds four hundred, and those of Denmark, which only amount to thirty-eight, we have a gross total of nearly a thousand, of which the larger

had been dug up in Norway it would have taken its place as one in a great series of the ordinary Viking type, and these brooches from the woman's grave would have matched exactly with some hundreds of similar pairs from Norwegian graves.[1] The whole group of objects would have corresponded with the special characters of many similar groups preserved in the Christiania Museum. The special forms of each of the members of the groups—as, for instance, the forge-tongs, the hammer, the adze, the axes,—are all forms that are abundantly represented in Viking graves there. Nicolaysen gives twenty-three instances of smithy-hammers, and seventeen instances of forge-tongs among the articles found in grave-mounds of the Viking time described by him, in Norway. Several of these grave-mounds contained more or less complete sets of smith's tools, including anvils, chisels, files, as well as hammers and tongs. Along with an interment of this period at Thiele, in Jutland, there were two anvils of different forms, four different kinds of hammers, four varieties of pincers or forge-tongs, two chisels, two implements for drawing wire, four files, two melting pans, a pair of scales and weights, and a quantity of other implements. It was natural that the smith's craft should hold a high place in the estima-

portion are from Norway. No archæological period in any country is marked by such a distinctly peculiar and characteristic type.

[1] In a letter to me acknowledging receipt of a copy of my "Notes of the Relics of the Viking Period of the Northmen in Scotland," Professor Rygh, Curator of the Museum at Christiania, says:—"Among the oval brooches which you have figured, there is not one that might not have been found in Norway. The brooch from Pierowall is of a form exceedingly common with us, of which I know no fewer than one hundred and eight specimens. The commonest form of all in Norway is that of the brooches from Islay and Tiree, of which we have one hundred and eighteen examples. The brooches from the Longhills at Wick belong to a variety of the last form well known with us, and that from Castletown in Caithness has many analogous examples here in Norway, although they are not so common as the two previously mentioned types."

tion of a people wholly devoted to the use of arms, and as famous for their skill in forging, tempering, and ornamenting weapons as for their prowess in using them. But such homelier objects as the pot and the saucepan of the Islay graves are common accompaniments of these interments in Norway, and the counterparts of the implement of black glass found in the woman's grave may be seen in the museums of that country, and their purpose demonstrated by specimens that are actually still in use. Nicolaysen describes them as lumps of glass formed like the bottom of a bottle, and the character of the objects usually associated with them may be indicated by the contents of one grave-mound in which this implement occurs. The mound was a large one, 44½ feet long, and 73 feet broad, set round the base with large stones. It contained an interment after cremation. The ashes were gathered into a bronze vessel, 8 inches high, and 17 inches in greatest diameter, over which was inverted a pot of steatite, both vessels enclosing a quantity of iron implements cemented into a solid mass of oxidation and burnt human bones. Among the implements were a lump of glass like the bottom of a bottle, a knife-blade, the rings of a bridle-bit, an axe, a sickle-blade, a whetstone, some bronze ornaments, and an ox-horn. Alongside of the bronze vessel were a spear-head and a frying-pan of iron, 8½ inches diameter, with 7 inches of the handle remaining, and all around were large quantities of clinker nails. Here the associations of the glass implement are similar in character to its associations in the Islay graves. Its purpose is demonstrated by the facts recorded by Nicolaysen and Lorange, who state that in Mandal Amt and in several remote districts on the west coast of Norway, the women still use them for giving a gloss to their white linen caps, and generally for getting up a gloss on linen by friction.[1]

[1] When showing the relics from the Ballinaby graves to a lady, she remarked that in her home in Caithness she remembered seeing a similar

It has thus been demonstrated that every feature of these two Islay burials, and every object associated with them, is clearly of Norwegian type, and of the heathen period of their Viking time—that is, of the period ranging between the beginning of the eighth and the end of the tenth centuries— and that the sword of this peculiar form and the bowl-shaped brooch of this remarkable type are the most characteristic objects associated with this class of burials.

The next question that presents itself for determination article of glass, which she was told was formerly used for a similar purpose. Though now resident in Edinburgh, she believed the implement was still preserved, and at my request she made search for it, found it, and sent it to the Museum. It is an implement so similar in form to the ancient specimen, that there can be no question as to the identity of type. It is of black bottle glass, 3 inches in diameter, and 1¾ inch thick, and is here engraved (Fig. 28) to the same scale as the specimen from the Ballinaby grave (Fig. 26). That the discovery of this lump of glass in a Pagan grave should

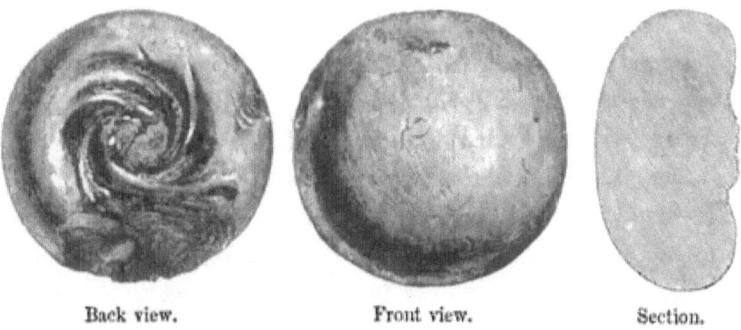

Back view.   Front view.   Section.

Fig. 28.—Linen Smoother of Black Glass, modern (3 inches diameter).

be the means of bringing to light the existence of similar implements in Scotland which had continued in use till within living memory, is a curious illustration of the rapidity with which the knowledge of special implements and special processes becomes extinct when the implement has been superseded by a new form and its use rendered obsolete by an improved process. The placing of this specimen (of the modern type) in the Museum has brought to light other three specimens of modern calendaring implements of glass. They are of larger size and furnished with handles, which are also of glass.

is, What is the range or area of this type of burial, associated
with these types of objects, in Scotland ?

On this same estate of Ballinaby, in Islay, a grave was
discovered under a large standing-stone in the year 1788.
There is no precise record of the circumstances beyond the
fact that a pair of oval bowl-shaped brooches (Fig. 29) were

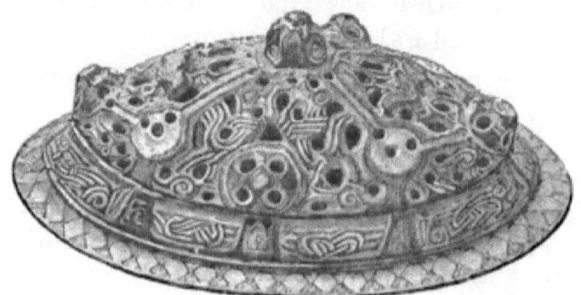

Fig. 29.—Brooch found at Ballinaby, Islay, in 1788.
One of a pair (4¼ inches in length).

found in it. They were presented to the National Museum,
and are thus preserved. They are of the same variety of
type as those previously described, but differing somewhat
in the patterns of their ornamentation. They are 4¼ inches
in length, 2⅞ inches in breadth, and 1¼ inch in height.
Their pins were of iron and are gone, but the hinge and catch
remain in both. The central ornament of the upper shell
is a raised boss, cast hollow in the metal, chased on the upper
surface, and pierced with four holes. The channels cut in
the bands of unpierced metal between the patterns of pierced
work, and the holes through which the plaited strands of
silver wires had passed, are visible, but the wires themselves
are gone. The holes for the pins that fastened the studs of
coloured paste on the circular spaces at the junction of the
bands are there, but pins and studs are both wanting. The
patterns of the ornamentation are zoomorphic, representing
winged, dragon-like animals placed face to face. The band

round the lower part of the under shell of the brooch is filled
with a suggestion of zoomorphic patterns in panels, and the
flange or flat border underneath it is divided into a series of
raised and sunk spaces, produced apparently by a triangular
punch.

In 1845 a similar burial was discovered in the strath
near Newton Distillery, also in Islay. No record of the circumstances is preserved, but two oval bowl-shaped brooches
(Fig. 30) and an amber bead, which were found in the grave,

Fig. 30.—Brooch found in a grave near Newton, Islay.
One of a pair (4¼ inches in length).

are in the possession of Mr. John Campbell of Islay. The
brooches are each 4½ inches in length, 2¾ inches in width,
and 1 inch in height. The pins had been of iron and are gone,
but the hinge and catch are still traceable. These brooches
differ from those that have been already described, inasmuch
as they are not double shelled but cast in one piece, that is,
they are made of a single shell, which is chased, but not
pierced in open-work patterns. The division and the arrangement of the patterns are much the same as in those first
described, but there are no channels in the partitions for
silver wires, and the partitions themselves are ornamented
with a species of fret. The circular spaces at the junctions
of the partitions have been ornamented with studs of paste
pinned on, but studs and pins are both gone. The patterns
of the ornamentation are executed with a graving tool, but

they exhibit so little coherency of design that it is impossible to call them zoomorphic.[1]

In the old Statistical Account of Tiree it is stated that, in digging at Cornaigbeg, there were found at different times human skeletons, and nigh them skeletons of horses. Swords, it is said, were also found, but diminished with rust,—silver-work preserved the handles; there were also shields and

Fig. 31.—Brooch found in Tiree.
1. Under Shell of Brooch, gilt.
2. Upper Shell of pierced and chased work.

helmets. In March 1847 an oval bowl-shaped brooch of this special character, which had been found in Tiree, was exhibited to the Society by Sir John Graham Dalzell, but it was not left in the Museum, and it is not now known what became of it. But in 1872, the late Rev. Dr. Norman Macleod presented to the Museum a brooch of this character found in Tiree (Fig. 31), which is almost precisely of the

[1] A similar grave was found in Mull, and the brooches are in the pos-session of Lord Northampton at Torloisk, but I have no further information regarding them.

same pattern as those first found in Islay. It is 4¼ inches in length, 2¼ inches in breadth, and 1½ inch in height. It is double, and is here figured with the upper and under shells separated from each other so as to show the manner in which they were fitted and pinned together, so that the smooth-gilded surface of the under shell might shine through the pierced work of the upper. This brooch also presents a peculiar appearance common to them all, but which, in this instance, is strongly marked. The interior of the under shell is impressed with the texture of coarse cloth so distinctly, that the size, number, and interweaving of the threads are as visible as in the web. The cloth seems to be coarse linen, and the appearance is really an impression cast in the metal. These under shells were probably cast in moulds prepared in this way—the side of the mould corresponding to the convex surface with its ornamental border was cut in soft stone, a thickness of wet cloth was then fitted into it corresponding to the thickness of the metal, and over this a lump of clay was rammed hard ; the clay was lifted and the cloth removed, thus leaving a cavity for the metal ;[1] the clay became one side of the mould and the stone the other, and, when the metal was run in, it produced a cast of the impression of the cloth retained upon the backing of clay. Thus these brooches present castings in metal of the textile fabrics of the eighth and ninth centuries, showing the thickness of its threads, the method of weaving, and the general finish of the fabric. But there is a still more interesting circumstance connected

[1] The metal of which these brooches are made is not bronze but a very soft brass. Professor Rygh has given the details of the analyses of four, and the composition of the metal is as follows :—

Analyses of bowl-shaped brooches.	Copper.	Zinc.	Lead.
1. From Stromsund, Norway	74·78	10·44	14·36
2. From Braak, Norway	72·85	11·90	15·71
3. From Gardness, Norway	88·00	11·90	...
4. From Denmark	84·44	11·00	3·77

with them in respect to the cloth of the period when they were made and worn. In some instances they have not only preserved casts in the metal of the impression of cloth in the clay of the mould, but have actually preserved portions of the dress in which they were worn, or in which they were fixed when committed to the grave with the body of the wearer. I have already stated that they have usually had pins of iron, now represented by a lump of oxidation. In this brooch from Tiree, and also in one which I brought from Hakedalen, near Christiania, I have ascertained by careful examination of this lump of oxidation that it has enclosed and protected from decay a minute portion of puckered cloth which had been caught between the point of the thick pin and the iron catch into which it slipped when the brooch was fastened on the dress. I have been able to remove and mount for microscopical examination some small scraps of this cloth. It appears to be linen, but with a partial admixture of another fibre, which may be hemp, and I can detect no material difference between the cloth in the specimen from Norway and that from the island of Tiree on our own western coast.

Continuing our inquiry as to the area over which these peculiar relics have been found in Scotland, we ascertain that there are other instances of their occurrence in the Hebrides. On the island of Barra a large grave-mound, crowned by a standing stone 7 feet high, was opened by Commander Edge in 1862. The grave contained a skeleton placed with the head to the west, and along with it there were found an iron sword, 33 inches in length, with remains of the scabbard, a shield-boss of iron and some remains of the shield, a whetstone, two oval bowl-shaped brooches of this type, and a comb of bone, 8 inches in length.[1] A similar burial was

---

[1] *Proc. Soc. Antiq. Lond.* 1861-64, p. 230. The comb is there said to have been of boxwood, but it seems more likely that it was of bone.

found "in the island of Sangay" (probably Sanderay) "between Uist and Harris." The grave contained a skeleton, and with it were found a pair of these brooches (closely resembling Fig. 48, from Pierowall in Orkney), together with a brass pin and a brass needle.[1] Even in remote St. Kilda the evidences of the occurrence of this typical form of burial are not wanting. A pair of these oval brooches found in that island are preserved in the Andersonian Museum, Glasgow.[2]

Coming now to the mainland of Scotland, we find that one of these brooches is preserved in Ospisdale House, Sutherlandshire, of which there is no precise record; but there is every reason to conclude that it is one of a pair found somewhere in the neighbourhood. Another pair were found in a grave in the neighbourhood of Dunrobin Castle, and the under shells of them are preserved in the Duke of Sutherland's museum there.

In Caithness there have been occasional discoveries of interments of this character, but unfortunately no one seems to have thought a burial which was associated with "rusty pieces of old iron" worthy of careful investigation. The Rev. Mr. Pope records, incidentally,[3] a remarkable discovery of swords "in a peat bank near the house of Haimar" in the neighbourhood of Thurso, and dismisses the subject with the remark that "they were odd machines resembling plough-shares, all iron." A pair of oval bowl-shaped brooches of great beauty were found at Castletown in Caithness in 1786. One of these (Fig. 32) is in the National Museum.[4] It is 4½

---

[1] One of these brooches is figured in the *Vetusta Monumenta of the Society of Antiquaries of London*, vol. ii. pl. xx., and it is there said that "the fellow of it is in the British Museum."

[2] One of these is figured by Worsaae in the *Aarbøger for Nordisk Oldkyndighed* for 1873.

[3] Pope's Translation of Torfaeus, Wick, 1866, p. 169.

[4] The other was given to Mr. Worsaae on the occasion of his visit to

inches in length and 3 inches in width. It is double-shelled, and the gilding, both on the under and upper shells, is still visible, although the "double row of silver cord along the edge," which is noted in the first description of the brooches when they were presented by James Traill of Rattar in 1787, is now gone. The centre of the convexity of the brooch is surmounted by a bold ornament, in form somewhat resembling a crown. The ornamentation is distinctly zoo-

Fig. 32.—Bowl-shaped Brooch, found with a Skeleton at Castletown, Caithness (4½ inches in length).

morphic, the four projecting ornaments below the centre-piece being carved into the form of animals' heads. These brooches were "dug out of the top of the ruins" of a Broch near Castletown, and were found "lying beside a skeleton, buried under a flat stone with very little earth above it." This evidently implies that the interment had been made in the upper part of the mound covering the ruins of the Broch.[1]

Scotland, and I had no difficulty in recognising it in one of the cases of the Museum at Copenhagen.

[1] It was the custom of the Northmen to bury their dead in mounds raised in their honour, but they also took advantage of mounds already raised, and of natural or artificial mounds which were convenient for the purpose. See also the remarks on the use of the mounds covering the ruins of Brochs as burial-places in the subsequent Lecture on Brochs.

Another pair of these oval bowl-shaped brooches from

Fig. 33.—Oval Bowl-shaped Brooch, found in a cist in the Longhills, Wick.

Caithness is also in the National Museum. They were found in a cist in the top of a natural mound of gravel called the Longhills, on the north side of the river, a little above the bridge of Wick, in 1840. Although found together they differ in pattern, one being nearly similar to the Tiree brooch, while the other (Fig. 33) differs from all the Scottish specimens in having eight bosses of open work arranged round the central boss. They retain portions of the twisted strands of fine silver wire which lay in the channeled depressions of the upper part.

Passing from Caithness to Orkney, we find abundant evidence of the same form of burial associated with objects of similar character. At Sweindrow, in the island of Rousay, there is a field in which there are many graves, from which objects of iron were occasionally turned up by the plough many years ago, when the soil had been less frequently disturbed. In the year 1826 a fine specimen of the peculiar type of sword associated with these burials (Fig. 34) was thus turned up by

Fig. 34.—Sword found in Rousay (39¼ inches in length).

the plough in close proximity to the spot where previously the iron boss of a shield had been similarly discovered.[1] The sword is a long, broad-bladed, double-edged weapon, with short straight guard and triangular pommel. It measures 3 feet 3¼ inches in total length, the blade being 2 feet 8 inches in length. The guard is 5 inches in length and 1¼ inch in depth. The grip measures 3½ inches in length. The pommel is 4¼ inches in width and 3 inches in height. The blade, which is 2⅛ inches wide at the hilt, has been in the scabbard at the time of its deposit, and blade and scabbard are now converted into a mass of oxidation. The scabbard has been made of thin laths of wood, the fibre of which is

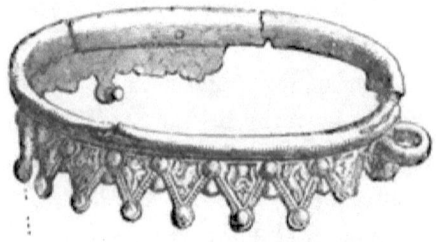

Fig. 35.—Silver Mounting of a Drinking-Horn found at Burghead
(2¾ inches diameter).

still visible, covered in some places with leather. There are also some remains of the side-plates of bone or horn which made up the grip, and the gilt metallic mounting which adorned both ends of the grip still remains. The ornament closely resembles that of the silver mounting of the rim of a horn or beaker (Fig. 35), which was dug up at Burghead some time previous to 1826, and is now in the Museum. But the ornament of the sword has a distinctly zoomorphic feeling, and still more closely resembles the decoration of a similar

[1] This fine sword, now broken in many pieces, was presented to the Museum in 1874 by the representatives of the late Professor Thomas S. Traill, through the Rev. G. R. Omond, Free Church minister at Monzie, one of the oldest Fellows of the Society.

mounting of the hilt of a sword of the Viking type dug up at Islandbridge, near Dublin, and preserved in the Museum of the Royal Irish Academy.

Except in the island of Westray (in which seven specimens have occurred), there is no record of the discovery of the oval bowl-shaped brooches elsewhere in Orkney. I shall describe the remarkable group of graves in Westray in connection with the phenomena of burial, merely remarking here that the presence of these brooches and this type of sword carries the area of this form of burial into the Orkney Islands.

Two oval bowl-shaped brooches, having the usual mark of cloth on the inside of their inner shells, are also in the museum at Lerwick. They were found at Clibberswick, in the north end of the island of Unst, the most northerly island of the Shetland group. Along with them there were found a plain silver bracelet, two glass beads ornamented with twisted streaks of white and blue, and a trefoil-shaped brooch of a type which is also peculiarly Scandinavian, covered with a zoomorphic ornament consisting of dragonesque forms, whose feet twist under and grasp parts of their bodies.[1]

The range of these burials, distinguished (among other features peculiar to themselves), by the presence of this peculiar type of sword and this remarkable type of brooch,[2]

---

[1] This trefoil-shaped brooch closely resembles one figured in the *Memoires de la Société des Antiquaires du Nord*, 1840-44.

[1] Including those found in the Viking cemetery at Pierowall, in Westray, Orkney, the total number of these brooches found in Scotland is thirty-two. The total number of Celtic brooches that I was able to enumerate was fourteen. The difference is striking, and the fact that the foreign form occurs in larger numbers than the native form is so opposed to what is naturally expected, that the explanation becomes of some interest. It is simple, but significant. The largeness of the larger number is an archæological result of Paganism. The smallness of the smaller number is an archæological result of Christianity. The effect of Paganism was that those who had brooches were buried with them. The effect of Christianity was that brooches ceased to be buried with

has thus been traced through the western and northern isles from Islay to Unst, in Shetland, touching the mainland only in the counties of Sutherland and Caithness. This area, established on archæological evidence, coincides exactly with the area established by historical record as that which was colonised and possessed by the Norwegians in the time of their heathenism.

I now proceed to notice other instances in which burials with grave-goods of a similar character, though differing more or less in certain special features, have been observed. It is but recently that they have attracted attention, and the interest and significance of their peculiar phenomena is only beginning to be understood.

About fifty years ago, a grave-mound situated between the chapel of St. Donan and the shore in the island of Eigg, was levelled by the tenant of the land. No observations of the phenomena of the burial were made, but the objects found were fortunately preserved.[1] The principal object found in this grave-mound was a sword-hilt of bronze (Fig. 36), 7½ inches in length. In its form it resembles the hilt of the Islay sword, but is greatly superior to it in the beauty of its ornamentation and the skill of its workmanship. Indeed, I know no finer or more elaborate piece of art workmanship of the kind, either in this country or in Norway. It is constructed in four pieces—the triangular pommel, the cross-

<hr>

those who had them. The tendency of the one system was to take all the brooches ultimately into the soil with the remains of the generations that wore them ; the tendency of the other system was to keep the brooches from going underground. Hence we see that the preponderance of these foreign relics in the soil of Scotland (which is almost destitute of native relics of the same age and purpose) is an archæological result which is directly dependent on the difference between Paganism and Christianity.

[1] They are now deposited in the Museum, and have been fully described by Professor Norman Macpherson, LL.D., in an elaborate paper, read before the Society, on the Antiquities of Eigg.

piece under it, the grip, and the guard. Each of these has been cast and worked separately, and they are all united by

Fig. 36.—Sword-hilt of the Viking time, from a Grave-mound in the island of Eigg (7¼ inches in length).

E

the tang of the blade which passes up through them. The decoration is difficult to describe, but it is not difficult to perceive the harmony, elegance, and fitness of the general design. Each of the four parts is treated with reference to its decoration as a separate whole, but they also combine to give to the entire object a completely harmonious design. The triangular pommel is placed upon a cross-piece answering in character to the cross-piece below the grip, and the grip answers in character to both. The ends of the pommel are formed as

heads of animals, the zoomorphism more suggested than expressed, and more distinct in the front view of the whole hilt (Fig. 36) than in the side view of the pommel alone as here represented (Fig. 37). The grip and the cross-piece below it are all decorated in the same style, with a beautiful pattern formed of a series of arcaded spaces with quadrate ornaments between. The patterns chased in the arcaded spaces are apparently zoomorphic in character, and the quadrate ornaments between them are plates of silver pinned on to the bronze, a circle being incised round every pin head, and each pair of circles connected by a line drawn from the right side of the one to the left side of the other, so as to resemble an S-shaped scroll. The edges of the grip (Fig. 38) are orna-

Fig. 37.—Side view of Pommel of Sword-hilt.

Fig. 38.—Edge of Grip of Sword-hilt.

mented with three sunk panels of interlaced work alternating with four plain panels. The upper side of the guard (Fig. 39) has two ornaments of similar character, each consisting of four loops round a pellet, the bands composing the loops crossing each other in the centre of the figure. There is nothing that is distinctively Celtic in the style of this interlaced work. Indeed, there is so little of it, that it would be difficult, from this specimen alone, to form any opinion as to the relations of interlaced ornament to the system of decoration characteristic of the Viking period. I have already stated that the mere presence of interlaced work is not a feature which can be relied on as a certain indication either of the Celtic or the Scandinavian character of the

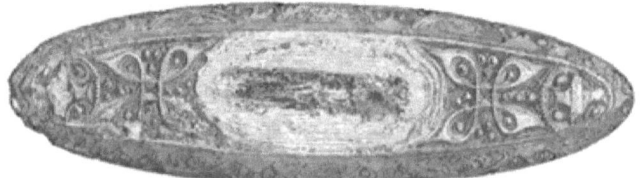

Fig. 39.—Upper side of Guard of Sword-hilt.

ornament of which it forms a part. In consequence of the close intercourse which subsisted between the areas of the two distinctive schools of art during the Viking time, the influence of the one upon the other is traceable in such transitional styles as that of the Manx crosses and the decorations of the Skaill brooches to be hereafter described. And the Celtic manner, with a Scandinavian spirit, is distinctly discernible in the decoration of a sword-hilt (Fig. 40) found in a grave-mound of the Viking time at Ultuna, in Sweden.[1]

[1] The tumulus contained the remains, still distinctly recognisable, of a ship in which a warrior had been entombed along with his arms and two horses. The iron nails which fastened the planks together were still visible in their places. The vessel appeared to be a galley of no great size, carrying a single mast. Alongside of the body, which was unburnt, was found a sword, the blade of iron, and the splendid hilt of gilt bronze decorated with interlaced patterns of extreme beauty and elegance. Remains of the wooden sheath and its gilt

In the grave-mound at Eigg there were found, along with the sword-hilt, a buckle or fastener of a belt of bronze or

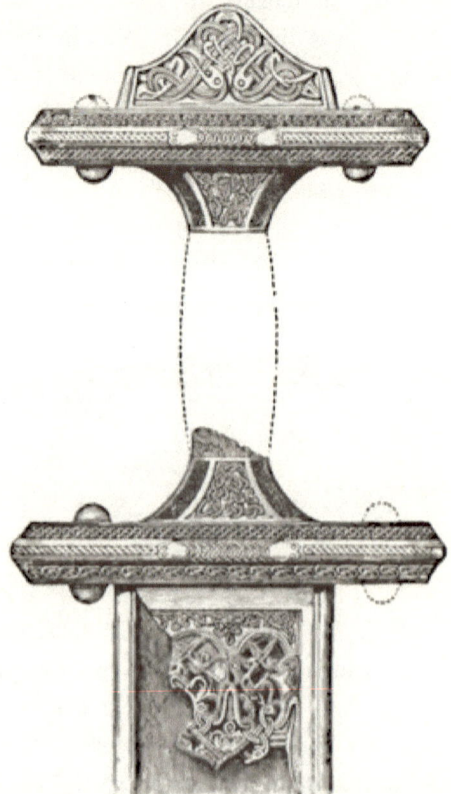

Fig. 40.—Sword-hilt found in a Grave-mound at Ultuna, Sweden.

mountings were also found. A helmet of iron was also found, having a crest or ridge of bronze, containing zinc as an ingredient—the only helmet of the Pagan period in Sweden hitherto known. There were also found a magnificent umbo or boss of a shield, in iron plated with bronze, and adorned with patterns of interlaced work, the handle of the shield, nineteen arrow-heads, the bits of two bridles, a pair of shears, all in iron ; thirty-six table-men and three dice, in bone. Besides these there was an iron gridiron and a kettle of thin iron plates riveted together, with a swinging handle, as also bones of swine and geese, probably the remains of the funeral feast.—*La Suede Prehistorique*, par Oscar Montelius, Stockholm, Paris, and Leipzig, 1864, p. 114.

brass (Fig. 41), attached to a thin plate of the same metal, and a solid lump of metal apparently of a similar alloy, 2½ inches

Fig. 41.—Buckle of Bronze (actual size), from a Grave-mound in the island of Eigg.

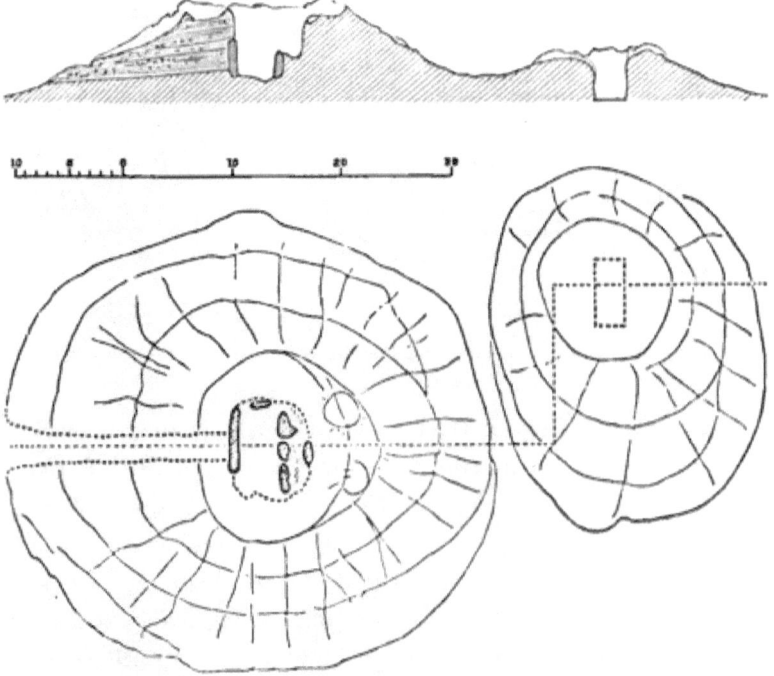

Fig. 42.—Ground-plan and Sections of Grave-mounds in Eigg.

in length, which appears to have been one of the feet of a
large three-footed pot.

Two other grave-mounds in the same neighbourhood were
excavated in 1875 by Professor Macpherson, and I had the
opportunity of seeing them subsequently. The ground-plans
and sections of them which are here given (Fig. 42), were
made by Mr. Arthur Joass. The largest mound was about
40 feet in diameter and from 6 to 7 feet in height, with a

Fig. 43.—Brooch of Bronze, silvered, from Grave-
mound in Eigg (2½ inches diameter).

Fig. 44.—Belt-Clasp
(actual size).

circular depression in the centre. In an enclosure roughly
formed of stones in the centre of the mound and on the
original level of the surface, there were found traces of an
interment, with grave-goods, of the usual Viking character.
They consisted of an iron sword in the sheath, similar to
that found in the Islay grave, an iron axe-head, a spear-head
of iron, a penannular brooch of bronze plated with silver
and ending in knobs of the shape of thistle heads (Fig. 43),

an agrafe or belt-clasp of bronze or brass, ornamented with a

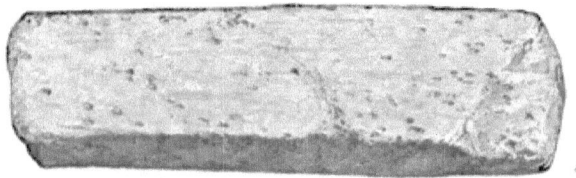

Fig. 45.—Whetstone (actual size).

scroll-like pattern in relief (Fig. 44); a small whetstone (Fig. 45), and several portions of dress consisting of cloth of three different varieties of texture (Fig. 46), one of which is trimmed with fur.

The smaller grave-mound, a few yards distant, contained the fragments of an iron sword, a whetstone, a plain penannular brooch with knobbed ends, of a slightly flattened form, in bronze or brass, and some beads of amber and jet.

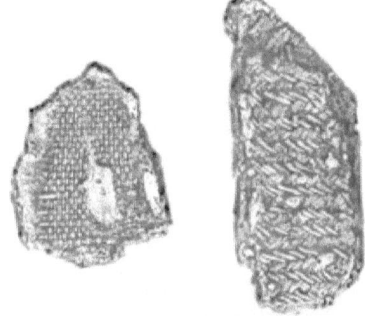

Fig. 46.—Specimens of Cloth found in the Grave-mound.

Perhaps the most remarkable cemetery of graves belonging to this intruded Paganism of the Norsemen was that excavated by Mr. William Rendall, of Pierowall, in the island of Westray, in Orkney, in 1849. The graves were situated in the sandy links at the north-west side of the head of the bay of Pierowall. Mr. Rendall's notes are brief and imperfect. I have twice gone over the ground explored by him, with the view of ascertaining certain points in connection with these interments, and I think there is evidence on the spot that each of them was placed on the original surface of the ground, that they were surrounded by roughly made enclosures of stones, and covered by a mound of greater or less bulk. Mr. Rendall explored two groups of these grave-mounds, the one containing four and the other five interments.

In the first group, grave-mound No. 1 contained a human skeleton laid on its right side, north and south, the skull cleft, apparently before burial, and only one half of it found. Deposited with it there were a number of iron weapons or implements, among which Mr. Rendall recognised an iron axe and what he calls the half of a helmet, which I have no doubt was half of the globular boss of a shield. Grave-mound No. 2 contained the remains of a man, a horse, and a dog. It is not said whether the whole skeleton of the horse was in the grave, but the remark is made that the horse was of small size, and the bridle-bit remained between its jaws. Many pieces of iron were found, among which were a buckle and a spear-head or part of a sword. Grave-mound No. 3 contained the remains of a man and a horse with fragments of iron implements. Grave-mound No. 4 contained a skeleton only.

At a little distance to the north-east of this group of grave-mounds was the second group. In grave-mound No. 1 was the skeleton of a man. At his head lay the cup-shaped boss of his shield; at his left side his sword. A whetstone, a comb, and several glass beads were also found, and many pieces of iron of whose form and purpose there is no suggestion. In grave-mound No. 2 was a skeleton, which Mr. Rendall concluded to be that of a female. Two oval bowl-shaped brooches of brass were found on the breast, and a little below them a circular ornament and a pin of the same metal. There were no traces of iron, or remains of iron implements or weapons. Grave-mound No. 3 contained a small skeleton with two oval bowl-shaped brooches and a small circular-headed pin on the breast, and two long single-edged, round-backed combs of bone (Fig. 47) lay on either side of the neck. No. 4 had been previously disturbed. In No. 5 were two brooches, two combs, and a pin similar to those in No. 3.

In 1851 Mr. Rendall presented to the National Museum the contents of a grave which is not described in these notes

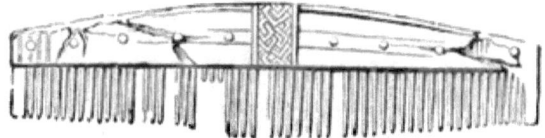

Fig. 47.—Round-backed Comb from a Grave-mound in Westray.

but was found in the same locality. It contained the skeleton of a man, with which there had been deposited an iron axe, a spear-head of iron, and the iron boss of a shield, an oval bowl-shaped brooch (Fig. 48), and a penannular brooch

Fig. 48.—Oval Bowl-shaped Brooch from a Grave-mound in Westray.

of Celtic form, ornamented with interlaced work of purely Celtic style.[1] In this remarkable cemetery we have the same type of burial and the same typical forms of weapons, implements, and ornaments, as in Islay and in Eigg. Of the whole group of objects found in all these graves there is but one, viz. the Celtic brooch last mentioned, that is of a type native to the soil in which they are found.

But a still more remarkable set of graves was found at Pierowall by Mr. Farrer and Mr. George Petrie. Unfortunately there is the same absence of any precise and detailed record of the phenomena. The first, which contained the

[1] Figured in the previous series of Lectures—*Scotland in Early Christian Times*, p. 29, Fig. 22.

bones of a man and a horse, had been found at the sands of
Gill by Mr. George Petrie in 1841, and the relics from it
were deposited in the Kirkwall Museum. When that museum
was broken up and its contents sold, they were purchased by
Colonel Balfour of Trenaby, and sent to the National Museum.
They consist of the bronze cheek-ring of a bridle with part
of the iron bit, and fragments of wood with iron rivets which
were supposed to be the remains of a shield. The second
grave was explored by Mr. Farrer in 1855. There is no
record of the phenomena of the burial, but the objects found
were sent to the museum. They are an iron knife, a small
sickle of iron, an iron key of peculiar form (Fig. 49), and a

Fig. 49.—Iron Key, from a Grave-mound in Westray (5¾ inches in length).

bronze mounting of a sheath or scabbard-end plated with
silver, and ornamented with an engraved pattern suggesting

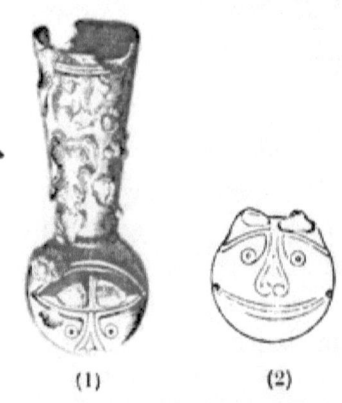

(1)   (2)

Fig. 50.—1. Sheath-mounting from a
grave in Westray, Orkney. 2.
Plan of its ornament.

a grotesque face (Fig. 50).
With these were found large
quantities of decayed wood
pierced with iron rivets which
were also supposed to be the
remains of a wooden shield.
The third grave-mound was
explored by Mr. Farrer and
Mr. Petrie in 1863. No record
of the phenomena exists, but
the articles found were two
iron buckles apparently of
saddle girths, and a quantity of
pieces of decayed wood varying

in thickness from 1 to 2 inches, pierced by iron rivets, and
also suggested to be portions of a wooden shield.

In these three instances the principal feature of the interment is the presence of quantities of wooden planks, sometimes as much as two inches thick, pierced by iron rivets.
When these are closely examined it is seen that the wood is
of oak, that the rivets are peculiar in character, having round
heads on one side and square heads on the other, and that
they frequently pass through the wood obliquely. These are
the characteristics of the clinker-nails which fastened the
planking of the Viking ships. They were square-headed on
one side and round-headed on the other. The fact that these
rivets pass through the wood obliquely is more suggestive of
a boat than of a shield. The thickness of wood between the
rivet-heads is more than twice that of any shield of the time
whose thickness is known. No shield-boss or handle was
found with any of these interments, and no shield of oaken
planks fastened with such rivets is known. In point of fact,
no shield could be used whose thickness was two inches of
solid oak, and the quantity of wood and iron found with the
interments seems much in excess of what would be required
for shields. I therefore conclude that, in these three instances,
the form of burial was that in which the Viking was laid in
his ship—drawn up on the strand, and set on even keel to
receive him and his grave-goods—and a mound raised over all.

The testimony of the earlier sagas is unanimous that the
common mode of sepulture in the heathen Viking time was
by raising a mound over the remains of the dead, who were
placed in their grave-mounds honourably, with abundance
of goods, weapons, ornaments, and costly garments, horses
and sometimes even thralls or slaves. Thus we are told that
great store of goods was placed in the grave-mound with
Hravnkel Freysgode, and all his war-suits and his good spear.
So also we learn that Skalagrim was laid in his grave-mound
with his horse, his weapons, and his smithy-tools, and Egil
was buried with his weapons and his clothing. Thorgrim,

priest of Frey at Sæbol was buried in his ship, over which they raised the mound after the ancient fashion. But the most striking of all the saga notices of heathen burial is that of the sepulture of King Harald Hildetand, who was slain on Braavalla Heath by his nephew Sigurd Ring, in the middle of the eighth century. After the battle the victor caused search to be made for the body of his uncle, which he placed in his chariot in the midst of the grave-mound; then his horse was slain and laid beside the dead; and Sigurd caused his own saddle to be placed beside the horse, so that Harald might have his choice and ride or drive to Valhalla as he had a mind. Then Sigurd made a great funeral feast, and the nobles threw massive rings and splendid arms into the grave-mound in honour of the dead king.

Thus we gather from the early literature of the Scandinavians a very vivid impression of the character and accompaniments of their heathen burial. Yet this literary evidence is characteristically defective on special points that are of paramount interest to the archæologist. Hence, when it is attempted to be used scientifically, the result is what might be expected of a scientific operation conducted with unscientific materials. For instance, Dr. Dasent, gathering the literary evidence into one generalisation, concludes that the burial took place in a how or cairn, and that the body was laid in the how with goods and arms, sometimes in a sitting posture, sometimes even in a ship, but *always* in a chamber, formed of baulks of timber or blocks of stone, over which earth and gravel were piled. Since it is the main object of our science to attain to great and wide generalisations from completed evidence, it is manifest that such a generalisation as this, which gives us what *always* was the special character of the sepulchral structure for a given period, would be one of the most precious and costly fruits of scientific research. Founded on purely archæological evidence, it could only be the result of the completed investigation of all the grave-mounds of the period. As here given, it is arrived at by a much shorter process, viz. the comparison and critical inter-pretation of a few texts, for it is not expressly stated in any text, but is an inference from incidental expressions in several of them.[1] And the interest with which we must regard the inference lies in the fact that this special form of sepulchral mound, which is deduced from the literary evidence as having been *always* the form in use throughout the Viking period, is a form which is almost archæologically unknown in that period.

It is to be observed also that the saga evidence is defective as to the customs connected with cremation.[2] The only literary evidence we possess in regard to them is to be found in the strange narrative by Ahmed Ibn-Fozlan, an eye-witness of the ceremonies attending the incremation of the dead body of a Northern chief.[3] The scene is on the banks of the Volga, and the date is towards the close of the Viking time. The narrator tells us that there was a temporary interment till all the preparations were made; that a female slave who had elected to die with her master was given in charge to an old hag, who as mistress of the ceremonies was significantly styled " the angel of the dead ;" that the dead man's ship was

---

[1] Sometimes the description of a burial mentions the digging of a grave instead of the raising of a mound. When Thorolf died, Egil took his body and prepared it according to the custom of the time, then they dug a grave and placed Thorolf in it with all his weapons and raiment, and Egil placed a gold bracelet on each of his arms, then they placed stones over him, and earth over all.

[2] Snorri says that the custom of burning the body was over before the time when the historical sagas begin their chronicle of events. The fact that it is represented in the mythological sagas as the burial rite of the Æsir, in the Twilight of the Gods, shows that it was out of memory as a human custom in Iceland.

[3] A translation of this narrative is given in the *Proceedings of the Society of Antiquaries of Scotland*, vol. ix. p. 518.

hauled up on the strand and prepared to be his funeral pile;
that, when all was ready, the corpse was taken out of its
temporary grave, arrayed in fur-mounted and gold-embroidered
garments, and laid in state on the deck, where a banquet was
spread for him; that his weapons were placed ready to his
hand, and two horses, two oxen, his dog, and two fowls were
hewn in pieces with swords and cast into the ship; that the
woman who was to die, after taking leave of her friends, was
first drugged with strong drink and then brutally slaughtered
with a big knife by the "angel of the dead," while two men
pulled the ends of a cord wound round her neck and the
crowd beat upon their shields to drown her shrieks; that she
was then laid beside her dead lord and the pile fired by his
nearest relative, and after it had burnt out a great mound was
raised over the ashes.

Turning now to the evidence derived from the grave-
mounds themselves, we find that it corroborates and supple-
ments the literary evidence in a remarkable manner. For
instance, close above the strand at Möklebust, in Norway,
there is a semi-globular mound 12 feet high and 92 feet in
diameter; round its base there is a ditch 12 feet wide and 3
feet deep, interrupted on the south and east by accesses on
the natural level. The whole base of the mound was covered
by a layer of burnt ashes. In an oval, about 28 feet long
and 14 feet wide, lay a quantity of iron rivets and nails as
they had settled down among the ashes when the planks they
had fastened were consumed. Around the circumference of
this oval, and among these rivets, were found no fewer than
forty-two shield-bosses, mingled with pike-heads, axes, swords,
knives, and other implements of iron. Near the centre of
the oval lay a large bronze pot or caldron, one-third full of
burnt human bones, over which were heaped the bosses of
thirteen shields, now firmly rusted to each other and to the
sides of the pot. The pot itself was splendidly enamelled

round the rim; in fact, an exquisite work of art. Among the bones within it was an iron pike-head, which M. Lorange, who explored the mound, concluded to have been the weapon by which the Viking met his death. Recounting the whole phenomena and circumstances of the burial as observed during the process of exploration, he says: "It seems that the sea-king's men had drawn his ship up on the strand, with all its fittings as it was on the day of his death, laid the dead man in it clad in his best and with his arms and horse; then they hung their shields round the gunwales as they used to do when going on a cruise, hoisted the sail, piled wood under and around, and fired the vessel as she stood. Then, when the fire had done its work, they gathered the burnt bones into this splendid pot, covered them with the bosses of the burnt shields, and placed them in the centre of the heap of ashes over which the great mound was finally reared."

But more frequently the vessel and its contents have not passed through the fire. One such ship I have seen. It was found under a mound at Tune, and is now preserved in connection with the museum at Christiania. The mound was 12 feet high and 80 yards in circumference. The vessel stood on the original surface on even keel. It is clinker-built; the planks of oak, the ribs of fir. The keel is 43½ feet in length, and the ship is low and narrow for her length, which is no more than that of a first-class herring boat of the present day on the east coast of Scotland. Each side was of eleven planks, an inch thick, fastened with clinker nails, having round heads outside and square heads inside. The seams were caulked with tarred oakum of neat's hair. The ribs, thirteen in number, are built of three different layers of wood fastened with oaken trenails and iron nails. The mode in which they are fastened to the skin of the boat is peculiar. The upper boards alone are fastened with oaken trenails, and the lower ones are merely attached to the planking by ropes of bast passed through holes in the ribs, and then through corresponding holes in wooden clumps on the planks. The mast was secured in a step on the bottom lining, and the vessel was steered by a side rudder. The Viking's body, which was unburnt, was placed on a wooden platform abaft the mast. Beside it lay the bones of a horse, with remains of the saddle. The rest of the grave-goods were of the common character, comprising merely a few beads of coloured glass, a few fragments of clothing, a sword of the ordinary Viking type, a spear-head, a shield-boss, a rolled-up coat of mail, and some tools and implements of iron.

Another of larger size was discovered last summer in a mound at Gokstad, near Sandefiord, and is now placed beside the Tune specimen. Its length is about 80 feet, with a breadth of beam of 17 feet. It is of oak, and clinker-built, the planks and the frame-timbers connected in the same peculiar manner as in the Tune ship. All the planks have planed and moulded edges both inside and out, but there is no trace of the use of the saw either in the planking or frame-work of the vessel. Her lines are well laid; stem and stern are alike sharp and finely modelled. She has neither deck nor seats for the rowers, although her sides are pierced for sixteen oars each. The oars, some of which were found on board, were 20 feet long. In rowing, they were passed through circular holes 18 inches below the gunwale, and having narrow slits cut on each side of them to allow the passage of the blade of the oar. Like all her kind, she had but one mast and one sail, square in form, and she was steered by a side rudder. The vessel, though showing signs of wear, had been comparatively new when drawn on shore to enhance the funeral honours of its owner. A sepulchral chamber was built of timbers in front of the mast reaching to the prow. In this chamber the dead Viking was laid, surrounded with his grave-goods, his arms, and ornaments. That these were numerous and costly there can be little doubt, but the mound was broken into at an early date, a great hole cut in the side of the ship, and the funeral chamber rifled. The few relics that were left, chiefly mountings of belts and harness, exhibit the finest art of the Viking time, and the completeness of the equipment of the vessel, from the row of painted shields round the gunwale down to her cordage and anchor, and the cooking utensils of the crew—together with the fact that the mound also contained the remains of three boats and the bones of eight or nine horses, as many dogs, and a peacock— testify to the wealth and consideration of the man whose burial rites were thus celebrated.

I have described these Viking burials found in Norway and in Scotland partly because they enable us most vividly to realise the peculiar characteristics of Pagan burial, but chiefly because I am unable to illustrate the burial pheno- mena of the Iron Age Paganism of Celtic Scotland from its own remains. The archæology of Scotland is absolutely destitute of recorded data for this purpose. The uninstructed excava- tors have some respect for stone and bronze, but old iron is shovelled into oblivion without a moment's hesitation.

LECTURE II.

(20TH OCTOBER 1881.)

NORTHERN BURIALS AND HOARDS.

IT has now been shown that the intrusion of the Norwegian
Paganism into the northern and western area of Scotland
produced an extension into this country of types and phenomena which are purely indigenous to the Scandinavian area.
But along with the types and phenomena that are purely
Norwegian we also find, within the area of this intruded
Paganism, a series of modified types—neither purely Celtic
nor purely Scandinavian, but partaking to some extent of
the distinctive characteristics of both. This has already been
demonstrated in so far as the products of this commingling of
distinctive styles and customs have been characterised by
indications of Christianity;[1] but there still remain to be
discussed a group of phenomena and objects of this mixed
character which either present no distinct indications of
Christian associations or exhibit characteristics that are
distinctive of Paganism.

I therefore proceed to describe a series of burials occurring
within the same area in which the distinctive form of burial
with arms, implements, and ornaments of purely Norwegian
types also occur, but differing from these, inasmuch as though
they present unequivocal indications of Paganism they do not
so distinctly indicate their origin. As we examine their

---

[1] *Scotland in Early Christian Times* (second series), pp. 226-232.

characteristics it will be seen that they form a group strictly local in its range, and possessing affinities which are rather Norwegian than Celtic.

In July 1869 the late Mr. George Petrie investigated the contents of a burial-mound, situated on the crown of a ridge overlooking the sea, at a place called Orem's Fancy, in the island of Stronsay, Orkney. The burial-mound is a low, elongated accumulation of stones and earth, partly indistinguishable from the natural ridge, and apparently about fifty yards in length. Several burials had been discovered in it from time to time in the process of bringing it under cultiva-

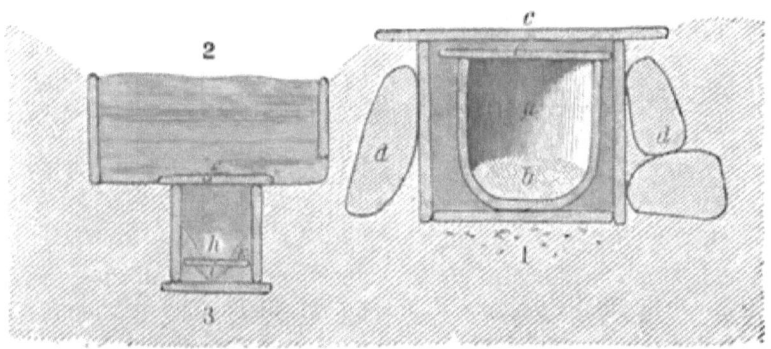

Fig. 51.—Sectional view of Burials in Stronsay, Orkney.
1. Section of Cist with Stone Urn.—*a.* Urn, seen in section, 17 inches deep. *b.* Burnt bones in the urn. *c.* Cist of flagstones, 2 feet square. *d.* Boulder stones supporting sides of cist.
2 and 3. Double cist with burnt bones, close to No. 1.

tion. One of these (Fig. 51, No. 1), which was carefully examined by Mr. Petrie, was contained in a cist of rough slabs, the sides being 25½ inches and 22 inches in length, and the width and depth of the cavity about 23 inches. The bottom of the cist was formed of a rough slab, and the covering stone of a larger slab of the same character. The cist contained a large and somewhat irregularly-shaped urn of stone, hollowed evidently by a metal tool. The urn (Fig. 52) stood on the bottom slab of the cist (as shown in the foregoing section) and was covered by a thin slab of clay slate, rudely dressed

at the edges to a circular shape. The urn was filled to a depth of about 5 inches with burnt bones, largely mixed with vitrified matter, and run together in masses. No fragments of implements, weapons, ornaments, or other articles were present among the bones. The fragments of bone were greatly comminuted, but portions of the long bones, vertebral processes,

Fig. 52.—Urn of Steatitic Stone from Cist No. 1, at Orem's Fancy, Stronsay (17 inches high).

and fragments of the skull were recognisable. The urn of stone was therefore the only remarkable feature of the interment. It is a rudely-formed vessel of irregularly-conical form, narrowing from the brim to the bottom. At the brim, which is oval in form, it measured 20¾ inches in its longer, and 18 inches in its shorter diameter. Its depth is 17 inches, and the greatest width across the bottom 15 inches. The rim is smooth and slightly rounded, and the marks of the tool by which the vessel was scooped out of the block of stone are distinctly visible. The stone is a soft and easily-worked steatite.

Adjoining this cist there was another 31 inches long, 21 inches wide, and 12 inches deep (Fig. 51, No. 2), which had been previously opened, and contained nothing but earth. Underneath it was a smaller cist, 13 inches long, 9½ inches wide, and 12½ inches deep (Fig. 51, No. 3). On the bottom stone of this under cist was a quantity of clay, in the centre of which there was a bowl-shaped cavity (i) nearly filled with burnt bones, and covered with a thin slab of clay slate, dressed to a circular form, over which was another layer of clay (*k*) about 2 inches thick, with a depression (*h*) in the middle, leaving a portion of the centre of the stone visible when the upper cover of the cist was lifted.

At a little distance another burial was discovered, placed simply in the mound without the protection of a cist. The deposit of burned bones was contained in an urn of stone similar to the first, but slightly smaller, measuring across the mouth 19 inches in the longer and 15 inches in the shorter diameter, and 15 inches in depth. The urn had been simply set in the ground, the mouth covered with a flat stone, and a quantity of stones and earth heaped over it, so that its covering stone was scarcely more than 18 inches beneath the surface.

Another urn of the same character was found, also set in the ground about a foot below the surface. It had no covering stone. Two small cists containing burnt bones and ashes, but no urns, were also found in the mound separately. At a distance of seven yards from one of these there was a circular enclosure, formed of oblong beach stones, each about a foot long, and standing on end about a yard apart. Within this circle two other cists were discovered, each containing the usual indications of a burial after cremation—burnt bones, ashes, and charcoal—but no urns and no deposit of arms, implements, weapons, or ornaments.[1]

In a large burial mound at Stennis, Orkney, excavated by Mr. Farrer[2] in December 1854, another burial was found, accompanied by an urn of stone of this special character. The mound was 62 feet in diameter, and about 9 feet high, circular and flat on the top, the sides sloping at a considerable angle. Near the centre of the mound, and at a height of about 3 feet above the original level of the ground, there was

---

[1] Described by Mr. Petrie in *Proc. Soc. Antiq. Scot.*, vol. viii. p. 367.

[2] *Proc. Soc. Antiq. Scot.*, vol. ii. p. 50.

a cist formed of massive side stones about 6 feet in length, and end stones about 2 feet in length, set in the middle of the space between the side stones, so that the cavity enclosed was only about 2½ feet long, 2 feet wide, and 2 feet deep. In the cist was an urn of steatitic stone (Fig. 53), 22½ inches

Fig. 53.—Large Steatite Urn, found at Stennis, Orkney (20 inches high).

diameter across the mouth, and 20 inches high. It was filled to about one-third of its depth with calcined bones, largely mingled with vitrified matter. It differs from the Stronsay urn in having a triply incised border immediately underneath the rim. The burial-mound also differs from the Stronsay mound in being higher and more regularly - shaped. Like the Stronsay mound, it contained more interments than one, although the excavation only revealed two.[1] The second burial was a little beyond the centre of the mound, to the northward of the first, and at about the same height above the original surface of the ground. It was contained in a cist formed of rough flagstones placed on edge, which measured 33½ inches in length, and 19 inches in width. A small urn of baked clay, 5 inches diameter, and 5 inches deep, stood in the north-west corner of the cist. It contained fragments of calcined bones, and was unaccompanied by any other relics

[1] The unscientific method of opening a burial mound by driving a trench across it cannot be too strongly condemned. No such investigation can be regarded as scientific which leaves any part of the mound or of the site beneath it unexamined ; and no one should touch a burial-mound who is not prepared both to investigate and record its phenomena in a scientific manner.

whatever. The urn fell to pieces, and has unfortunately not been preserved. In his account of it Mr. Petrie does not state whether it was plain or ornamented, and we are thus left with no more definite indication of its characteristics than that it was made of clay.

Quite recently a cluster of burial mounds at Corquoy, in the island of Rousay, Orkney, was examined by Mr. George M'Crie. The largest mound was about 50 feet in circumference, and 5½ feet high. It contained a cist in the centre, and on the level of the surrounding ground, composed of four side stones, a bottom stone, and a covering stone, the joints being coated with tempered clay. The cavity of the cist measured 2½ feet in length, by 2 feet in width, and 18 inches in depth. It was almost filled with clay, ashes, and fragments of bones. In the centre was an urn of steatite (Fig. 54), oval in shape, with a slightly bevelled rim. It measures 9¾ inches in its longer, and 8 inches in its shorter diameter, across the mouth, and stands 7 inches high.

Fig. 54.—Urn of Steatite, found at Corquoy (7 inches high).

The other mounds contained cists, but no urns or remains of any kind except comminuted fragments of bones.

There is in the Museum another urn of this material (Fig. 55) also from the island of Rousay, but unfortunately there is no record of the circumstances of its discovery. It is of steatite, oval in shape, the sides bulging from the bottom upwards. It measures 11 inches by 10 across the mouth, and stands 7½ inches high. It is rudely ornamented by incised lines cut round the outside immediately under the rim, and is still about one-third full of calcined human bones.

Fig. 55.—Urn of Steatite from Rousay, Orkney (7½ inches high).

An urn of the same character (Fig. 56) was recently found in making a road through a sand hill about a mile north-east of Balfour Castle, in Shapinsay, Orkney. It was enclosed in a cist in a small tumulus, the cist being composed of four slabs for the sides and ends, and a slab for the bottom, with another flat stone for a cover. When found the urn was in fragments, but the fragments

Fig. 56.—Urn of Steatite found in Shapinsay, Orkney (4 inches high).

had been united by some kind of string, the fibrous texture of which was discernible in the holes which had been bored on either side of the fractures, and through which the cord had been passed to repair the breaks.

In 1874 a small burial mound, about 8 feet in diameter and

2½ feet high, was removed in the course of the construction of a road between the North and South Havens in Fair Isle, lying midway between Orkney and Shetland. In the mound there was found a large, oval-shaped, rudely-formed, and unornamented urn of baked clay. Although imperfect it measures upwards of 12 inches in height. Beside it there was a smaller urn of steatite (Fig. 57), also oval in shape, but much more neatly formed. It measures 5½ inches in its longer diameter, and almost 5 inches in its shorter diameter across the mouth, and stands 4 inches high. Under the rim is a bevelled band, giving it something of an orna-mental character. Close by this mound, in a flat space, there were

Fig. 57.—Urn of Steatite, found in Fair Isle (4 inches high).

found at intervals a number of flat stones, from 6 to 12 inches under the surface, and below each stone there was observed what is described as "a carefully-rounded hole, about 6 inches deep by 10 inches broad, very smooth in the inside, and lined with about an inch thick of a soft, black, adhesive substance, resembling a mixture of peat-moss and clay, and containing in the bottom a whitish substance resembling bone ash." These phenomena thus imperfectly observed indicate in all probability a small cemetery of urns set in the ground, with stone covers, and having no mounds heaped over them.

In 1821 a mound in the island of Uyea, in Shetland, yielded a group of six interments, each consisting of an urn of this character filled with burnt human bones and ashes. Hibbert describes one of the urns as a well-shaped vessel, constructed of a soft magnesian stone, having the bottom made of a separate piece, and fitted into its place by a groove.[1]

[1] Mr. Petrie notices a similar instance in Orkney, the bottom being

In the month of August 1863, when some excavations were being made on the summit of an eminence called the Meikle Heog, at Haroldswick, in the island of Unst, Shetland, for the purpose of planting a flag-staff as a fishing signal, the labourers broke into a place of sepulture formed of upright flagstones, and enclosing a number of skulls and bones. Further examination disclosed another cist similarly formed. Unfortunately there is no record of the dimensions of these cists. In the one last mentioned there were found a human skull, some bones of the ox, and six urns or vessels of chloritic schist or steatite.[1] They were of different shapes and sizes, as follows :—

No. 1, a flat-bottomed vessel, with an unsymmetrical four-sided outline, the corners slightly rounded, and the sides bulging from the bottom upwards, about 7 inches high.

No. 2, a tolerably symmetrical four-sided vessel of similar form, but thinner and better made, measuring 5½ inches in length, 5¼ inches in width, and 3½ inches high.

No. 3, a rude thick-sided vessel of the same form, 6¼ inches long, 4½ inches high, and 4½ inches wide.

No. 4, a rudely-made and unsymmetrical vessel, oval in outline, flat-bottomed, the sides bulging from the bottom upwards, and slightly contracting towards the rim, about 4 inches in length, 3¾ inches in width, and 4 inches high.

No. 5, a small cup-shaped vessel, oval in shape, 4½ inches long, 3 inches broad, and 2¾ inches high.

No. 6, a rather neatly-made oval vessel, 4½ inches long, and 4 inches wide at the brim, contracting to 2½ inches long, and 2 inches wide at the base. It is the only one in the group which bears any ornament, the ornament consisting of

formed of a lozenge-shaped piece of stone, fitted into its place by a groove cut round its circumference.

[1] These vessels are figured and described by Mr. G. E. Roberts in the *Mem. Soc. Anthrop. Lond.*, vol. i. p. 296.

two incised lines scored round the upper part of the vessel, immediately under the rim.

These burials in the Meikle Heog differ from all the others that have been described, inasmuch as they are burials unburnt. The character of the vessels is also different, inasmuch as they are not cinerary urns placed in the grave for the purpose of containing the burned bones of the interment. But the general form of the vessels is similar to that of those which are found in Orkney and the Fair Isle, containing burnt bones, and the character of the ornament and the nature of the material of which they are made is identical.

Two vessels of stone, of the same irregularly oval shape, but slightly more ornate in character (Fig. 58), were turned

Fig. 58.—Vessels of Sandstone, found at Aucorn, Caithness (13 inches and 8 inches high).

up by the plough on the farm of Aucorn, in the parish of Wick, in Caithness, in 1853. The larger vessel is flat-bottomed, oval, and furnished with handles projecting from its ends. It measures 17 inches in its longest diameter, and 16 inches in its shortest diameter at the mouth, and stands 13 inches high. The smaller vessel is without handles, measures 10 inches in greatest, and 9 inches in its least diameter at the mouth, and stands 8 inches high. The ornamentation of both these vessels is similar in character to that of all the others, consisting of incised lines drawn round the outside, immediately below the rim. Unfortunately their contents were neither examined nor preserved, but Mr. Rhind states that it has been observed that the grain grows greener and richer on the spot where they were turned up than anywhere else in the field; and he infers from this, as well as from the character of the vessels themselves, that they were deposited with an interment or interments after cremation.

The largest vessel of this description which has been recorded is one which was presented to the museum in fragments in 1834. It was dug out of a mound called Wilkie's Knowe, in the island of Westray, in Orkney, and an account of its discovery, which has not been preserved, was read to the Society in April 1835. The form of the vessel is oval, narrowing from the brim downwards. The circumference of the upper part is about 6 feet, and the thickness of the sides of the vessel 1½ inches. The material is the same chloritic or steatitic stone of which the others are formed.

These examples will suffice to show the general characteristics of this peculiar class of interments. They are interments of bodies usually burnt, but sometimes unburnt; usually placed in cisted mounds, sometimes singly, at other times in groups; and generally unaccompanied by any manufactured article except the urns. The character of the urns is peculiar. They are not of clay, but of stone. They are not circular, but oval or irregularly four-sided in shape. They vary extremely in size, the largest known being 6 feet in circumference, and the smallest less than 5 inches long and 3 inches high. They are characterised by extreme simplicity of form and decoration. When they are ornamented the decoration is confined to the scoring of two or more lines underneath the rim, and rudely parallel to it. Their range, so far as is at present known, is confined to Caithness, Orkney, and Shetland, the area proper of the old Norwegian Earldom of Orkney.

Urns of steatitic stone are of common occurrence in the burial mounds of the Viking time in Norway.[1] But they are rarely placed in cists of stones, and they are usually accompanied by such deposits of arms, implements, and ornaments, as have been described in the previous Lecture. This form of burial, which is found in the area of the Norwegian colonisation of the north of Scotland, is not completely comparable to the common form in Norway. But it presents as its characteristic feature the single point in which Norwegian burials of that period differ from all others. Nowhere else in Europe are urns of steatite the characteristic feature of any class of burials. In this respect, therefore, these northern interments in Scotland link themselves with interments of

[1] A few notices of these are appended to show the character of the burials :—At Hof, in the district of Hedenmarken, round the church are several grave-mounds. In some of these there were found, in 1842, four axe-heads, three spear-heads, fragments of two double-edged swords, a pair of stirrups, two bridle-bits, ten arrow-points, a fire-steel, fragments of a shield-boss, a ring, a kind of pincers, and other fragments, all of iron, along with two vessels of steatite, the one having an iron handle, and the other containing burnt bones and oxidised iron fragments.—*Nicolaysen's Norske Fornlevninger*, p. 59. In a circular grave-mound at Gaarden, Ostre Alm, Hedenmark, there was found an urn or vessel of steatite with remains of its iron handle, a two-edged sword contorted and broken into three pieces, a bent spear-head of iron, an iron axe-head, two shield-bosses of iron, a bridle-bit, a pair of stirrups, a strap-buckle and two iron tags, a portion of a comb of bone, pretty long, and toothed only on one side, made of small pieces of bone held between two slips of bone riveted together, two hemispherical tablemen of bone, and a small figure in bone of an animal resembling a dog. In the urn lay ashes.—*Foreningen for Norske Fortidsmindesmærkers Bevaring*, 1866, p. 88. At Nordby Sagbrug, Akershus, there were found in a small low grave-mound, the pieces of a bowl-shaped urn of steatite, 7 inches diameter, in which were ashes and burnt bones, and along with it a two-edged sword of iron, the blade 30¼ inches long, a spear-head, an axe-blade, and other iron relics.—*Foren. for Norske Fortids. Bev.*, 1867, p. 49. At Elset, in Solum parish, province of Bratsberg, there was found a bowl-shaped urn of steatite of the kind so commonly occurring in graves of the later Iron Age. It had an iron hank round the rim and an iron bow-handle, and was full of burnt bones.—*Foren. for Norske Fortids. Bev.*, 1868, p. 115.

the Viking time in Norway. But they are so far differentiated from the common Norwegian type as to constitute a
distinct variety of that type peculiar to the area proper of the
Norwegian colony which founded the earldom of Orkney in
the time of the Scandinavian Paganism.

I now pass to the description of another series of objects,
having no distinct connection with interments, but possessing
associations and characteristics which also link them with the
intrusion of the Norwegian element into the northern districts
of Scotland.

In the month of March 1858 a boy, chasing a rabbit into
a hole in the links of Skaill, in the parish of Sandwick,
Orkney, found a few fragments of silver which had been
unearthed by the rabbits at the mouth of their burrow. The
news of this discovery soon spread in the neighbourhood, and
a number of people having joined in the search, a large
quantity of silver articles were found in the sand. Mr.
George Petrie of Kirkwall (a zealous corresponding member
of the Society of Antiquaries of Scotland) was speedily upon
the spot, and fortunately succeeded in securing the bulk of
the articles, which had become dispersed in various hands,
and they finally found their way through the Exchequer to
the National Museum. The aggregate weight of silver thus
recovered amounted to 16 lbs. avoirdupois.

The hoard, which had apparently been deposited in one
spot, consisted of three classes of objects—personal ornaments,
ingots of silver, and coins. The personal ornaments formed
the bulk of the deposit. They were of three varieties—
brooches, neck rings, and arm rings, all of silver.

The brooches are of great size, and unusually heavy and
massive in their construction. The metal is brittle, and most
of them are more or less broken. The largest of those that
are entire (Fig. 59) consists of a plain penannular ring, formed

of a solid cylindrical rod of silver, ¼ inch thick, the ring forming an incomplete circle 6¼ inches diameter, and terminating in bulbous knobs, which are furnished with expansions giving them a strong resemblance to thistle heads. These knobs are each 1¼ inches in diameter. They have been cast hollow, with a short cylindrical collar at either side, through which the ends of the ring of the brooch pass, to be riveted at their terminations. A similar knob with similar collars at either side fits loosely on the ring of the brooch. Its upper part terminates in the conventional thistle head, and its lower part is prolonged into a stout pin of great length. This pin, which is fitted by a socket at its upper end upon a projection of the bulbous head, is, like the ring of the brooch, a solid rod of

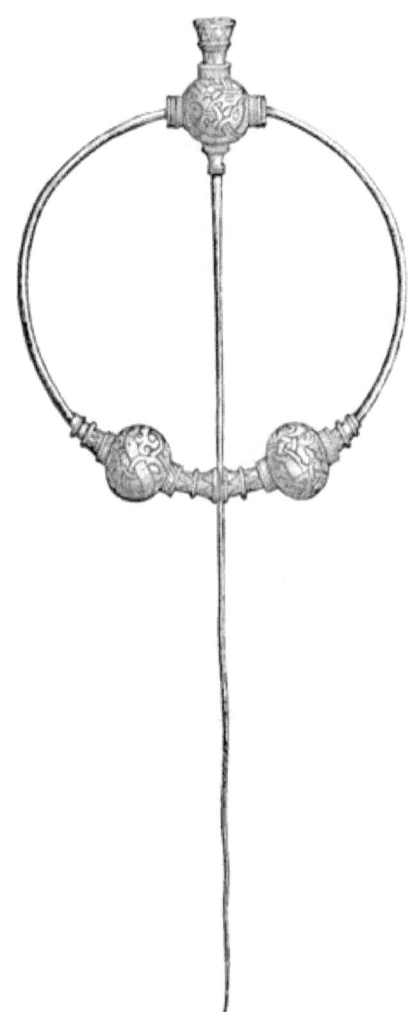

Fig. 59.—Silver Brooch found at Skaill (15 inches long).

hammered silver, cylindrical in the upper part, passing into a squarish section in the middle of its length, and tapering gradually to a bluntish point. The total length of the pin from head to point is 15 inches. The only parts of the brooch that are ornamented are the knobs and their collars, and the terminal expansions which give their suggestive resemblance to thistle heads. The spherical surfaces of the knobs are plain on one hemisphere, and the other is decorated with engraved designs of zoomorphic character (Figs. 71-73), to which I shall direct attention at a subsequent stage, for the purpose of determining the typical relationship of the style of ornament. The collars are decorated by a series of bands of engraved parallel lines, passing obliquely across the spaces they fill. The terminal expansions are decorated with triangular spaces, filled with parallel lines, and alternating with spaces that are plain.

Another brooch, the pin of which is gone, is a similar ring of hammered silver, ¼ inch thick, and 6¾ inches diameter, with bulbous knobs, which are plain, though the collars and terminal expansions are ornamented with a T-like fret, and with bands of triangles filled with parallel lines.

Among the other brooches there are three which present a different variety in the ornamentation of their bulbous extremities. The largest of these is formed of a solid cylindrical bar of silver, ⅜ of an inch in thickness, bent into an incomplete circle 8 inches in diameter, and terminating in bulbous expansions 1½ inches in diameter. The pin of this brooch is gone, but if it bore the same proportion to the diameter of the ring as is exhibited by that of the brooch first described, it could not have been much under 20 inches in length. The bulbous knobs of this brooch are differently ornamented on their opposite hemispheres. The surface of the one hemisphere is covered with a peculiar prickly ornamentation, which intensifies their suggestive resemblance to thistle heads. These prickles have been cut out of the solid. They are square at the base, cylindrical, and slightly tapering at the points. They stand somewhat over an eighth of an inch in height, and each has been separately finished in the upper part by a hollow drill. The opposite hemispheres of the bulbs are ornamented by engraved circular patterns of interlaced work (Fig. 68), and the collar of the expanded part is also ornamented with a running pattern of interlaced work (Fig. 70.)

The second of these three brooches (Fig. 60), is equally massive and handsome, though smaller. The ring is a solid cylindrical bar of silver, $\frac{3}{4}$ inch in thickness, bent into an incomplete oval $5\frac{1}{2}$ inches in diameter. The bulbous ends of the penannular ring are decorated on the one hemisphere with the prickly ornament which has just been described, and on the other hemisphere by a T-shaped fret, enclosed in a circle placed in a lozenge-shaped space, bordered by incised lines, as shown in the woodcut under the figure of the brooch.

The third of these brooches consists of a penannular ring, formed of a solid cylindrical rod of silver $\frac{1}{4}$ inch thick, and $6\frac{1}{2}$ inches diameter. It wants the pin, but the head, which is still on the ring, is furnished with a

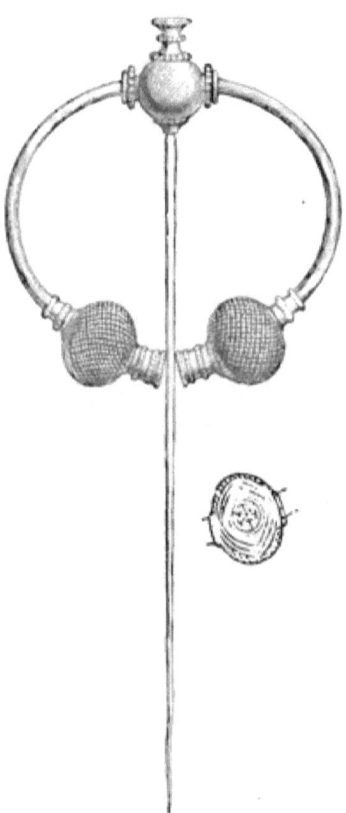

Fig. 60.—Silver Brooch found at Skaill (5¼ inches diameter).

tapering projection, which fitted into a socket in the upper end
of the pin. The bulbous extremities are not ornamented on
one hemisphere with the prickly ornament, but have the one ·
hemisphere plain and the other decorated with patterns of
zoomorphic character (Figs. 75 and 76), while the bulbous
head of the pin, which still remains on the ring of the brooch,
has the remarkable anthropomorphic ornamentation shown in
Fig. 77, and on the circular top of the pin-head is seen the

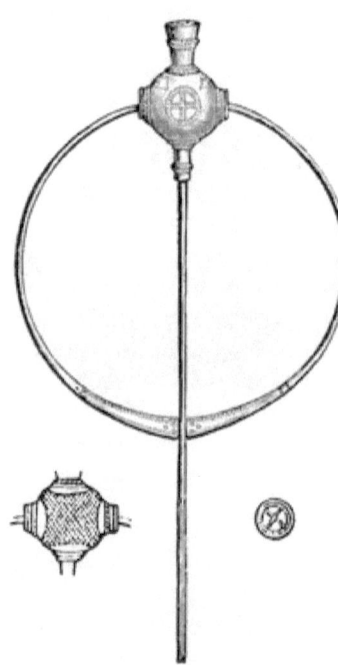

interlaced ornament shown
in Fig. 69.

Another brooch with bul-
bous extremities, which also
wants the pin, has its bulbs
plain. Along with these
bulbous ring-brooches there
are other three examples of
the same type which present
variations in the form of the
extremities of the pin and
the penannular ring.

The largest of these (Fig.
61) consists of a solid cylindrical rod of silver, ¼ inch
in thickness, bent into an
incomplete circle 5 inches in
diameter. The pin, which
wants the point, has a bulbous head of the same cha-
racter as those previously

Fig. 61.—Silver Brooch found at Skaill
(5 inches diameter).

described, but the prickly ornamentation is merely indicated
by incised lines crossing each other diagonally. The other
hemisphere of the bulbous head of the pin is decorated with
a circle enclosing an equal-armed rectangular cross. The
top of the pin presents a similar ornament, which might be

described as a St. Andrew's Cross; but there is nothing in the character of either of these figures which might not be present in a purely geometric ornament, and they need not therefore be supposed to possess a symbolic significance. The ends of the penannular ring of the brooch, instead of being furnished with bulbs, are slightly flattened and expanded, and their ornamentation consists of a simple dotted margin, with a triplet of larger dots placed in triangular form at the extremities of the expansions of the ring.

Other two brooches of this form are smaller, and their pins have no bulbous heads, but are simply looped on to the ring of the brooch. The smaller of the two is perfectly plain; the larger has the expanded ends of the ring ornamented with zoomorphic interlaced work, slightly engraved in the silver with a very fine point.

It is thus evident that the special peculiarity of these brooches is their excessive size, their massiveness and solidity of construction, the bulbous form of their terminal expansions, and their prickly and engraved ornamentation.

We pass now to the examination of the neck and arm rings found with them. The commonest form of the neck rings is a circlet of about 5 inches diameter, composed of a series of thicker and finer strands, twisted spirally together, and passing at the ends into flattened expansions, terminating in hooks. One, 5¼ inches diameter (Fig. 62), is composed of two thick strands, spirally intertwisted with two sets of finer wires, each set consisting of a plait of two very thin wires, bordered by a single fine wire on each side. These lie in the hollows of the twists between the thicker strands, and add greatly to the beauty of the necklet. The ends of all the strands are united together, forming terminal flattened expansions, which are provided with recurving hooks to fasten the ring when worn. There are ten examples of this type, differing only in the arrangements of thicker strands, with twisted wires of various degrees of fineness.

Another variety, an example of which is shown in Fig. 63, is formed of seven hammered rods of equal thickness, closely

Fig. 62.—Neck Ring of Silver found at Skaill (5¼ inches diameter).

interplaited like the thong of a whip. The central portion of the ring is a solid knob, oval in shape, from which the strands decrease in thickness towards the extremities, where they are soldered together and drawn out into a cylindrical tapering rod, which is coiled into a spiral termination, and the two ends recurved so as to hook into each other when the ring was worn.

Another of these interplaited rings (Fig. 64) is formed of three plaits of two strands each, spirally twisted together,

Fig. 63.—Neck Ring of Silver found at Skaill.

and intertwisted with double strands of very small wires, also plaited together, which lie in the interstices of the larger plaits. The thicker wires taper slightly towards the extremities, where they are soldered into solid flattened ends, one of which terminates in a hook, while the other is furnished with an eye to fasten the ring when worn. The flattened ends are

ornamented with punched triangular depressions, having a
raised dot in the centre.

There are two of the arm rings which are of the same

Fig. 64.—Neck Ring found at Skaill (5¼ inches diameter).

construction as the neck rings.   Both are closed rings, though
both are treated with respect to their ornament as if they
were penannular.   One is formed of a series of thick strands
and finer wires, spirally intertwisted.   The other (Fig. 65) is
of more elegant design.   It is 3¼ inches in its inner diameter,
and is formed of four sets of two strands of wire, each set
being separately twisted, and the four double twists intertwisted spirally.   The strands decrease in thickness from the
middle of the armlet towards the ends, where they are soldered
to a bar, formed into the semblance of two animal's heads,
grasping in their mouths the part which forms the junction
between the penannular ends of the ring.

Besides these neck rings and armlets formed of inter-twisted rods and wires, there were in the hoard twenty-five solid penannular rings of silver, bent to an elongated oval,

Fig. 65.—Armlet of Silver found at Skaill (3¼ inches diameter).

and tapering slightly towards the extremities. They vary in size from 2½ to 3¼ inches in the long diameter, and are thus of a size sufficient to enclose the wrist. They are either

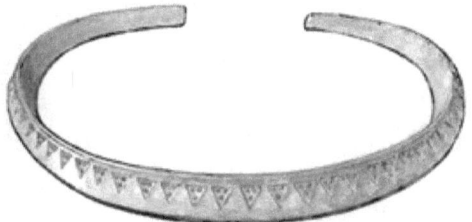

Fig. 66.—Armlet of Silver found at Skaill (3¼ inches diameter).

quadrangular or circular in section, and, except in one instance, they bear no ornament whatever. The solitary exception (Fig. 66) is ornamented by a series of triangular markings impressed by a punch, having three dots in the field. Another armlet of a different form (Fig. 67) is a flat

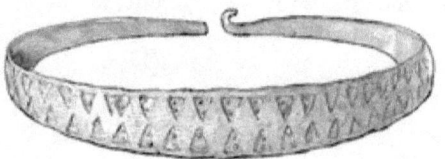

Fig. 67.—Flat Arm Band found at Skaill (2¾ inches diameter).

thin band of silver, wider in the middle than towards the ends, and terminating in a hook at one extremity, the other being broken. This example is the only one of its kind in the hoard. It is also ornamented with a double row of impressed triangles, having two dots in the field.

With these personal ornaments of various kinds, which constituted the bulk of the hoard, there was a small quantity of bullion, and a few coins.

The bullion consisted of a number of ingots of silver, some entire, others cut, and a quantity of fragments of brooches and arm-rings chopped up into small pieces, as if with an axe or chisel. The largest ingot is 3¼ inches in length, and weighs 1089 grains.

The coins were few—at least few were recovered—although from their small size and thinness they were more liable to be overlooked in the hasty and promiscuous grubbing of many treasure-seekers. One is a St. Peter's penny struck at York, of tenth century date. Another is a penny of King Æthelstan (A.D. 925), struck at Leicester. All the others are Asiatic, of the time when the seat of the Mohammedan Caliphate was at Cufa or Bagdad. Three of these Cufic coins belong to the Abbaside Caliphs, and seven to the Samanian dynasty. They range in their dates between A.D. 887 and 945, and the places of mintage, still legible, are Al-shash, Bagdad, and Samarcand.

Let us now group the characteristics of this deposit. It is a hoard buried in the earth, but with no indication of its having been in any way connected with the rites of sepulture. It is a large hoard, altogether amounting to 16 lbs. in weight. It is entirely of silver, and consists of personal ornaments, ingots, and coins. The ornaments are brooches, neck rings, and arm rings. The brooches are of penannular form, but differ · in their character from those we have learned to recognise as distinctively Celtic. The neck rings and arm rings present no features of a specially Celtic character. The coins are Cufic and Anglo-Saxon, dated mostly in the end of the ninth and the first half of the tenth centuries.

No similar hoard has been discovered in any other part of Scotland. But in its general composition the Skaill hoard resembles a considerable number of other hoards of similar articles which have been found in other countries. They are most abundant in the eastern parts of Sweden, less common in Norway, and of occasional occurrence in Denmark. In none of these countries has there been found a hoard consisting of such a large number of personal ornaments as that found at Skaill, but the forms and the character of the ornaments found in these hoards of silver, associated with mintages of the ninth and tenth centuries, are always the same. The specialty of these hoards so found in Scandinavia is that they are largely composed of Cufic and Anglo-Saxon coins.[1] The personal ornaments associated with them consist for the most part of large rings for the neck, formed of intertwisted rods and wires; arm rings of similar character, or of solid bars, circular or quadrangular in section, bent into a penannular oval, and ornamented with the peculiar triangular patterns impressed by a punch, with dots in the field. The brooches, with long pins and bulbous ends like thistle

---

[1] Upwards of 20,000 Cufic and 15,000 Anglo-Saxon coins have been enumerated from hoards of this period in Sweden alone.

heads, are less common, but occur occasionally in such hoards in all the three Scandinavian countries. In many of the hoards there are also ingots, and dismembered ornaments cut and hammered into lumps of mere bullion. "This fact," says Hildebrand, "shows that they had no value with the people who possessed them, except the intrinsic value of the metal." Weighing scales and weights are sometimes also found with them, and close examination reveals the fact that the ornaments and portions of ornaments have been often tested with a cutting instrument to try their purity. This again reveals the trafficker rather than the plundering Viking, who carries off his spoil without any such careful examination; and, according to this view, Mr. Hildebrand concludes that the silver ornaments and the Cufic coins must be considered as equally foreign to Scandinavia. "There can be no doubt," he says, "that these ornaments, ingots, and lumps of silver were brought with the coins from Asia, where silver is more easily obtained than in the northern parts of Europe." With reference to this conclusion it may be remarked that while the derivation of the Cufic coins needs no demonstration, and while it may be admitted that other products of the Arab civilisation of the time were brought by the same stream of commerce through Russia to the Scandinavian countries, and thence to Scotland, England, and Ireland, it still remains to be shown that these silver ornaments are Oriental in their origin. This can only be demonstrated by showing that they are allied by their forms and ornament to the Oriental types of that period; or, if this cannot be done, it must at least be shown that they differ so widely in form and ornament from the types of the western lands in which they are found as to forbid the supposition that they may be of western origin.

We have no knowledge of the types of personal ornaments in use in Asia at the time indicated by the dates of mintage of these Cufic coins. It is impossible, therefore, to

establish the Oriental origin of these silver ornaments by
demonstrating their identity of type with Oriental ornaments
of that period. The question which remains for discussion,
therefore, is, whether their forms and ornament present such
relations to the forms and the ornament of any of the western
countries in which they are found, as will correlate them with
known types of native origin.

In 1840 a large hoard of silver ornaments, weighing
upwards of a thousand ounces, along with a quantity of silver
coins, from six to seven thousand in number, was discovered
concealed in a leaden chest, and buried in the soil at Cuerdale,
near Preston, in Lancashire. The coins consisted chiefly of
Anglo-Saxon pennies, with a few of French and some Cufic
mints, and the inference from the data they afford is that the
deposit was probably made at some time subsequent to the
commencement of the tenth century. The personal ornaments in the hoard consisted chiefly of rings of various sizes
and of similar character to those that have been described
as occurring in the deposit at Skaill. Some of the larger
rings were composed of interplaited rods and twisted wires
like those from Skaill, and the solid rings were also ornamented with patterns produced by impressions of a triangular
punch, with dots in the field. There were also some fragments of the peculiarly-shaped brooches, with bulbous knobs
and prickly ornamentation. One object in the hoard was
distinctively Scandinavian—a small Thor's hammer of silver,
such as were commonly worn as amulets in the heathen time.
Among the fragments described at the time as incapable of
being determined, there are four which may now be said
with certainty to be portions of penannular brooches of the
distinctively Celtic form. This Celtic relationship was not
perceived by Mr. Hawkins (who described them), except in
one instance, which he recognises as "so much resembling
the patterns on early crosses and architectural remains, that

it is difficult to assign to it any other than a Northern origin."
But his general conclusion is that " it is scarcely consistent
with sound reasoning upon all the facts of the case to assign
any but an Oriental origin to these objects." In this he is
supported by Mr. Worsaae, who says that as these silver
ornaments are not found in the west of Europe except in
association with Cufic coins, and do not occur at all in the
interior or southern parts of Europe, he regards it as without
doubt that Mr. Hawkins has been perfectly right in giving an
Oriental origin to at least a great part of the silver ornaments
found at Cuerdale.

Setting aside these conclusions, in so far as they are
merely conjectural, it appears established that the area over
which these deposits of silver ornaments are found is limited
to the three Scandinavian countries and the British Isles. It
is certain that among the ornaments so found some are
distinctively Scandinavian, and others distinctively Celtic,
while the remainder, which constitutes the bulk of the
deposits, is of unknown derivation, but has been conjecturally
assigned to an Oriental origin, on account of its association
with the Cufic coins. I therefore proceed to the examination
of these objects which are of undetermined origin, with the
view of ascertaining the special characteristics and relations
of their form and ornament.

I have already remarked that the form of these bulbous
brooches is that which is distinctive of the Celtic brooch—
penannular, with expanded ends. Its special peculiarities
are exaggerations of the specialties of form by which the
Celtic type is distinguished from all others; and in this
respect the form assumed by these bulbous brooches, though
Celtic in type, is so strongly differentiated from the purely
Celtic form, that it may be regarded as a distinct variety. No
other form of brooch is so huge and massive, with such a
length of pin. The Celtic brooch-maker was so much more

of an artist than the mere silversmith that he flattened the ring of the brooch and broadened its terminal expansions in order to provide space for the elaborate surface decoration in which he delighted. The maker of these bulbous brooches, on the other hand, is so much more of the silversmith than of the artist that the bulk of his work is merely finished with the hammer—the ring and the pin are beaten into form, and the expansions made globular instead of flat. The form of these brooches, therefore, agrees with the Celtic form in its main features, its penannular character, and its length of pin, loosely looped on the ring of the brooch.

But if the form of these brooches be thus closely allied to the Celtic form, their ornament is no less closely allied to the Celtic system of ornamentation. The peculiar prickliness of the bulbs, which is the most marked feature of their character, is not distinctively Celtic, but a suggestion of it is occasionally found on Celtic silver-work, as, for instance, on the almost globular head of a Celtic brooch in the National Museum, and on a gold brooch found near Coleraine.[1] But the reverse hemispheres of the bulbous terminations of the Skaill brooches, which present this prickly ornamentation on the obverse, are also decorated with engraved designs. These are of two varieties, simple interlaced ribbon patterns and zoomorphic patterns. The character of the interlaced work so closely resembles the Celtic style that it may be said to be more Celtic than Scandinavian. The character of the zoomorphic work, on the other hand, is more Scandinavian than Celtic, and is suggestive of the style and treatment of the designs on the Manx crosses, while it more closely resembles some of the more characteristic designs of the purely Scandinavian metal-work of the heathen time.

The interlaced work is present on the reverse hemispheres of the bulbs of one of the largest of the prickly brooches, in the

[1] The gold brooch is figured in the *Ulster Journal*, vol. iv. p. 1.

form of a circular pattern (Fig. 68) which is common in Celtic work, and may be seen on several of the sculptured monuments of the east coast of Scotland. Another circular pattern of interlaced work (Fig. 69), differing in its construction, but

Fig. 68.—Circular pattern on reverse of the bulbs of the brooch described p. 80 (actual size).

Fig. 69.—Circular pattern on the head of the pin of brooch, described pp. 81-82 (actual size).

possessing the Celtic peculiarity of the divided bands, is found on the head of the pin of another brooch. The collars of the first-mentioned example are also surrounded by bands of interlaced work in a running pattern (Fig. 70), which is common on Celtic stone and metal work.

Fig. 70.—Pattern on the reverse of the bulbs of the brooch described p. 80 (actual size).

The zoomorphic patterns consist mostly of animal forms, which are treated in a freer manner than is usual in Celtic work. One of these occupying the reverse of a single bulb with prickly ornament, is shown in Fig. 74. The irregularity of the design, its want of balance and symmetry, and the tendency of the interlacements of the intertwisted members to break off in scroll-like terminations, are all features which are usually present in Scandinavian work, and as usually absent in the work of the pure Celtic school. The body of the beast, seen sideways, is outlined with a double line, as is usual in the Celtic style. Its head is thrown back, its mouth open and tongue protruding; a single tooth appears in each

Fig. 71.—Zoomorphic pattern on bulb of the brooch in the Skaill hoard, shown as Fig. 59.

jaw. Its feet are furnished with two toes, and its tail and crest, convoluted with the body and limbs, terminate in irregular scrolls. The patterns on the bulbous terminations of another brooch (Figs. 71, 72, 73), have a curious resem-

Fig. 72.—Ornament on bulb of brooch, shown as Fig. 59 (actual size).

blance to this one, while presenting points of difference. It is the same beast, almost in the same attitude, but differing in the treatment of the details in both representations. In Fig. 72 the body of the beast is covered with scale-like markings, and the same tendency of the convolutions of the crest to break off in scroll-like terminations is visible in both. The figure

on the bulbous head of the pin of this brooch (Fig. 73) differs
from those on the bulbous terminations of its ring in being

Fig. 73. — On the pinhead of
brooch, shown as Fig. 59
(actual size).

Fig. 74.—On a single bulb of a brooch
in the Skaill hoard (actual size).

more bird-like than beast-like, and its convolutions more
broken into indefinite scrolls and whirls. It is noticeable,
however, that the crest, the eye, and the two-toed foot of this
bird-like figure are the same as those of the beast which
appears in the patterns previously described, and re-appears in
conjunction with a more remarkable figure on another brooch
(described pp. 81-82) in the Skaill deposit. The figures on its
bulbous terminations (Figs. 75, 76) are finely engraved. They

Fig. 75.—On one of the bulbs
(actual size).

Fig. 76.—On one of the bulbs
(actual size).

represent the same beast which is figured on the others, with
but slight variations of detail, but the bulbous head of the pin

shows quite a remarkable deviation from the general form of these representations. Instead of the conventional beast, we see here (Fig. 77) a quasi-human figure worked up into a pattern of interlacements. The treatment of this anthropomorphic form is peculiar. It presents a bearded face, which is curiously elongated and triangular in outline; the nose is represented by a curved line, and the eyes are connected by double lines

Fig. 77.—On the bulbous head of the pin (actual size).

across the upper part of the nose. The hands are bound with interlacements, and the body is treated as the bodies of the beasts commonly used for zoomorphic patterns. This bearded, broad-nosed, goggle-eyed figure has no Celtic relations, but we meet with the same typical face in Scandinavia, occasionally placed in association with zoomorphic patterns, which are almost identical with those of the Skaill brooches in motive and style.

For instance, the motive and the style of the decoration of an

Fig. 78.—Axe-head inlaid with silver, from the Mammen How, Denmark.

iron axe-head (Fig. 78), inlaid with silver, which was found in a grave-mound of the heathen time called the Mammen How, near Viborg, in Denmark,[1] are almost identical with those of the engraved designs on the Skaill brooches. There is the same scale-covered beast, in the same attitude, rendered with the same conventionality of treatment, and the convolutions of the tail and crest which interlace with the limbs and body of the creature exhibit the same tendency to break off in scrolls. In the upper part of the axe we have the same triangular, broad-nosed, goggle-eyed face which also appears on one of the brooches from Skaill. The same face appears on the pendants representing Thor's Hammer, which are occasionally found in hoards of personal ornaments of the heathen period in Scandinavia. They are usually of silver, sometimes parcel-gilt, and decorated with

[1] In this remarkable sepulture the body was found in a pit 6 feet beneath the natural surface, under the centre of the mound, laid in a chest constructed of oaken planks, axe-dressed, and fastened together with large round-headed iron nails. The chest had somewhat of the form of a closed bedstead, for it was supported by six posts driven into the soil at the bottom of the pit. On the bottom planks of this rough bedstead the skeleton lay extended on cushions filled with feathers, with the head to the north-east. It had been clothed in garments worked with gold thread, of excessive richness and beauty. The fragments preserved include portions of a girdle of silk, ornamented with fretwork and gold tissue; a mantle of woollen cloth, with a band of foliageous scroll-work interwoven with figures of human heads and hands, and further ornamented with figures of animals, and patterns worked in gold thread; and portions of cuffs or bracelets, also of silk, ornamented with gold thread. In the interior of the chest or bedstead, along with the skeleton, there were found the fragments of a sword and scabbard, with its mountings, inlaid with silver, and two axes, of which the one was plain, the other inlaid with zoomorphic patterns in silver, as shown in Fig. 78. On the lid of the chest there stood at the one end a cauldron of thin brass, two buckets, constructed of oaken staves hooped with iron, and at the other end lay a wax candle, 22 inches in length, which had burned for some time, probably during the funeral ceremonies.—La sepulture de Mammen, par J. J. A. Worsaae, in the *Memoires de la Societe Royale des Antiquaires du Nord:* Copenhagen, 1870.

filigree work. One of these (Fig. 79), found in Skane,
Sweden, bearing the typical
face with the goggle-eyes and
the bar between them, is here
figured of the actual size.[1]
The same face occasionally
occurs on Runic monuments
of the heathen time. It is
seen on a stone 5 feet high
by 3 feet broad, and from 2 to
16 inches thick, at Skjern, in
North Jutland (Fig. 80), which
is here reproduced from the
engraving given by Professor
Stephens, who thus describes

Fig. 79.—Thor's Hammer in silver,
from Skane, Sweden (actual size).

the figure :—" In the centre is the head of Thor, wild and
bearded. There is no manner of doubt that he is here introduced and invoked to bless and protect the deceased and his
tumulus, grave-stone, and funeral-marks." That the face is
really intended for that of Thor appears to be demonstrated
by its occurrence upon the small amulets representing Thor's
Hammer in silver, and by such monumental sculptures as
that on a stone at Aby, in Sodermanland, Sweden (Fig. 81),
where a similar face, though less conventional in treatment,
occurs in association with a sculptured representation of a
Thor's Hammer. But it is quite immaterial to our present
purpose to determine whether this peculiar type of face is
more of a mythological conception than a conventionality of
art. The point which concerns our inquiry is that we have
localised the typical form definitely within the Scandinavian
area, and demonstrated its association with the art of the monuments and the metal work of the Scandinavian heathen time.

[1] This and the two following figures are copied from Professor Stephen's
Thunor the Thunderer: Copenhagen, 1879, folio.

The general result of this examination of the typical form and ornamentation of these bulbous brooches is that they are found to possess features that are Celtic, in combination with features that are distinctive of the art of the Scandinavian

Fig. 80.—Runic Monument at Skjern, North Jutland, with Thor's face
(5 feet high).

heathen time. The obvious inference is that the birthplace of the type is to be looked for in an area in which the population were partly Celtic and partly Scandinavian in their extraction. At the period indicated by the range in date of these silver hoards,[1] and for a considerable time previous to the earliest date assigned to them, this was the character of the mixed race of the Gall-gael of the Western Isles, and it was also to a certain extent the character of the inhabitants of the northern isles of Orkney and Shetland, though there the Celtic element was feeble and the northern element strong. But this is precisely the nature of the mixed art of these brooches. It is more northern than Celtic, and seeing that the deposit is found in the very area where

Fig. 81.—Runic Monument at Aby, with representation of Thor's Head and Hammer.

this was the special character of the population, the conclusion seems irresistible that the type is the product of the area in which it is found. There is no evidence whatever of its having come from the east—no evidence of its having come from Scandinavia itself. The only other example of the type that has occurred in Scotland—the plain bulbous brooch of silvered bronze—which was found with a heathen burial in the island of Eigg (Fig. 43), also occurs within the area of the mixed population. A few specimens have occurred sporadically in England,[2] but there they are confined to the north-western area—that is, the portion adjacent to the

---

[1] The approximate dates of the hoards are indicated by the coins found with them.

[2] Besides the fragments that occurred in the Cuerdale hoard, two entire brooches of this type have been found in England—one near Kirby Lonsdale, in Westmoreland, 5½ inches diameter; and one near Penrith, in Cumberland, which is the largest on record, the ring being 8½ inches in diameter, the pin 21 inches long, and the weight of the whole brooch 25 ounces avoirdupois.

insular territories possessed by the Norse colonists of the
Western Isles. A few specimens have been found in Ireland,
chiefly isolated, but in one remarkable instance associated
with brooches and other metal work of pure Celtic types.[1]
In Scandinavia itself they do not occur in such abundance as
to suggest that they were common ornaments characteristic
of the people or the time. While, therefore, they are partially
Scandinavian in the character of their art, they occur so
sparsely in the Scandinavian countries that they cannot be
considered as products that are characteristic of that area, or
indigenous to it, and their presence in such limited numbers
in the archæological deposits of Norway, Sweden, and Denmark, is not inconsistent with the conclusion that the type
may have had its birthplace in the Scandinavian colonies
planted in Celtic soil, between whom and the fatherland
there was always such a closely-knit connection and continuous intercourse.

In passing finally from the examination of these brooches,
it may be desirable to refer briefly to the materials composing
the dress in which such gigantic ornaments were worn. The
perishable nature of these materials precludes the possibility
of obtaining such specimens of them as would suffice to show
the form and appearance of the garments themselves. But
there are occasional instances in which the natural circumstances of the deposit have been more than usually favour-
able to their preservation, and there may be cases in which
exceptional carefulness in the examination of these circumstances may preserve not only the texture but even the form

---

[1] One of these brooches occurred in the remarkable hoard of silver objects
found in the Rath of Reerasta, Ardagh, in Limerick, in 1868. The hoard
consisted of a silver chalice of exquisite beauty, one other vessel of bronze,
three brooches of pure Celtic type, decorated like the chalice with interlaced
designs in panels, in the best style of the art, and a fourth brooch of the
bulbous or " thistle-headed " form.—*Transactions of the Royal Irish Academy*,
vol. xxiv. p. 433.

and appearance of the garment. I have already alluded to
the fact that small portions of the dress from a grave of the

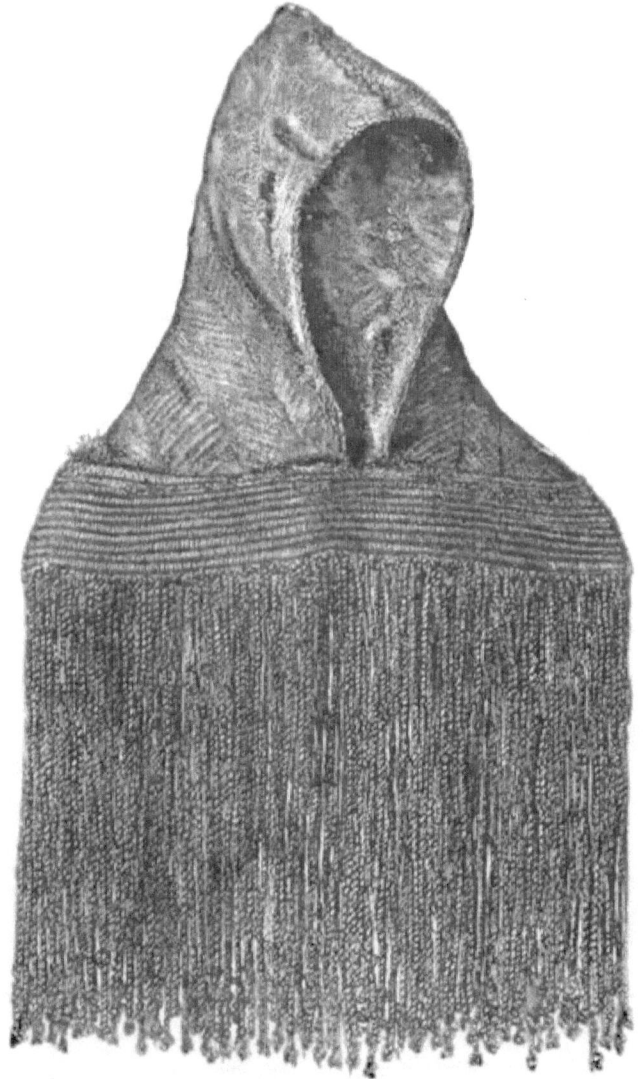

Fig. 82.—Hood found in a Moss in St. Andrew's Parish, Orkney.
(27 inches in length.)

Viking time in the island of Eigg exhibit distinctly the

texture of the woollen fabric, and retain portions of its mountings of fur. Similar discoveries in Denmark and Norway have established the truth of the Saga narratives, which testify to the excessive richness of the ornamentation, and the costly nature of the materials of the dress of this period.

The fact that a few examples from Scottish graves have shown the possibility of obtaining even from these perishable materials the tangible evidence of the form and fashion of the garments that clothed the men and women who made and wore these ornaments, gives room for hope that with increasing interest and greater care the products of future investigations may complete this evidence. In the meantime we have but one piece of dress which retains its form, and which may with some degree of probability be attributed to the mixed population of the Scandinavian colony. It is a hood of a coarse woollen fabric (Fig. 82), woven with a peculiarly twilled texture, and decorated with a long fringe of pendent and knotted cords, formed by twisting the doubled end of a thread with two contiguous threads of the warp. It was dug up in a peat moss in the parish of St. Andrews, in the mainland of Orkney, many years ago, and came into the possession of the late Mr. George Petrie of Kirkwall, after whose death it was acquired for the National Museum, along with his general collection. It measures 32 inches in height and 17 inches in greatest width. The border to which the fringe is attached is 3 inches in width. The fringe itself is 15 inches in depth. The fabric of which the body of the hood is composed is worked in alternate stripes, presenting at their junction the appearance shown in the woodcut (Fig. 83). The fringe of two-ply cords (Fig. 84), which is its most peculiar feature, presents a striking similarity to the fringe (Fig. 85) of a portion of the dress of a woman whose body was discovered in 1835 in digging peats in the Moss of

Haraldskjaer, in Jutland. The body, which was stretched on its back, was pegged down in the moss by hooked branches

of trees driven into the peat so as to fasten down the legs and arms at the knees and elbows, and further secured by other branches placed across the breast and abdomen, and staked down at the ends. The dress was well preserved when first discovered, but only a few fragments were saved, and among them is a portion

Fig. 83.—Portion of the Fabric of the Hood.

with a fringe of two-ply cords (Fig. 85), bearing a suggestive similarity to the fringe of the Orkney hood. This similarity,

Fig. 84.—Part of the Border and Fringe of the Hood.

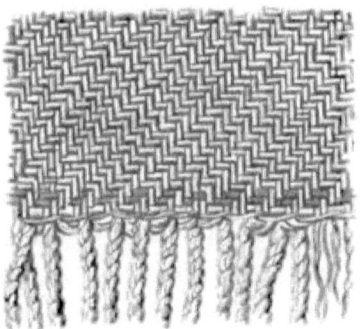

Fig. 85.—Woollen Fabric from the Moss of Haraldskjaer, Jutland.

so far as it has any value as an indication of relationship, links the Orkney specimen with the Scandinavian, and thus gives apparent ground for the inference that the hood may belong to the period of the Scandinavian colonisation of the islands, and that, like the brooches, it may represent a typical variety of head-dress peculiar to the colony.

The typical form of neck ring and arm ring (Figs. 64, 65),

Fig. 86.—Gold Rings found at Stenness (actual size).

which is associated with the bulbous brooches in these hoards, composed of hammered rods and intertwisted wires of silver plaited manifoldly, and formed into a circlet by soldering the ends, does not occur again in Scotland. But it has obvious relations with a group of personal ornaments in gold, which present similar features of form and construction. They are of smaller size than the silver rings, all that are known being obviously finger-rings.

Two of these (Fig. 86, Nos. 2 and 3) were dug up in the month of August 1879, in a field near the shore of the Loch of Stenness, in Orkney, and are now in the National Museum. The largest is formed of two double twists of gold wires, hammered round, and tapering to the small ends, which are connected by a lozenge-shaped bezel. The smaller of the two is composed of three strands of gold wire, similarly shaped by the hammer alone, and intertwisted, and the small ends soldered together. With them there were also found two plain flat hoops or circlets of gold, of about an inch in diameter, ¼ inch wide in the widest part, and tapering to the ends, which are unjoined (Fig. 86, No. 1).

There is also in the Museum a hoard of gold objects of this character, consisting of six finger-rings of plaited wires,

a plain solid ring formed of a tapering rod (Fig. 87), with
the ends unjoined, two portions of plaited rings cut off, and
two portions of plain solid rings similarly cut.   Two of the
plaited rings (one of which is shown in Fig. 87) are formed

Fig. 87.—Gold Rings found in the Hebrides (actual size).

of three wires each, intertwisted, and the ends soldered
together; the wires or rods are simply rounded by the
hammer and tapered to either end.   The other four rings are
slightly larger.   They are composed of eight wires, each
similarly fashioned by the hammer alone, and ingeniously
interplaited, so that two strands of the plait form a ridge
all round the convexity of the ring, the ends united and
worked flat to form a bezel.   Unfortunately we are unable to
localise this hoard more closely than that it was found somewhere in the Hebrides.

Another hoard of somewhat similar character was found
in June 1863, in the island of Bute, about 300 yards distant
from the old church of St. Blane, in Kingarth.   The hoard,
which was deposited beneath
a large stone, consisted of
two gold rings, three long,
narrow fillets of thin gold,    Fig. 88.—Ingot of Silver (actual size).
a small ingot of silver (Fig.
88), weighing 228 grains, and a number of silver coins,
of which twenty-one were pennies of David I. of Scotland, three of King Stephen, and one of King Henry

I. of England.   Of the two gold rings, one (Fig. 89, No. 1) is
a plain solid ring, formed of a rod rounded by the hammer,

Fig. 89.—Gold Rings found in Bute (actual size).

and tapered to both ends, and the ends unjoined.   The other,
shown in Fig. 89, No. 2, is composed of three similarly-
hammered rods or wires twisted together, and the ends joined
into a lozenge-shaped bezel.   The largest of the three fillets
found with them is (Fig. 90) 17 inches in length, and about

Fig. 90.—Terminal portions of two Gold Fillets found in Bute (actual size).

$\frac{3}{16}$ inch wide in the centre, tapering to both ends until it
expands into a small terminal loop.   The others are similar
in form.   They are scarcely thicker than stout writing-paper,
and the largest, though 17 inches in length, weighs only 55
grains.   Their ornamentation consists of zig-zag running
patterns, and beaded work in *repoussé*.

It is thus evident that this typical form of construction of
personal ornaments in the precious metals by interplaiting
and intertwisting slender rods of metal, rounded and tapered
by the hammer alone, and their ends soldered together, comes

down at least to the twelfth century, and appears in associations in which there is no suggestion of an Oriental origin. Its area, so far as our present knowledge enables us to define it, appears to be limited to the northern and western isles, no well-authenticated instance having been recorded from the mainland of Scotland. On the other hand, the area of the type extends eastwards into Scandinavia, but there the type itself is regarded as one which is not indigenous.

The type of penannular arm ring, which is of rounded or quadrangular section, with tapering or slightly flattened ends, of which so many examples were associated with the twisted rings and bulbous brooches in the Skaill hoard, has not occurred in any other metal than silver. Like the other types associated with them, they have not been found in Scotland beyond the area of the Scandinavian colonisation. Within that area, however, they appear not unfrequently. Wallace records the discovery of a hoard of nine in one of the mounds at Stennis, in Orkney. Another hoard, of which the precise number is not given, was found in 1774 at Caldale, near Kirkwall, with a horn containing 300 silver pennies of Canute the Great. In 1830 six or seven were found at Quendale, in Shetland, with a horn full of Anglo-Saxon coins of Ethelred, Ethelstan, Edwy, and Edgar.

In 1850 a hoard of at least six were found in the island of Skye, but in circumstances of which there is no record.

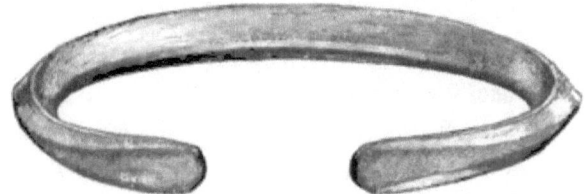

Fig. 91.—Penannular Arm-ring of Silver, one of a hoard of eight, found at Burn of Rattar, Caithness (3½ inches diameter).

In 1872 a hoard of eight were found in a cist of stones in or close to an ancient burying-ground near where the burn of

Rattar enters the Pentland Firth, in Caithness. One of these is shown in Fig. 91.

All these are similar in form to each other, and to the rings of the same type found in Scandinavia in association with the other types of silver ornaments previously described. They are more frequently plain than ornamented, and when ornamented their decoration consists simply of a series of impressions formed by a triangular punch, with one, two, or three dots in the field. This species of ornamentation is only found on these silver ornaments in Scotland, but in Scandinavia it is common to them and to the oval bowl-shaped brooches of brass which were the characteristic personal ornaments of the closing period of the Scandinavian Paganism.

It follows from this enumeration of the characteristics of form and ornament exhibited by the different varieties of these silver ornaments which have been deposited in hoards within the area of the Scandinavian colonisation of Scotland, that they possess a character which is distinctive and peculiar, being neither wholly Celtic nor wholly Scandinavian, but owing its individuality to an intermixture of characteristics derived from forms and systems of ornament which are peculiar to each of these racial areas.

The deposit of such hoards of ornaments and coin is a custom more characteristic of the Scandinavian than of the Celtic area. Deposits of this character may have been placed in the soil for simple concealment at any time, but they are much more frequent in this particular period than in any other, and there was a motive connected with the Pagan faith of the people which may have operated to increase their abundance. We learn from the Saga of Egil Skalagrimson that there was a belief among the Pagan Northmen that treasure thus buried during their lifetime would be available for use or display in the life to come.

But whatever may have been the manner or the motive

of their concealment, the fact, which is of special importance
for the purpose of the present investigation, is that they are
for the most part relics which, by their forms and the
characteristics of their art, are but feebly linked with the
forms and art of the Celtic area in which they are found, and
strongly linked by their art characteristics with the art of the
Scandinavian Paganism, which was contemporary with the
art of the Christian Celtic school. The soil in which they are
found is within that area of Scotland which was occupied by
a mixed population, composed of the two races whose special
art instincts are visible in the mixed art of the objects—the
dominant race, moreover, being that whose art is dominant in
their decoration.

The colonisation of the northern and western coasts of
Scotland by the heathen Northmen forms an episode in the
history of our country only second in importance to the
earlier colonisation of its southern districts by the Romans,
and far surpassing it in the interest of its historical annals.
Its archæological interest may be estimated by the number
and variety of the relics which have now been shown to
belong to the Viking period of the Northmen in Scotland—a
period of singular interest alike in connection with its history,
its archæology, and its art.

LECTURE III.

(October 24, 1882.)

THE CELTIC ART OF THE PAGAN PERIOD.

In this Lecture I shall deal with certain groups of relics which present in their forms and their decoration features which we have learned to recognise as distinctively Celtic.

About the year 1820 a singular object was found in a morass on the farm of Torrs, in the parish of Kelton, Kirkcudbrightshire. Having passed into the possession of Mr. Joseph Train, it was presented by him to Sir Walter Scott, and it still remains in the Museum at Abbotsford.[1] It is of the form of an elongated mask (Fig. 92), somewhat resembling the frontal of a horse. It measures 10½ inches in total length, but the tip is apparently imperfect. Its breadth in a straight line across the lower margin is 3⅝ inches, and about 8½ inches on the round outside. Its greatest breadth in a straight line across the back is 6 inches, and 11 inches on the round outside, immediately above the insertion of the

---

[1] This and many of the other objects referred to in this Lecture have been described in the *Proceedings* of the Society of Antiquaries of Scotland by Dr. John Alexander Smith, who has specially illustrated the interesting relics which I regard as belonging to the closing period of Scotland's Paganism. They have been referred by Mr. Franks and others to a special school of art which they have denominated the "Late Celtic," but from my point of view I must regard them as the work of the early Celtic school, which was the precursor and parent of the greater school of Celtic art of the Christian time which I have already described.

horns.   At a height of 3 inches above the lower straight
margin are placed two circular holes, one on each side, each
measuring 2 inches in diameter.   From between these eye-
like holes, and a little above the level of their centres, two

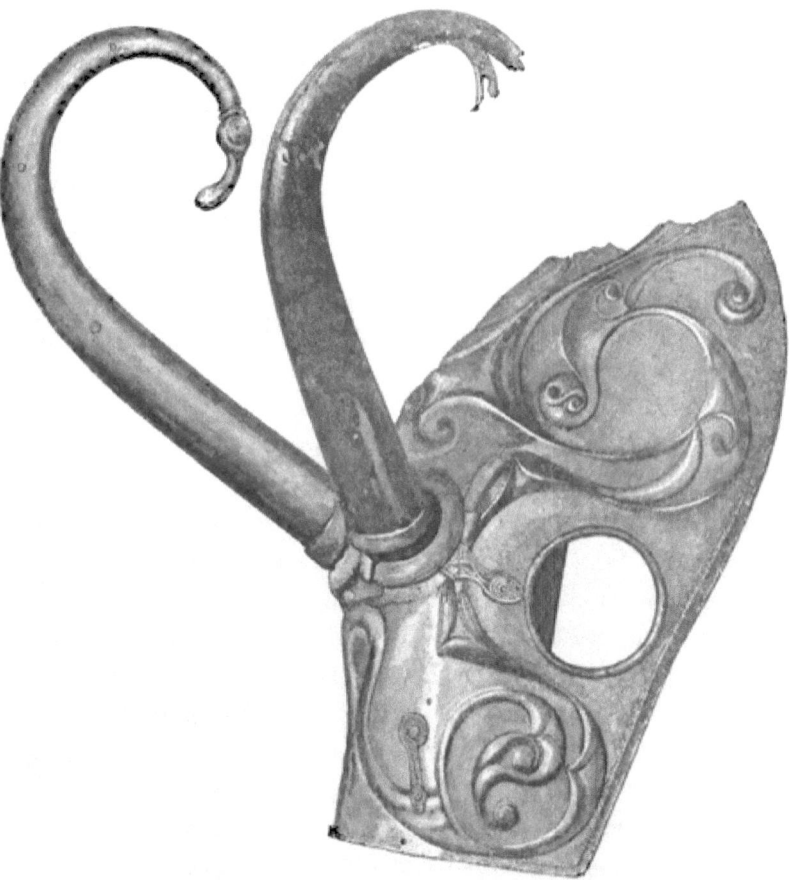

Fig. 92.—Bronze object found at Torrs, Kirkcudbrightshire (10½ inches in
length).

curiously curved, cylindrical, tapering horns spring close
together on either side of the median line.   The diameter of
each of the horns at the base is 1¾ inch, and they rise to a

I

height of 8¾ inches to the top of the curve, the whole length
of the perfect horns along the curve of the outer edge being
16½ inches. The horns are hollow, the whole object being
formed of thin beaten bronze.

Its ornamentation is as peculiar as its form. It consists
of a series of irregularly divergent spirals in *repoussé* work
repeated symmetrically but not identically on either side of
the median line of the front of the object. These spirals or
scroll-like figures are formed of curves which are long and
flattened, passing suddenly into curves of quicker motion,
and ending in volutes. These curves, though proceeding in
the same direction, do not proceed at parallel or regular
distances from each other, but converge and diverge so as to
enclose between them alternate spaces of varying extent of
surface. The spaces enclosed between the curves are raised,
and the spaces enclosed by their convolutions are flat, but
the raised spaces are modelled so as to express the confluence
of solid curves of the peculiar forms already indicated. These
trumpet and spiral scrolls, as they are called, enclosing irregularly formed curvilinear spaces, and producing designs
which are similar but unsymmetrical, are repeated in different
varieties of pattern on the outer sides of the horns (Fig. 93).
In the terminal convolutions of the scrolls the curves are
sometimes arranged so as to produce a zoomorphic effect,
which differs from the later zoomorphism of the metal-work
of the Christian time and of the later manuscripts, in being
more geometrical in form and character. The zoomorphic
termination of the horns has also more of a geometric character than is usual in the Christian period.

The object being incomplete, its purpose is not obvious.
But it is suggestive of the probability of its having formed
part of a helmet that Diodorus Siculus, writing only a few
years after the conquest of Gaul by Julius Cæsar, describes
the military equipment of certain Gallic tribes as including

" bronze helmets with lofty projections rising out of them,
which impart a gigantic appearance to the wearers ; for
upon some are fixed pairs of horns, upon others the shapes
of birds and beasts wrought out of the same metal." These
horned helmets are represented on some of the consular

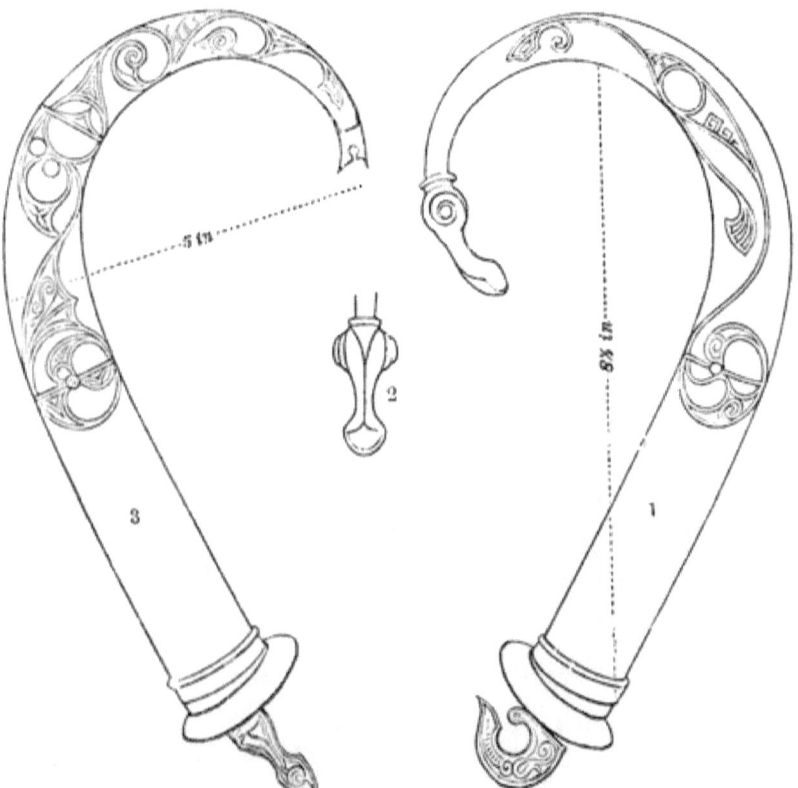

Fig. 93. — Plan of the Horns and their Ornament.   (1) The right horn.   (2) Zoomorphic termination of the right horn seen frontwise.   (3) The left horn.

medals, and the whole description of the Gallic equipment
is so similar to what we know of the habits of the Celtic
tribes of Britain, that it may be concluded that in this
respect their customs may not have been greatly dissimi-

lar.[1]   And, in point of fact, there is in the British Museum a
bronze headpiece found in the river Thames, near Waterloo
Bridge, which, from its peculiar form, was at first considered
to be a jester's cap.   But Mr. Franks has shown that it is a
military helmet of native workmanship.   It consists of a cap of
thin bronze, with an additional plate at the back, decorated
with scrolls of this peculiar character in low relief, among
which are cross-hatched discs once coated with red enamel.
From each side of the cap projects a conical horn terminating
in a moulded button, and upon one side of the horn runs a
string of small projecting studs.

It is therefore not improbable that this object at Abbotsford may have been
the front part of a
military helmet, or
of a headpiece used
for display.   Such
a   headpiece with
similarly large and
curving horns, ter-
minating in similar
zoomorphic endings
is seen (Fig. 94) on
the head of a warrior
who appears to be
engaged in mimic
combat with another
accoutred as fantastically as himself, and whose grotesque
headpiece bears a resemblance still more remarkable to

Fig. 94.—Bronze Plaque found in Oland
(actual size).

---

[1] The common denarius of the family Furia exhibits a trophy formed of
the horned helmet, the tunic of mail, the peculiarly ornamented oval shield,
and the large war trumpet.   On a denarius of Servilia a Gaul wearing the
horned helmet appears aiming a back-handed blow with his long sword at a
Roman antagonist.   The name "Cornuti" itself is suggestive of this peculiarity.

another bronze object of the same character which I have next to describe. These representations occur on a bronze plaque dug up in the island of Oland, and they have therefore no necessary connection with the usages of the Celtic people. They merely show that in assigning such a purpose to these objects we are not attributing to them a purpose to which they were never applied. But the special use of the object is really of no great moment for the pur-

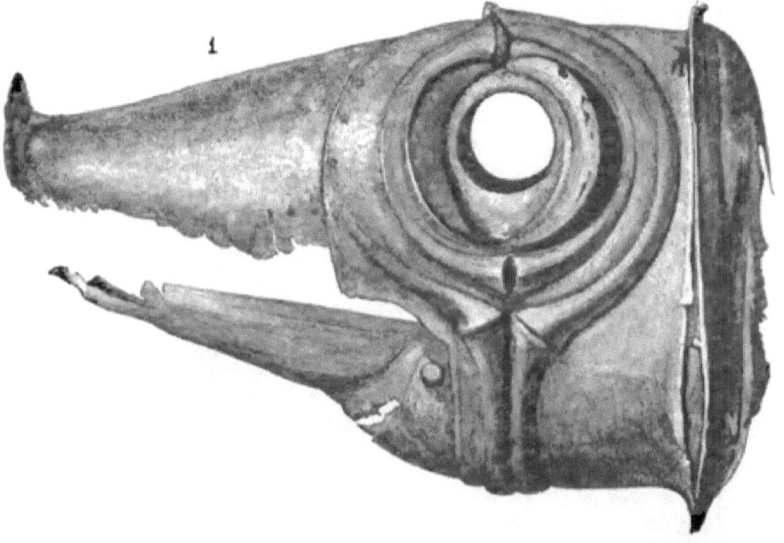

Fig. 95.—Bronze object in the form of a swine's head found at Liechestown, Deskford, Banffshire (8¼ inches in length).

pose of the present investigation. That purpose is fulfilled when we are enabled to say, from an examination of its special characteristics, that it has certain typical relations linking it with other objects, forming a distinct group and occupying a definite place in the series of types which characterise the area now termed Scotland. I therefore proceed to the description of other objects distinguished by the same characteristics.

At Liechestown, in the parish of Deskford, Banffshire, about the year 1816, a remarkable relic (Fig. 95), now in the Banff Museum, was found in a mossy piece of ground, at a depth of about 6 feet, and resting on a bed of clay at the bottom of the moss. This object, which is equally peculiar

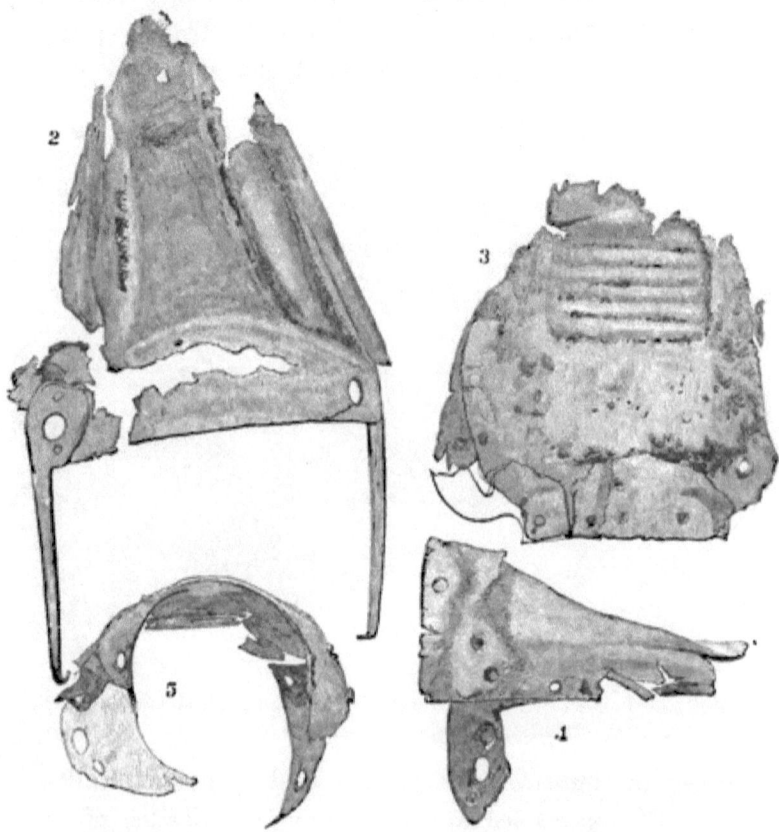

Fig. 96.—Plates of thin bronze forming separate parts of the swine's head. (2) The lower jaw. (3) The palate. (4 and 5) Posterior and lateral views of the palate.

alike in respect to its form and ornamentation, is in the shape of a boar's head of thin beaten bronze 8½ inches in length by 5½ in greatest breadth. The lower jaw is movable. The eyes are circular holes 1¼ inch in diameter. The whole head is formed of four plates of bronze, the snout, the palate, and the lower jaw (Fig. 96) having been each made separately, and attached to the posterior part of the head, which consists of an embossed plate bent to the shape. A disc-like plate, which was found with it, is now attached to the open back of the head, but does not quite fit, and it is doubtful whether it had been so placed originally. The ornamentation of this singular object is of the same character as that of the Torrs bronze, but simpler, being merely a series of trumpet-shaped ridges in *repoussé* work round the eyes. But this ornament, simple as it is, is quite sufficient to determine the relations of the relic to that general group of objects of which it and the bronze from Torrs are the most remarkable specimens.

It is obvious that if these objects had any relation to military equipment, we ought to find the very peculiar art which is so conspicuous in their decoration, also exhibiting itself in the decoration of the weapons and other war-gear in use among the same people. Diodorus, in fact, informs us that the Gauls used oblong shields as tall as the man, and painted after a peculiar fashion. Some of these shields, he also says, had figures of animals in relief of bronze, not merely for ornament but also for defence, and very well wrought. It has been already remarked that it is probable that the military equipment of the Gallic tribes resembled that of the British ; and it is the fact that oblong shields, decorated with the peculiar patterns characteristic of the style of art exhibited by the two headpieces which have been described, having these patterns further adorned by coloured enamels, and also possessing the distinctive feature of figures of animals in relief in bronze, have been found in England.[1]

---

[1] A bronze shield, found in the river Witham, 3 feet 8½ inches long, and nearly 14 inches wide, with straight sides and rounded ends, is decorated with

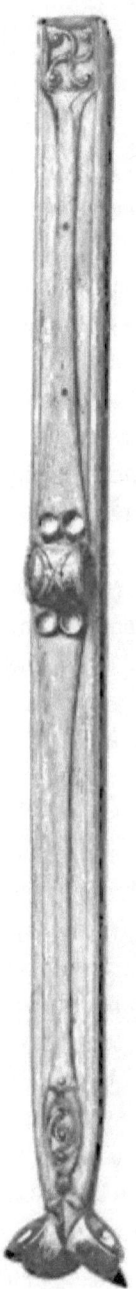

Fig. 97.—Sword-sheath found near Mortonhall (23½ inches long).

No shields of this character have yet been discovered in Scotland, but there are other objects of a military kind which exhibit the same peculiar art in a sufficiently character-istic manner. One of these is a sword-sheath (Fig. 97) of bronze, 23½ inches in length by 1¼ inch in width, which was found at the foot of the Pentlands, near Mortonhall, and is now in the Museum. It is formed of thin beaten bronze; the ornamental cup-shaped expansions at the lower end are solid castings, and the ornamental strap carrying the loop in front is fastened on with pins. The back of the sheath is a thin slip of bronze sliding in grooves in the inner margins of the two sides. This is the only example of a sword-sheath of this style and period known to have been found in Scotland. Several sheaths of the same character have been discovered in Eng-land. Perhaps the most characteristic of these is one in the collection of Canon Greenwell at Durham, which exhibits, in a very special manner, the peculiar style of ornament of which I have given so many illustrations. The swords which these sheaths contained were of iron and have perished. One found in the

studs of red coral, and had the figure of an animal attached to it by rivets. Another, found in the Thames, 2 feet 6½ inches long and 14¼ inches wide, is ornamented with enamelled patterns in this peculiar style, and of singular beauty and remarkable excellence of design and workmanship. They are figured in colours of the ori-ginals in the *Horæ Ferales*, edited by A. W. Franks, of the British Museum (4to. London, 1863), Plates XIV.-XV.

Thames has the blade still within it, 3 feet 1½ inch in length, but a mere mass of oxide.[1]   These swords differ greatly in the length and form of the blade from the leaf-shaped swords of bronze which were in general use at an earlier period, and their sheaths differ still more widely in form and ornament from the sheaths of the leaf-shaped swords.

Another class of objects, which are more of the nature of harness-mountings or horse-furniture, also exhibit this peculiar style of ornamentation, in some cases combined with the

Fig. 98.—Mountings of Cast Bronze (5 inches in length).

remarkable feature of having their sunk spaces filled with coloured enamels.

[1] The specimens of these iron swords with bronze sheaths found in different parts of England are enumerated by Mr. Franks in the *Proceedings of the Society of Antiquaries of London*, vol. iv. p. 166 ; and several are figured in *Horæ Ferales*, Plates XIV.-XVIII.

A pair of massively-formed objects (Fig. 98), the precise use of which is not apparent, were found in a bank of clay on a spur of the Cheviots at Henshole on Cheviot. They are of cast bronze, and consist of an oblong body, hollow, rounded at one end and flattened at the other; the upper and lower surfaces inclined towards the small end, which is narrower than the width at the middle. A stout tang of about 2 inches in length is carried on a bar which crosses the open part of the small end, and the convexity of the larger end bears the mark of hammering as if to drive the tang home. They are destitute of surface decoration, but they seem to be allied by the characteristics of their form to other objects which are less indefinite in the indications of their art.

In a large cairn on the farm of Hillock Head, in the parish of Towie, Aberdeenshire, which covered an interment placed in a cist with an urn, there were found a number of bronze objects, all of which were lost except two (Fig. 99),

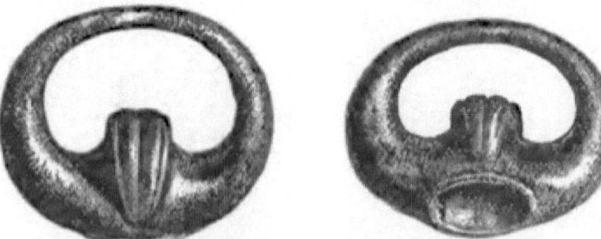

Fig. 99.—Bronze Ornaments found in a Cairn at Towie, Aberdeenshire.

which are now in the Museum. They are in the form of oval hollow rings, expanding on the inferior side, and having an oval opening in the under part, which shows the remains of an iron pin fastened at each side of the opening with lead. Their general appearance is suggestive of the mountings of horse-harness, but their precise purpose is not obvious, and the articles found in association with them are undescribed. Although the testimony is singularly defective on that point, it is not probable that they had any connection with the interment in the "short cist" which contained bones and an urn. A similar object in bronze, also presenting the remains of iron fastenings in the lower part, was found under a large stone on the hill of Crichie, near Kintore, along with a number of globular balls of shale each about 1¼ inch in diameter, slightly flattened on one side, and having the remains of iron loop-like fastenings in the flattened side.[1] A number of rings and harness-mountings found at Middleby, in Annandale, in 1737, and now preserved in Penicuick House, exhibit the same style of decoration in a more pro-nounced and characteristic manner.[2]

A mounting in cast bronze (Fig. 100), 2 inches diameter, the sunk spaces of which had probably been filled with enamels, was recently found in the dry bed of the loch of Dowalton, which was drained about eighteen years ago. It

Fig. 100.—Mounting in Cast Bronze from Dowalton Loch (2 inches in diameter).

is formed of a combination of segmental spaces, the curves of which are those of the divergent spiral, each space being surrounded by a raised border, and the sunk surfaces rough-ened with a tool.

A bridle-bit (Fig. 101), found in a moss at Birrenswark, in Annandale, before 1785, and now in the National Museum, exhibits the characteristics of this peculiar phase of art in a very striking manner. It is no less peculiar in its design

[1] *Proc. Soc. Antiq. Scot.*, vol. v. p. 111.

[2] They have been figured by Dr. Daniel Wilson in *The Prehistoric Annals of Scotland*, vol. ii. p. 156.

and construction than in the character of its ornamentation.

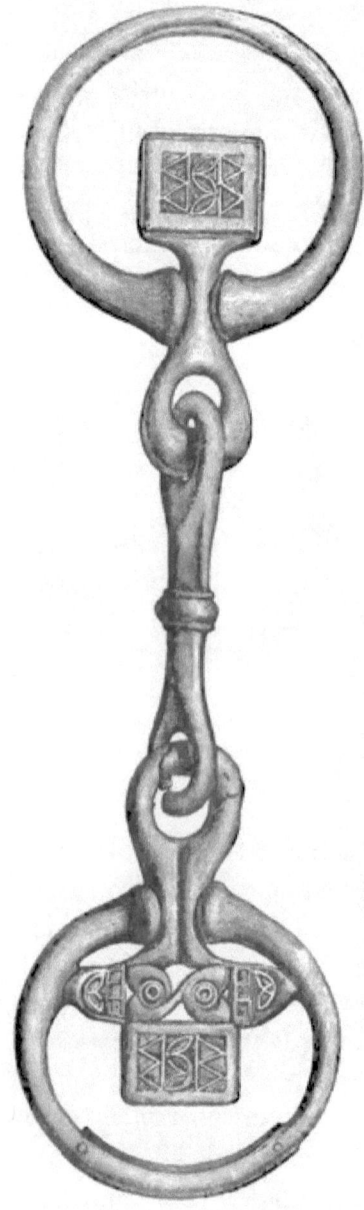

Fig. 101.—Bridle-bit found in a Moss at Birrenswark, Dumfriesshire (6¾ inches in length).

It is a single casting of bronze. The loops of the cheek-rings have been cast within the loops of the centre-piece, an operation implying technical skill and experience of complicated processes of moulding and casting. The design, however, is the most remarkable feature of the object. It is designed as carefully as if it were a piece of jewellery. The rings, though cast in one piece with the loops, are penannular in form, grasping the neck of the loop between their expanded ends. The two rings differ slightly in size, and the loops differ greatly in form. The one is treated as a loop formed of a cylindrical rod bent to the shape of a loop, and carrying the ornamented open-work of its terminal part as between its extended ends. The other loop is treated as a solid form, and in its ornamental termination there is no open work. The two rings are similar, but not identical.

The idea of openness suggested by the modelling of the one loop is carried into the construction of the terminal portions as open work, and the idea of solidity is similarly carried out in the other loop. The surface decoration of the terminal portions of the loops is of the same character in the parts of both that are similar, and is partly carried also into the parts of the one which are wanting in the other. It consists of red and yellow enamel *champlévé*, the colours alternating in alternate rows of triangular and oval spaces. A double spiral and trumpet pattern appears in the open work of the one loop. The loops and rings are greatly the worse for wear, and have been strengthened by thin pieces riveted on.

It is certainly a peculiar feature of an art so singularly decorative that it was applied so largely to the ornamentation of objects that were appropriated to the commonest uses. Enamelled horse-trappings of the most finished and beautiful workmanship have frequently been found in England, sometimes associated with the remains of chariots.[1] Not only is the use of enamel in the decoration of such objects unknown beyond the area of the British Isles, but the special system of design which accompanies its use is also confined within that area. And it is an interesting fact that there is historical evidence as to the nationality of these remains. The only classical author who mentions the art of enamelling is Philostratus, a Greek sophist in the household of Julia Domna, wife of the Emperor Severus. In a notice of the variegated trappings of the horses in a painting of a boar-

---

[1] They have been found at Polden Hill, near Bridgewater (*Archæologia*, vol. xiv. p. 90) ; at Hagbourn Hill, Berkshire (*Archæologia*, vol. xvi. p. 318) ; at Stanwick, Yorkshire, with chariot-wheels (York Volume of the Archæological Institute, p. 10) ; at Arras and Hessleskew, in the same county, with chariot-wheels and the bones of horses (*Ibid.* p. 28), and other places. A synopsis of the whole group of objects characterised by this decoration is given by Mr. Franks in *Horæ Ferales* (4to., London, 1863), pp. 172, 196, and many figures in the coloured plates (Plates XIV.-XX.).

hunt he accounts for their peculiar appearance as follows :— "They say that the barbarians who live in the Ocean pour such colours on heated brass, and that they adhere to it, become as hard as stone, and thus preserve the designs that are made in them." It is matter of inference what people they were who are thus styled "barbarians in the ocean," but it is matter of fact that horse-trappings of bronze (or brass) decorated with coloured enamels have hitherto been found in the British Islands alone.

But this peculiar style of art was not confined to the decoration of such objects as parts of military equipments or harness of horses. It was largely employed in the decoration of personal ornaments and objects of personal use.

In the parish of Balmaclellan, in Kirkcudbright, a number of bronze articles were found in draining a bog. It is stated that they were found about 3 feet under the surface in four

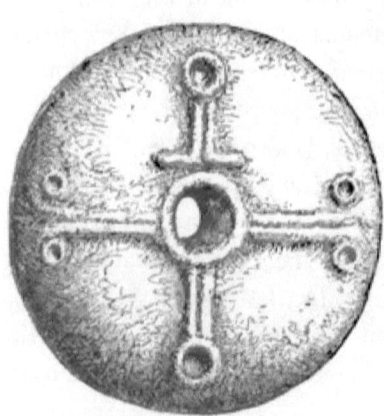

parcels, each wrapped in coarse linen cloth. Close by them the upper stone of a quern was also found. The quern stone (Fig. 102) is ornamented, but the ornament possesses none of the distinctive features of the decoration of the bronzes. They consisted of a circular mirror with handle, and a number of thin plates of bronze, some being long narrow bands, others

Fig. 102.—Quern-Stone of sandstone found at Balmaclellan (14 inches in diameter).

curved and cut into various shapes. The mirror (Fig. 103) is of the form so commonly seen on the sculptured monuments of the Celtic Christian time in Scotland. The circular part is 8 inches in diameter, and the handle 5 inches in projection from the circumference of the circular part. The body of the mirror is a thin plate of bronze, surrounded by a plain-rolled edging. The handle, which is also a thin plate of bronze similarly edged, is attached to the circular plate by rivets, and the junction is concealed by a finely-ornamented plate (Fig. 104), presenting a pattern composed of those peculiar raised surfaces formed by the meeting of curves rising from the flat at different angles, and traversing the ground also in curves, which converge and diverge in a manner pleasing to the eye, but difficult to describe. The upper part of this ornamental plate is tri-lobate, the lobes bounded by curves

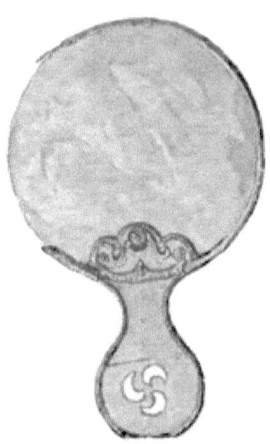

Fig. 103.—Bronze Mirror found at Balmaclellan (8 inches in diameter).

of peculiar form, and bordered by an edging of studs embossed on the metal. The central ornament of each lobe is a circular

Fig. 104.—Ornamental Plate of thin bronze, embossed, at the junction of the mirror with its handle (actual size).

device, with a central boss surrounded by a circle of oval-raised surfaces, and presenting a nearer approach to the effect of a floral decoration than is usually seen in this style of

ornament. The handle of the mirror is pierced with three
segmental openings formed of the curves of the divergent
spiral. A crescentic collar-shaped plate of bronze (Fig. 105), 13

Fig. 105.—Half of the Crescentic Collar-like Plate of Bronze found with
the Mirror at Balmaclellan.

inches in diameter, and 2 inches in the width of the band, is
decorated with a chased pattern of similarly convergent and
divergent curves, the spaces enclosed by the curves being
hatched with parallel lines. The remaining plates (Fig. 106),
of which there are a considerable number, are of various
forms. Some have straight outer edges, and the interior edges
cut into curves, meeting each other with long and short points;

others are triangular pieces, with one convex and two concave edges, while others again are long narrow bands with
straight edges. They are all bordered with an edging of thin
metal doubled over and pinned on, and they seem themselves
to have been attached by pins to some object of a more
perishable nature. What their precise purpose was—whether
they were mountings on wood or leather, or whether they
formed parts of some object constructed wholly of thin plates
of metal (as the two objects previously described are constructed)—it is not necessary to conjecture since the form and

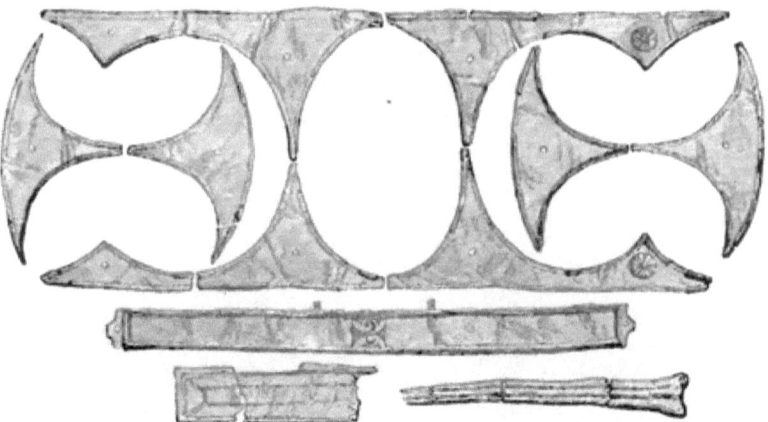

Fig. 106.—Form of the Bronze Plates found with the Mirror at Balmaclellan
(26 inches in length).

condition of the objects themselves give no definite indications on these points. Their being wrapped in cloth in
separate parcels may imply that they are not all parts of the
same object, and their local association with objects of such
incongruous purposes, as a mirror and a quern, may imply
that they were not necessarily even associated with each
other when in use. There is no evidence that the deposit
was in any way connected with sepulture, although the
mirror of this form, and bearing precisely the same kind of

K

ornamentation, has been found associated with interments of
Pagan time in Britain.

At Mount Batten, near Plymouth, a series of graves were
discovered in 1865,[1] which presented phenomena of a very
peculiar character. They were pits 4 or 4½ feet in depth,
one foot of which only was soil, the remaining three feet
being sunk in the disintegrated surface of the underlying
rock. They were very numerous, sometimes close together
and irregular in form, and had mostly been refilled with the

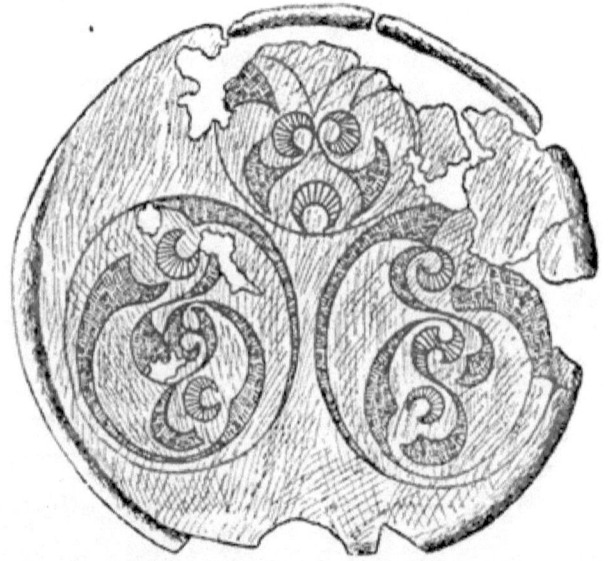

Fig. 107.—Bronze Mirror found in a grave at Mount Batten, Plymouth
(8 inches in diameter).

materials removed in making them. They contained fragments of pottery of black and yellow ware, and wheel-made.
Some fragments of glass vessels, portions of iron implements,
among which were a pair of shears, bronze rings and fibulæ,
and jointed armlets of bronze, with a knife or dagger in a
sheath of thin bronze, were also found. But the most in-

[1] Described in a paper by Mr. Spence Bate in *Archæologia*, vol. xl. p. 500.

teresting part of the discovery was the circular plate of a bronze mirror (Fig. 107), 8 inches in diameter, which lay on its face at the bottom of one of the graves. It is a very thin plate of bronze, with a rolled edging. The back is ornamented with three circular engraved patterns of spirals formed of the same peculiar curves, converging and diverging, the spaces between the lines forming the curves being filled with hatching. So closely do the patterns resemble those on the collar-like object from Balmaclellan, and so similar is the style of the work, that the conclusion is unavoidable that the two objects belong to the same school of art, and cannot be very far apart in time.

Another mirror, which is almost precisely similar in form and ornamentation, was found in 1833 at Trelan Bahow,[1] in the parish of St. Keverne, Cornwall. In the course of the construction of a new road a group of graves was discovered. Each grave was formed of six slabs set on edge, two forming each side of the grave, and one at each end. They were from two to three feet under the surface, and covered with large stones. In one of the cists, apparently with the remains of a female, there were found the bronze mirror almost perfect, some rings of bronze or brass, fragments of fibulæ, and other personal ornaments, and several beads of variegated glass. The mirror is circular, 6 inches in diameter, with a looped handle 2½ inches in length. The back of the mirror plate has a marginal ornament of triangular spaces alternately plain, and filled with short parallel lines struck by a punch. Across the central line of the mirror are two circles enclosing smaller circles and curvilinear spaces alternately plain, and filled with punched lines in a style similar to that of the ornament on the collar-like object from Balmaclellan.

Another mirror of the same character, found at Birdlip on

the edge of the Cottiswold Hills, near Gloucester, in 1879,[1] exhibits the same style of ornamentation. Three cists were discovered in a group, containing skeletons placed with their

Fig. 108.—Back of a Bronze Mirror found in a grave at Birdlip, near Gloucester (10¾ inches in diameter).

feet to the south. The first and third were apparently adult males, and with them no manufactured objects were found.

[1] *Proceedings of the Bristol and Gloucester Archæological Society*, vol. v. p. 137, and Plate XIV., from which the figure here given is copied by permission.

The second was apparently a female. On the face of the skeleton was placed a large bronze bowl, 9 inches in diameter, inverted; and among the other contents of the cist were a smaller bowl of bronze, 4 inches in diameter, a harp-shaped fibula of silver plated with gold, a bracelet and four rings of brass, a key-handle, a knife-handle terminating in the head of an animal, a string of large beads of jet and amber, and a mirror made of a massive bronze plate, weighing $38\frac{1}{4}$ ounces. The back of the mirror (Fig. 108), which is of a slightly oval form, measures $10\frac{5}{8}$ inches in its greatest, and $9\frac{3}{4}$ inches in its least, diameter, and is beautifully ornamented with a triple scroll-like pattern of flowing curvilinear spaces filled with hatchings of short lines in chequers, or groups disposed at right angles to each other. The pattern is so managed that the hatched spaces and the plain spaces alternate and form symmetrical arrangements, producing a pleasing effect. At the lower part, where the handle supports the mirror, is a triple arrangement of trumpet-shaped scrolls in relief, enclosing spaces which are similarly decorated. The handle is elegantly formed from a prolongation of the marginal beading of the mirror, which gradually thickens towards the lower margin to trumpet-shaped endings on either side of the handle, which takes the form of a double-loop, drawn out from the marginal bead, and terminating in a ring partly filled by an ornamented disc.

These mirrors all differ in their form and in the composition of the metal from Roman mirrors, and they differ in certain characteristics of their ornament still more widely from the Roman style. But the peculiar characteristics which form the special features of their decoration are identical with those of a large class of objects which we have now learned to recognise by the character of their art as distinctively Celtic.

The same character is exhibited by the ornamentation of

a series of spoon-like objects[1] found in England and Ireland, of which Fig. 109 is a characteristic example. Four of

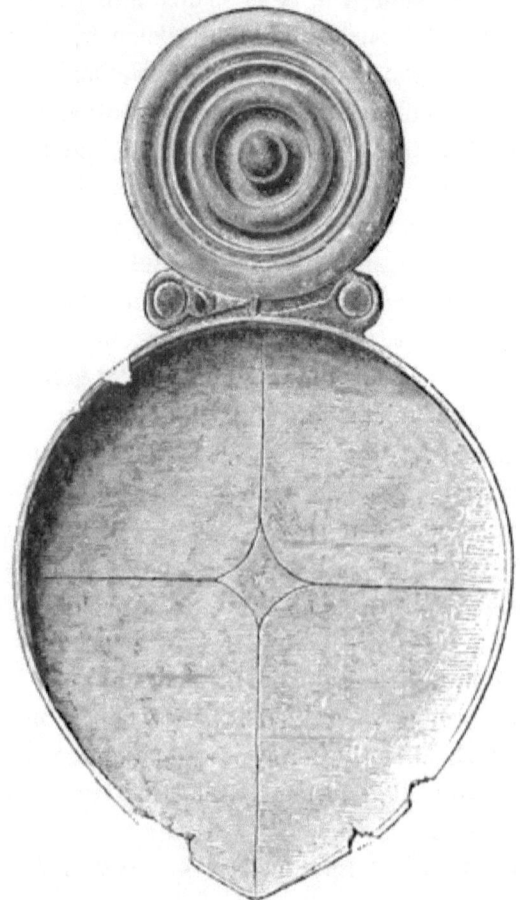

Fig. 109.—Bronze Spoon-like object (one of a pair) found at Weston, near Bath (actual size).

these are in the National Museum, and though no specimens

[1] These have been conjectured to be of Christian time, and to have been used in connection with the celebration of the Eucharist, but the evidence is insufficient to carry this conclusion. See the papers by Albert Way in *Archæological Journal*, vol. xxvi. p. 52 ; and by Rev. E. L. Barnwell in *Archæologia Cambrensis*, vol. viii. (Third Series) p. 208, and vol. x. p. 57.

have yet been met with in Scotland, I notice them here, because their decoration is so nearly related to that of the Scottish school. In the case of the pair of these peculiar objects found in excavating for a quarry at Weston, near Bath, the backs of the circular projections or handles (Fig. 110) are ornamented with patterns of this character in relief.

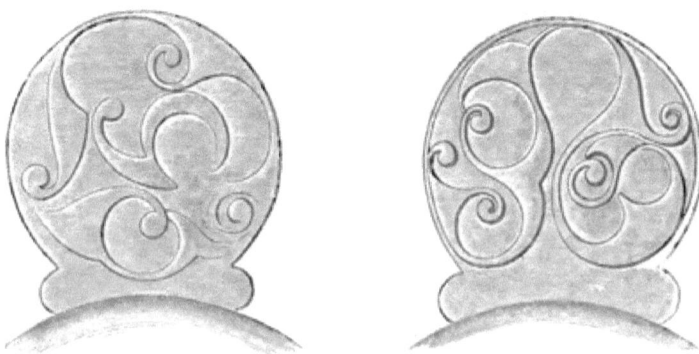

Fig. 110.—Backs of the Handles of the pair of Spoon-like objects found at Weston, near Bath (actual size).

The front of the disc is ornamented with a series of circular concentric mouldings, and the bowl of the spoon is quartered by incised lines. It is a peculiarity of these objects, that though found in pairs, the two members of the pair, though similar, are not identical. In some cases it is apparent that they have even been cast in different moulds. Usually one of the pair has its bowl quartered by incised lines, while the other has a small hole pierced near the edge of the bowl. Another pair, also in the Museum, were found in 1861 in a railway cutting in Llanfair parish, Denbighshire. They are slightly smaller in size, and differ in the ornamentation of the front of their discs. One of them (Fig. 111, No. 2) is here shown along with the second of the Weston specimens.

The same characteristic style of art is seen in the decoration of a massive collar of cast bronze (Fig. 112), which was found

in digging a well at Stitchell, in Roxburghshire, in 1747, and
is now in the National Museum.   Like the armlets found in

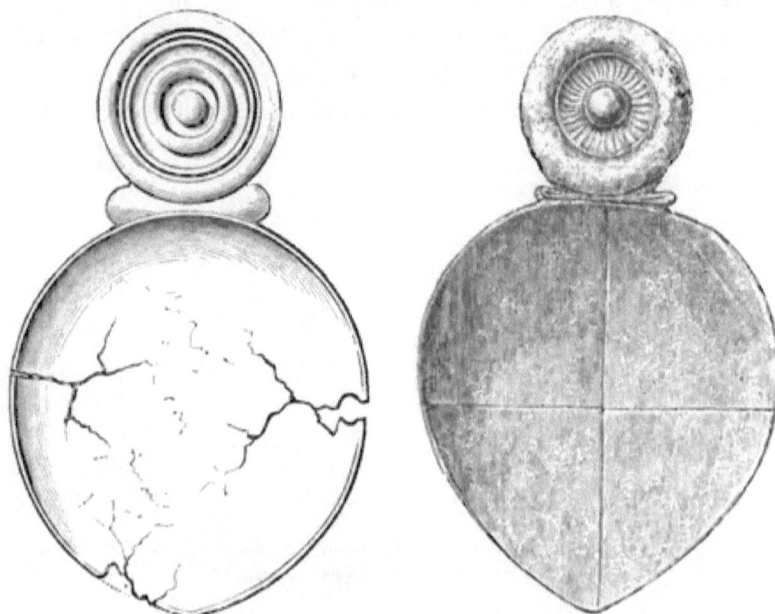

Fig. 111.—Bronze Spoon-like objects found at Weston and Llanfair.

Fig. 112.—Jointed Collar of Bronze found at Stitchell, Roxburghshire.

the Plymouth graves, this collar is jointed, opening on a hinge in the centre, and fastening in front by a pin and socket. It is a very massive and heavy ornament, the width of the opening being 6 inches by 5, and the breadth of the flattened ring varying from 1¾ inch to ¼ inch. The character of the ornament is simple, but highly peculiar, and bearing a strong family likeness to the double escaping and divergent spirals of the later Celtic art. All the patterns are in relief and cast in the solid, except those on the two panels on either side of the central opening, which are in *repoussé* on a thin plate of bronze fastened to the collar by pins at the four corners.

Closely akin to this jointed collar in the idea of its construction and the form of its ornament is an elegant armlet of thin bronze (Fig. 113), found in 1826 near Plunton Castle, in

Fig. 113.—Bronze Armlet found in the Parish of Borgue, Kirkcudbright.

the parish of Borgue, in Kirkcudbright. It is of thin beaten bronze, 1½ inch wide and 2½ inches in diameter, and, like the collar, it is made to open on a hinge in the centre, and close by a pin and loops. It is ornamented by three raised mouldings, beaten up from the back, which pass round it horizontally, but these are concealed on either side of the hinges by two plates of thin bronze of quadrangular form, ornamented in *repoussé* by trumpet-shaped ornaments connected by peculiar curves, and having studs placed in the concavities of the curves. These plates are fastened to the armlet at the four corners by pins, and bordered by a single row of small studs.

In the month of March 1806 a herd boy, passing along the side of the Shaw Hill, near the House of New Cairnmuir, in the parish of Kirkurd, Peeblesshire, saw something glitter in the ground, and on scraping the place with his foot he unearthed a hoard of gold objects, consisting of two twisted arm-rings, each weighing 8 oz. 12 dwt., a broken ring of the same form weighing 8 oz. 10 dwt., forty small studs, each weighing about half a sovereign, and a hollow spherical ornament weighing 4 oz. 5 dwt.—the bullion value of the whole being about £110. One of the twisted arm-rings passed into the possession of Sir George Montgomery of Macbichill; the spherical ornament and two of the small studs were obtained by Mr. John Lawson of Cairnmuir and placed in the National Museum; the rest of the hoard is believed to have been melted. The three arm-rings are spirally twisted rods of gold, with flat circular ends bent round to encircle the arm. The studs or pellets are nearly spherical, about the size of a large pea, and marked on the surface with a cruciform ornament in relief. The spherical ornament (Fig. 114) has some resemblance to the pommel of a sword, although its form gives no obvious indication of its purpose. It is 2½ inches in length by 2 inches in width, and about 1¼ inch in thickness. It has been cast hollow, with an opening through the centre of the rounded part, and must have been made by a very skilful workman. One side of it is plain, the other ornamented in *repoussé* work of great beauty. The style of the ornament is simple, elegant, and highly effective. The surface to be decorated is broken up into irregular spaces by a system of the peculiar curves, which are so characteristic of the style of art of the bronzes which have been already described. Some of these spaces are further ornamented by a peculiar pitting of the surface seen in some of the decorated stone balls (Fig. 146); others are raised in solid curves of the same peculiar form, while the interspaces follow the form of the object itself. Studs and prominences,

Fig. 114.—Gold Ornament found on the Shaw Hill, near Cairnmuir, Kirkurd.
Front and back views (actual size).

with spirals in relief, are introduced to give emphasis to the general design, which commends itself at once to the eye of taste as one of the most fitly beautiful and unaffected forms of surface-decoration which could be applied to such a purpose.

In this group of objects in bronze and gold we have characteristic examples of the work of this early school of decorative art, which in some of its features bears certain relations to the work of the later school of Celtic art of the Christian time. But the elements of its decoration are fewer. It has no interlaced work and no fret—nothing but curves and spirals. It does not systematically break up its surfaces in panels, but distributes its decorative effects in spaces that are circular or oval, or bounded by intersecting curves. Its prevailing features are not the production of intricately symmetrical and geometrically regulated patterns, but the production of effects of balance and beauty by the rhythmic recurrence and variation of curves and spaces with solid forms which, though not symmetrical, are similar. Their characteristic curves, as seen in the outlines of their figures and the sections of their solid forms, are specially peculiar, while the marked preference for relief in metal-work is in striking contrast to the general prevalence of chased and engraved designs in the later school.

It is to this characteristic treatment of the decoration of their metal-work by this early school of Celtic art that Mr. Kemble refers in the following remarks :—" When, as is often the case in metal, this principle of the diverging spiral line is carried out in *repoussé*—when you have those singularly beautiful curves, more beautiful perhaps in the parts that are not seen than in those that meet the eye, and whose beauty is revealed in shadow more than in form—you have a peculiar characteristic, a form of beauty which belongs to no nation but our own, and to no portion of our nation but the Celtic portion. It deals with curves which are not arcs of a circle ; its figures are not of the class we usually designate by the term geometrical ; and above all it calls in the aid of enamel to perfect its work—not *cloisonné* like the enamel of the East ; not mosaic work of tesserae like so many so-called enamels of the Romans, but enamel *champlevé* as Philostratus has described the island barbarians to have invented it. The engraved spiral line, with double winding, is found from America to the Baltic, from Greece to Norway, but the divergent spiral *repoussé* in metal and ornamented with *champlevé* enamel, is found in these British Islands alone.

I now proceed to notice another group of objects in metal

possessing peculiar features still more strongly marked, but exhibiting also the distinctive characteristics of the same style of art.

A pair of these objects were found imbedded in the earth over the entrance to a curious underground structure in the garden at Castle Newe in Aberdeenshire. The structure was a long narrow curved subterranean gallery about 50 feet in length and 7 feet wide on the floor. What remained of the walls was only 4½ feet high, but showed that it had been roofed over by bringing the walls gradually towards each other as they increased in height, till the space could be covered with flat stones of moderate length. This form of structure, as we shall see in a subsequent Lecture, is typical, and extends over the Celtic area. The pair of objects found in association with this typically Celtic structure are of quite a remarkable character. They are massively formed, but highly decorated objects of cast bronze. It is obvious from their form and decoration that they are designed for an ornamental purpose. It is impossible that they could have been worn as personal ornaments either with comfort or convenience, but that impossibility does not necessarily invalidate the conclusion that they were personal ornaments, because such things have been

Fig. 115.—Bronze Armlet, with enamelled ornaments (one of a pair), found at Castle Newe, Aberdeenshire. Front view (5¾ inches in diameter).

worn in all ages, although they have entailed discomfort and inconvenience to the wearers. The special form of the objects and the circumstance that a pair of them were found together are suggestive of their use as armlets. Their form, as shown in Fig. 115, is the typically Celtic form—penannular, with rounded and slightly-expanded ends. These terminal expansions have circular spaces in the centre, bordered by a double raised edging, and filled with plaques of bronze

ornamented with chequered patterns of red and yellow enamels. These bronze plaques are fixed in their places by iron pins. The body of the armlet (Fig. 116) is divided longitudinally into three distinct ridges or bands with convex surfaces, separated by narrow bands

Fig. 116.—Bronze Armlet, found at Castle Newe, Aberdeenshire. Back view (5¾ inches in diameter).

of a tooled chevrony ornament, which lie along the furrows between the ridges. At intervals there rise from the ridges solid, flattened, and curvilinear projections of about ¾ inch in length, placed obliquely across the ridges, and standing in rows from side to side of the armlet. These are connected longitudinally by less highly raised trumpet-shaped scrolls, slightly curved, and passing obliquely across till they meet in the centre. The median ridge stops short at the circular spaces in the terminal expansions, while the exterior ridges on either side pass round to form the border of the expansion on which the projecting ornaments are continued in a less pronounced form. The general contour of the armlets is that of an oval slightly compressed from front to back. Their greatest diameter is 5¾ inches, their greatest depth 4½ inches, and the weight of each is 3¾ lbs. They do not commend themselves to our notions of elegance and comfort as articles of personal decoration, but they possess a strong individuality of character, combined with an ingenious and highly-effective style of decoration which is not met with on any other class of objects in metal.[1]

Another pair of similar armlets found within a few feet of each other, and slightly covered with earth, on the farm of Pitkelloney, near Muthil, in Perthshire, are now in the British Museum. They are not exactly similar in size, though their forms are similar, and their ornamentation almost the same. One measures 16 inches in circumference, the other only 15 inches, but the smaller is the heavier of the two, weighing 3 lbs. 10 oz., while the larger only weighs 3 lbs. 3 oz. The circular spaces in the expanded ends of the armlet are filled with enamelled plates, fastened in their places by iron pins. The enamels are *champlévé* in flat plates of bronze, the colours

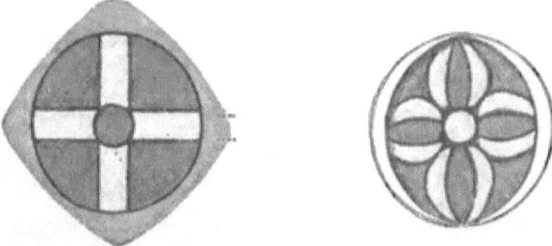

Fig. 117.—Enamelled Plates of each of the pair of Bronze Armlets found at Pitkelloney, Perthshire.

red and yellow. The patterns (Fig. 117) are not chequered like those in the Castle Newe armlets. One presents a plain rectangular cross-like figure in yellow on a red ground, with a

[1] A denarius of the Emperor Nerva was subsequently found close by the place where the armlets were discovered. The underground structure appears, like many of its class, to have been associated with an overground habitation, the site of which was marked by fire-burnt pavement, remains of querns, beads, etc., found near the present surface.

circle of red in the centre. The other has a double quatre-foil in yellow and red on a red ground, with a yellow centre.

An armlet of similar character was ploughed up in a field on the farm of Mains of Auchenbadie, on the estate of Mont-

blairy, in Banffshire, in 1866, and is now in the National Museum. Seen in front (as in Fig. 118) it is penannular and oval in shape, measuring 6½ inches in its longest diameter, and 4 inches from front to back. Its width across the middle of the back

Fig. 118.—Bronze Armlet found at Auchenbadie, Banffshire.   Front view (6½ inches in diameter).

(where it is narrowest) is 3¾ inches, and its greatest width across the terminal expansion is 5¾ inches. Its weight is 3 lbs. 9 oz. Like those already described, it is a solid casting of bronze, having its exterior surface (Fig. 119) divided longitudinally into three bands—convex exteriorly, concave interiorly—the middle band stopping short at the circular aper-

Fig. 119.—Bronze Armlet found at Auchenbadie, Banffshire.   Back view (6½ inches in diameter).

ture in the centre of the terminal expansion, the others passing round it and uniting at the completion of the

circle. A boldly chased pattern of zig-zag ornament lies in the furrow between each contiguous pair of bands, and along the slightly depressed furrow at the edges of the
outer bands. The con-
vexity of the exterior surfaces of the bands is studded
at equal intervals with bold
projections nearly an inch in
length, placed transversely
across the ridges, and standing in rows from side to side
of the armlet. From the
outer edges of each of these
to the inner edge of the next
a slightly curved and highly
raised projection passes
obliquely across the ridge,
those on the two outer
ridges running parallel to
each other, and those on the
central ridge in the reverse
direction. The circular
spaces in the terminal expansions (shown in Fig. 118)
have lost their enamelled
plates, but the traces remain
of the pins and fastenings
by which they were secured
in their places. The accompanying plan in outline (Fig.
120) of the form and ornamentation of the armlet,

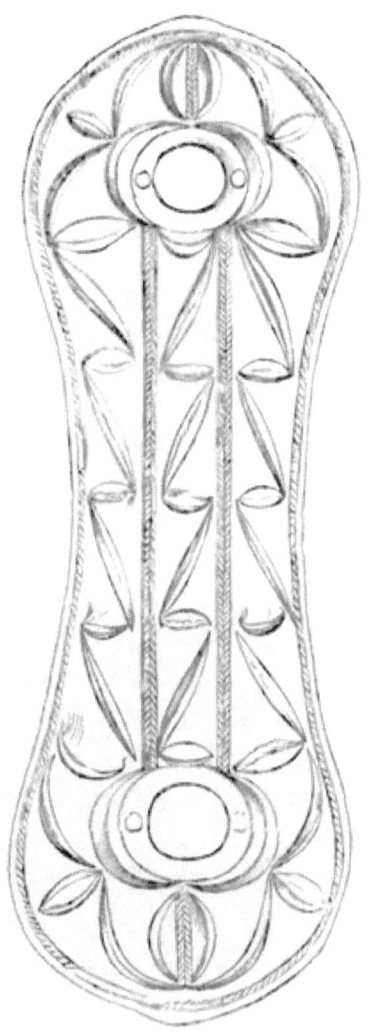

Fig. 120.—Plan of Ornamentation of Bronze Armlet found at Auchenbadie, Banffshire.

shown as it would appear if completely flattened out and

seen from above, will render these details more intelligible. From this it appears that the system of arrangement of the

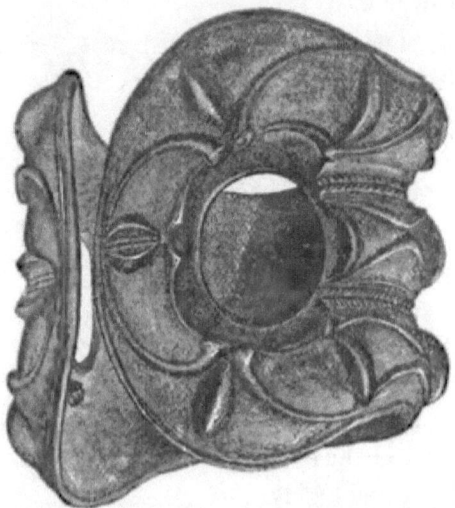

Fig. 121.—Bronze Armlet found at Drumside, Belhelvie, Aberdeenshire. Front view, seen sideways (4½ inches in diameter).

Fig. 122.—Bronze Armlet found at Drumside, Belhelvie, Aberdeenshire. Back view (4½ inches in diameter).

members of the ornament is that of the escaping double spiral, while the solid forms of the projecting masses are bounded and outlined by curves of the same formation.

An armlet of similar character, found 6 feet under the surface at Drumside, in the parish of Belhelvie, in Aberdeenshire, is also in the National Museum. It is considerably smaller in size (though it is here shown in Fig. 121 to a larger scale), and measures 4½ inches in its longest diameter, and 4½ inches in greatest width across the centre of the circular expansion of the terminal portion. Its weight is only 28 oz. Like the others, it is a solid casting in bronze, the exterior surface (Fig. 122) triply ridged and studded with projections of the same flattened oval character as those previously described. The less highly raised ridges that pass obliquely from projection to projection are more distinctly trumpet-shaped on the circular terminal part than on the middle portion of the armlet, and a comparison of their forms with the ornament round the eye-holes of the swine's head from Banff-shire (Fig. 95) will show their relationship at a glance. In its form, and the disposition of the members of its ornamentation (as shown on the accompanying plan in outline, Fig. 123), this armlet presents a striking similarity to the one from Achenbadie. It wants the chased border round the exterior edges of the outer bands, but the furrows between the ridges of the contiguous bands are

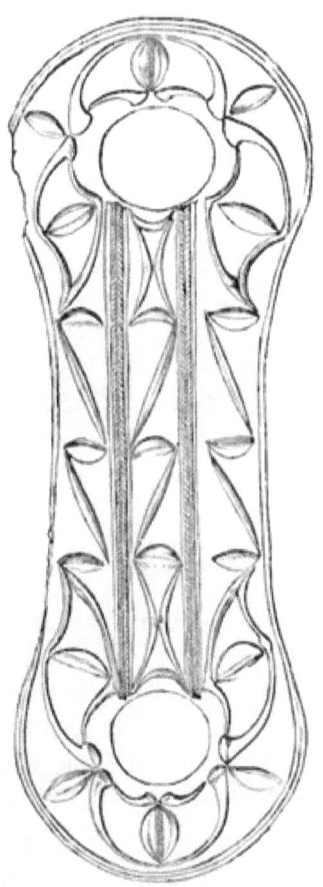

Fig. 123.—Plan of the Ornamentation of Bronze Armlet found at Drumside, Belhelvie, Aberdeenshire.

similarly ornamented in both. Like the Castle Newe and Pitkelloney examples, this armlet is one of a pair which were found together. It is not known what became of the other specimen of the pair.

Three others were found in ploughing a piece of new land three miles north-west of Aboyne, in Aberdeenshire, and are now in the possession of the Dowager-Marchioness of Huntly. Two of the three are similar in size and pattern of ornament, though not identical, one being slightly smaller than the other. One (Fig. 124) measures 4¼ inches in the

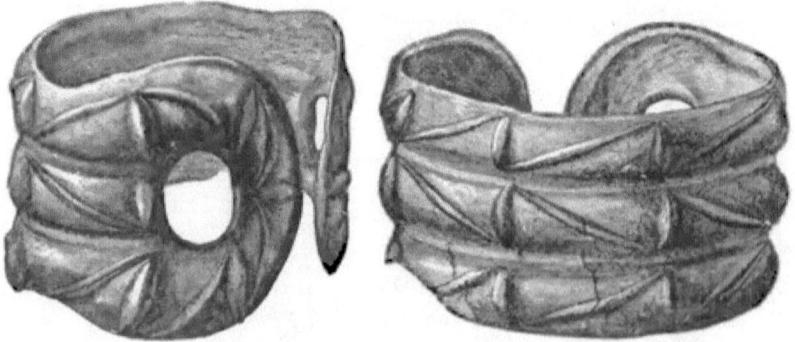

(1)   (2)

Fig. 124.—Armlet of Brass found near Aboyne (4¼ inches in diameter).
(1) Front view, seen sideways.   (2) Back view.

longer and 3¼ in the shorter diameter internally, 2¼ inches in width or height in the middle of the back, and 3 inches across the middle of the rounded extremity. Its weight is 20 ounces. The other, which is precisely similar in the pattern of its ornamentation, measures 4 inches in the longer and 3 inches in the shorter diameter internally, and weighs 14¼ ounces.[1] Both these examples show an

[1] These armlets were analysed by Professor Church, and the composition of the metal determined as follows :—

			Armlet No. 1.		Armlet No. 2.
Copper	.	.	86·49	.	88·19
Tin	.	.	6·76	.	3·64
Zinc	.	.	1·44	.	9·13
Lead	.	.	4·41	.	—
Loss	.	.	·90	.	—
			100·00		100·96

excess of wear at the edge on one side, where fully half the width of the outer band is worn away. The third armlet (Fig. 125) is broken and slightly twisted. It is much

Fig. 125.—Armlet found near Aboyne. Back and side view.

plainer, and wants the bold projecting parts of the ornament which are so conspicuous on the others.

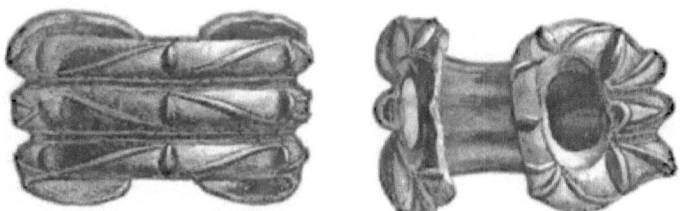

Fig. 126.—Bronze Armlet in the National Museum. Back and front views
(4½ inches in diameter).

An armlet of the same class, preserved in the National Museum (Fig. 126), has both its ends considerably cut away, so as to widen the opening. It measures 4½ inches in greatest diameter, and 3¼ inches in greatest width across the circular extremity. The locality in which it was found is unknown, although there is some probability that it may be one of two said to have been found in the neighbourhood of Bunrannoch, Perthshire. In the pattern and arrangement of its ornamentation it has a strong resemblance to the one next to be described. In all the previous cases these remarkable objects have been found unassociated with other articles, but in the case which follows there was an association which is suggestive of the period of the type.

In 1876, Mr. Lindsay, the tenant of the farm of Stanhope, in Peeblesshire, in searching for a rabbit underneath a large flat stone on the hillside, found the following articles among smaller stones underneath the larger one :—(1) a bronze armlet of the special character of those that have been described ; (2) two flat circular buckle-like articles of bronze ; and (3) a well made saucepan of bronze with a long side handle. The place where they were discovered is a small hollow close to the brow of a crag some 400 feet high,

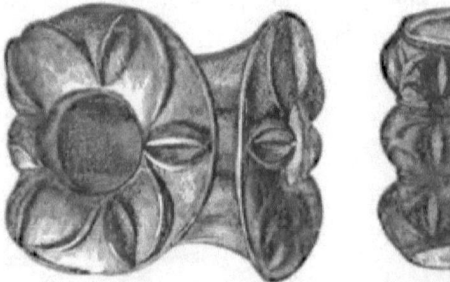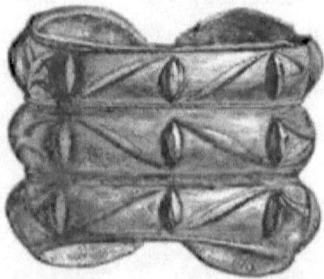

Fig. 127.—Bronze Armlet found at Stanhope, Peeblesshire.   Front and back views (4½ inches in diameter).

and lying below the summit of the hill, so that it cannot be seen unless by coming close to the brow of the hill overlooking it.

The armlet (Fig. 127), which is similar in form and ornamentation to those which have been described, measures 4½ inches in greatest diameter internally, and 4 inches from front to back. It is 3 inches wide across the middle of the back where it is narrowest, and 4½ inches across the centre of the terminal expansions. Its weight is 1 lb.

14¾ oz. The enamels which usually filled the circular spaces in the terminal expansions are absent, and there is no trace of the fastenings which held them in their places. The analysis of this armlet by Dr. Stevenson Macadam shows it to be a true bronze consisting of :—

Copper	.	.	.	90·69
Tin	.	.	.	9·29
Loss	.	.	.	·02
				100·00

The buckle-like objects (Fig. 128) are slightly oval in shape, formed of a single casting in bronze, consisting of an oval penannular ring 2¾ inches in diameter, convex exteriorly, and slightly hollow behind. It is decorated with two oval ornaments, with bosses at one side, and furnished with a somewhat rectangular projection, having a loop at the back. The ornamentation

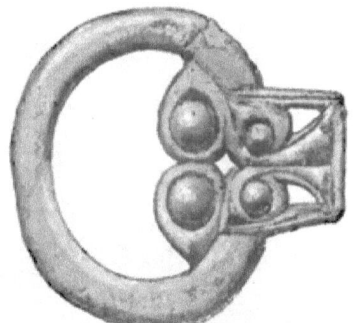

Fig. 128.—Buckle-like object of Bronze found at Stanhope, Peeblesshire.

presents the same character as that of the armlet, but is lower in relief, consisting of curved and trumpet-like forms projecting from the surface.

The saucepan (Fig. 129) is also a single casting in bronze, thin and beautifully finished, and tinned inside. The bowl of the pan is 6 inches wide at the mouth, the sides slightly bulging in the middle, and contracting to a diameter of 3¾ inches across the bottom. Its depth inside is 3⅞ inches. The bottom of the vessel is ornamented on the outside by four projecting concentric bands which give it strength, while the

thinning of the metal in the interspaces would serve to trans-
mit the heat quickly. It is furnished with a flattened side
handle 5½ inches in length, having a circular expansion at
the end. This special form of saucepan of tinned bronze,
with the long flat side handle terminating in a circular ornamented and perforated expansion, is found all over the area of
the Roman Empire.[1]   They seem to have spread over the area
of the Roman colonisation with other products of Roman manufacture, and when they are found in association with objects
that are not Roman in form and style of decoration, their pre-

Fig. 129.—Saucepan of Bronze found with the Bronze Armlet, etc., at Stanhope,
Peeblesshire.

sence is an indication that the period of the deposit cannot be
widely distant from the time of the Roman occupation.   The
conclusion drawn from the association of this saucepan with
these objects of native workmanship decorated in this purely
indigenous style of art, is plainly that this native style of art
was already in the period of its highest development at or
about the time of the Roman occupation of the southern portion of Scotland.

All these armlets are of one special variety of form, penannular, with expanded ends, having the exterior surface

---

[1] Another saucepan of this form found in the Loch of Dowalton, and
bearing the maker's name stamped on the handle, is described in connection
with the relics from Crannogs in Lecture VI.

divided into three parallel bands, the middle band stopping short at the circular opening in the expanded extremity, and the bands on either side of it passing round the openings to unite as one endless band.

There is another variety of form exhibited by some armlets of this character, which constitutes a link of connection between them and an equally remarkable class of armlets characterised by the same style of art, but exhibiting in their form a more distinctly zoomorphic feeling. Of this intermediate variety there are two specimens known in Scotland. The locality of the first specimen

Fig. 130.— Bronze Armlet, locality un-known, but probably from Bunran-noch, Perthshire (4½ inches in diam-eter).

(Fig. 130) is unknown, although there is some probability that it may be one of the two previously mentioned as having

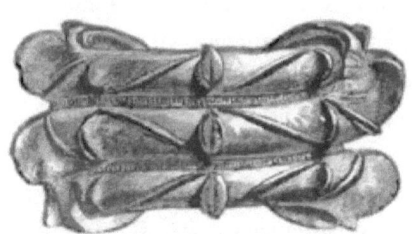

Fig. 131.—Bronze Armlet.   Back view.

been found at Bunran-noch, in Perthshire. It measures 4¼ inches in its greatest internal diameter, and 3 inches in greatest width across the middle of the cir-cular expansion at the extremity. Its weight is 31¾ oz. The openings in the terminal expansions are smaller than in the other armlets, and the projecting ornaments bolder and less uniform in character. Seen from the back (Fig. 131) it presents an appearance so similar to the form of those previously de-scribed that it is difficult to detect the variation. But on comparing the plans of the armlet given in outline (Fig. 132) with those of the other armlets (Figs. 120 and 123), the difference is apparent at a glance.   By throwing the furrows obliquely, which in the other armlets are parallel to the major axis of the form, and by cutting off the marginal ridges abruptly at the expansions of the rounded ends, the form of this armlet is changed into the similitude of a continuous band folded back upon itself from the two ends in opposite directions.   Although it possesses no distinctly zoomorphic character, it thus assumes a suggestively serpentine appearance.   This special variety of form is also exhibited by an armlet (Fig. 133), found near Seafield Tower, in the neighbourhood of Kinghorn, in Fife, which is at present exhibited in the Museum.   Its ornament (Fig. 134) is somewhat different in character, and the projections less prominent.   It measures $5\frac{1}{4}$ inches in its longest diameter internally, and $2\frac{7}{8}$ inches across the middle of the circular expansions at each extremity.

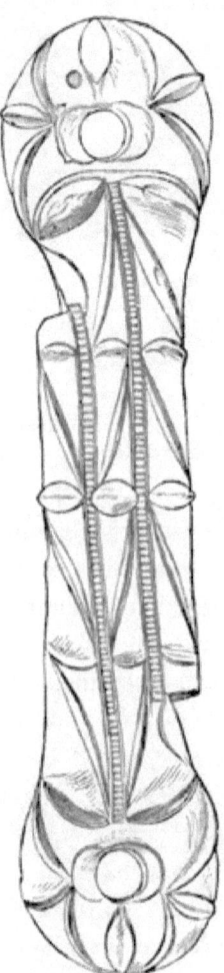

Fig. 132.—Plan of Ornamentation of Bronze Armlet.

From these descriptions it appears that there are two distinct varieties of one strongly-marked typical form of massive bronze armlet, decorated in a style of art which is remarkable for the special Celticism of its characteristics. It is a form which is found over a wide area in Scotland, and has only been once found out of Scotland.   The single example which carries the area of the form beyond the bounds of this country was found near Newry, in County Down,

Ireland (Fig. 135). It is 5 inches in its greatest diameter, and 3½ inches in height, and belongs to the transitional

Fig. 133.—Bronze Armlet found near Seafield Tower, Fife.   Front view, seen sideways (5¼ inches in diameter).

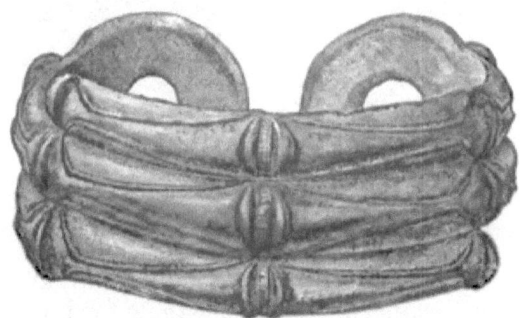

Fig. 134.—Bronze Armlet found near Seafield Tower, Fife.   Back view (5¼ inches in diameter).

Fig. 135.—Bronze Armlet found near Newry, County Down, Ireland (5 inches in diameter).

variety, which links this typical form with the zoomorphic type, which I next proceed to describe.

Some time before 1827 a man shooting over that wide waste of sand known as the Culbin Sands, near the mouth of the Findhorn, accidentally lost his gun-flint. He knew, how-

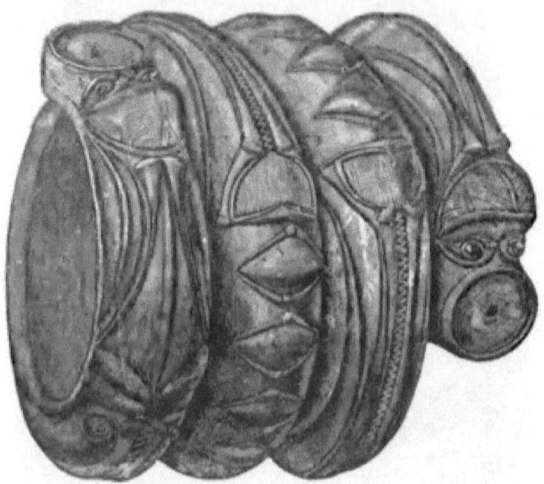

Fig. 136.—Bronze Armlet found in the sands of Culbin.   Front view (3½ inches in diameter).

ever, that in a special locality among these sand hills there is, on the site of an ancient settlement of the hunters of pre-historic times, a spot which is thickly strewn with fragments of flint, which these early hunters, who also used this material, had accumulated in the manufacture of their arrow-heads and other implements. Accordingly, he proceeded to this ancient flint factory to furnish himself with a new gun-flint, and when looking about for a suitable flake for his purpose he found a large and finely-made armlet of bronze (Fig. 136), which he carried with him and sold to a shopkeeper in Forres for half-a-crown. It subsequently passed into the possession of Lady Cumming of Altyre, by whom it is now exhibited in the Museum. It was described by Sir Thomas Dick

Lauder, and engraved in the *Transactions* of the Society so long ago as 1827. At that time it stood alone, and was regarded more as a curiosity than as a work of art. Now it stands as the representative of a peculiar class of art-products, which, so far as we know, are confined to Scotland alone. Its form is that of an armlet, formed of a coiled, double-headed serpent. It measures 3½ inches in diameter, and the

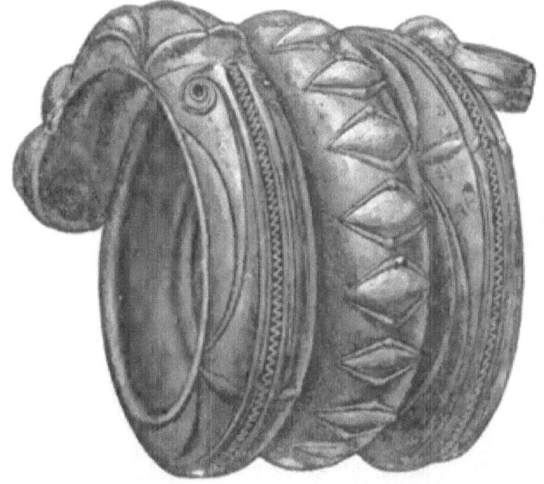

Fig. 137.—Bronze Armlet found in the sands of Culbin, Elginshire.   Back view.

same in depth externally. Its internal diameter is 2½ inches, and its weight 2 lbs. 9½ oz. It is a single casting in bronze, convex externally, concave internally, throughout the length of the coils, which, though closely contiguous, are completely separate, so that a sheet of paper can pass between them. There are three complete coils, and the middle coil (as seen in Fig. 137) is symmetrically ornamented with lozenge-shaped spaces, bounded by curves, and of considerable prominence. Each end terminates in a snake-like head, the eyes of which are set with blue glass. In front of the eyes is a round disc, sunk in the metal, which has probably been filled with enamel. The upper part of the head and neck is ornamented with raised trumpet-shaped scrolls, and about three inches behind the terminal head there is a simulation of a second head, the eyes of which are also set with blue glass. Speaking of it as a work of art, Sir Henry Ellis unhesitatingly calls it Roman work of the very best period, while Sir Thomas Dick Lauder observes that its workmanship is most beautiful. The taste which it displays, he says, is exquisite, and the detail executed with the greatest delicacy. And he further remarks that the natural form of the serpent has not been servilely and awkwardly copied, "as one might expect that a workman in an infant state of society would have done." But there is nothing in the character of the work, or in the nature of the art, to suggest that the workman belonged to an infant state of society. The technical skill displayed in modelling and casting such a difficult piece of work is undoubtedly of a very high order, and he would be considered a good workman to-day who could turn out an equally well finished casting of the kind. As to the design of the decoration there can be but one opinion. It possesses the merits of originality of conception, boldness of treatment, purity of style, and freedom of execution. It is decoration, also, of that complex kind which unites the effects of colour with those of form, and deals harmoniously with the results of such diverse processes as modelling in relief, chasing and engraving, the setting of jewels, and the fixing of enamels. The qualities of brain and hand that conceived and executed this piece of metal-work are not to be estimated solely by the results they have obtained in this single example. The man who did this was capable of much higher work if higher work had come in his way, and this solitary specimen of the work of an unknown artist is at least as interesting for the potentiality which it reveals as for the actual ability which it so clearly displays.

In the same year in which this armlet was first exhibited to the society (*i.e.* in 1827) another of similar character (Fig. 138) was presented to the Museum by the Dowager-Countess of Morton. It had been found at Pitalpin, near Dundee in 1732 ; but no record of the circumstances in which it was found is now extant. It is smaller than the one previously described, though still of greater size and weight than

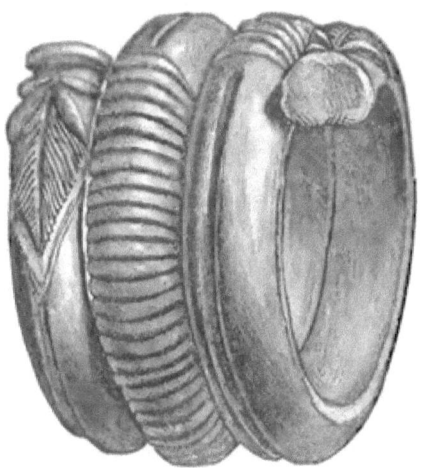

Fig. 138.—Bronze Armlet found at Pitalpin, near Dundee.

would now be considered convenient for wear as an article of personal adornment. It measures 3 inches in diameter, and about 3¼ inches in width externally, and has an internal diameter of 2½ inches. Its weight is almost 2 lbs. It is a single casting of bronze, consisting of three coils, of a serpentine form, convex externally and slightly concave within. The serpent-like body of the armlet is ornamented with transverse grooves on either side of a double furrow, running from end to end along the centre of the coils. The terminal portions are formed into the similitude of heads, but there are no settings for the eyes, and the zoomorphic character of the work is but feebly expressed. Nevertheless it is clearly an example of the same typical form and character of art as the Altyre specimen.

Another example, of smaller size (Fig. 139), is also in the Museum, but unfortunately nothing is known regarding its locality and the circumstances in which it was found. Like the others it is a single casting of bronze, of three coils of a

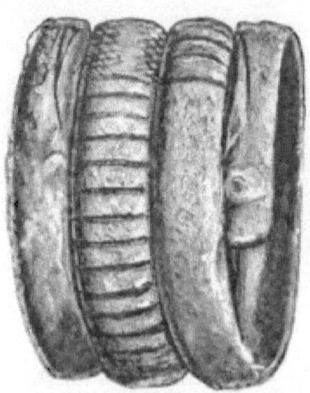

serpentine form, closely contiguous but not joined to each
other by their edges. The coils
are ribbed or banded transversely, with smoothly rounded
sections on the surface between the bands. The ends are
formed into the similitude of
animals' heads. The metal is
thin and finely patinated, and
the size and weight of the armlet are not excessive. Its internal diameter is 2½ inches,
its depth across the coils 2¼

Fig. 139.—Bronze Armlet (locality
unknown).

inches, and its weight 9¾ oz.

A fourth of these armlets (Fig. 140), closely resembling
the last in form and charac-
ter, but slightly larger in
size, was found in 1874 in
the course of the excavation
of an underground struc-
ture at Grange of Conan,
near Arbroath, in Forfar-
shire. The structure was of
the same character as that
in connection with which
the pair of massive bronze
armlets with enamels (Figs.
115, 116) were found at
Castle Newe, in Aberdeen-
shire. The special features

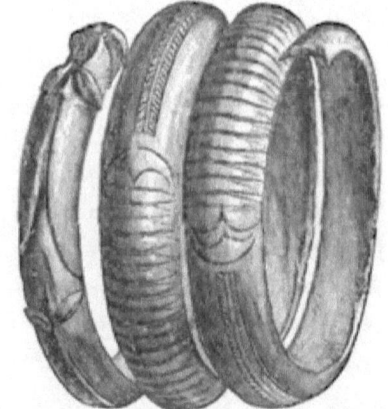

Fig. 140.—Bronze Armlet found at Grange
of Conan, near Arbroath, Forfarshire
(2¼ inches in diameter).

of these structures with their contents, and their relations,
will be discussed in a subsequent lecture, and it is only

necessary in this connection to mark the association of the two forms of armlets with the one type of structure. The armlet itself (Fig. 140) is a single casting of bronze, consisting of three coils, of a serpentine form, divided from each other by a somewhat wider interspace than in any of the other instances, and slightly more convex externally. The metal is thin, and the size and weight of the armlet are not excessive. Its internal diameter is $2\frac{5}{8}$ inches, and its depth across the coils $2\frac{1}{4}$ inches, its weight being about 10 oz.

In these spiral snake-like armlets, we have a class of objects exhibiting a distinct and strongly marked typical character. They are articles of personal adornment, possessing a very special form and style of ornament. Both by the peculiarity of their form and the specialty of their style of ornament they are closely allied to the class of more massive and more peculiar articles of adornment previously described. Like them also they are peculiarly restricted in range. The area over which they have been found, so far as we know, is confined to the eastern portion of Scotland, between the Moray Firth and the Firth of Tay. No specimen. is known beyond the bounds of Scotland.

In this connection, also, there falls to be described a class of objects of peculiar type, presenting features of decoration which are essentially Celtic in character. They are mostly carved in stone, but there is one example in bronze which supplies the link between them and the metal-work to which by their decoration they are most closely allied.

This object (Fig. 141) is a ball of cast bronze, found at Walston, Lanarkshire, long in the collection of the late Adam Sim, of Coulter, and now in the National Museum. It is $1\frac{1}{2}$ inch in diameter, divided into hemispheres, which differ considerably in the colour of the metal. Each hemisphere has a different variety of ornament, although the arrangement is the same in both. The surface of the ball is divided into six discs, three in the one hemisphere and three in the other. The discs

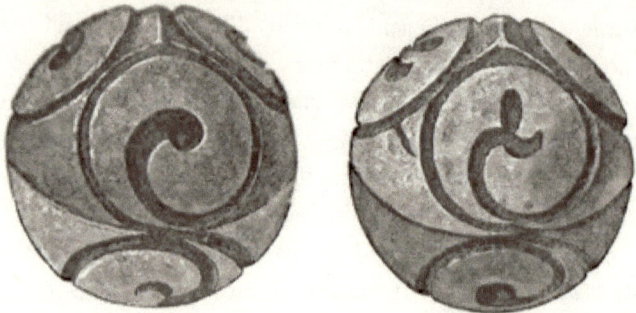

Fig. 141.—Ball of cast bronze, found at Walston, Lanarkshire (actual size).

are separated from each other by deeply hollowed grooves, and each disc in the upper hemisphere is ornamented by a spiral

Fig. 142.—Ornamented Slate Ball, from Elgin (actual size).

groove, terminating in a zoomorphic ending. The lower hemisphere is similarly treated, except that the spirals are simply geometric in their character.

A ball of clay slate, 2¾ inches diameter, from Elgin (Fig. 142), of which there is a cast in the Museum, has its surface divided into four projecting discs of considerable convexity, one of which is completely covered with a double spiral pattern, from which smaller spirals escape, but not in the regular manner so characteristic of the double spirals of the Celtic manuscripts and monuments of the Christian time. Another disc shows the commencement of an unfinished spiral. The two remaining discs are plain.

At the Glas Hill, in the parish of Towie, Aberdeenshire, in 1860, a finely ornamented ball of this description (Fig. 143) was found in digging a drain, and is now in the National Museum. It is of clay slate, fine-grained in texture, and dark in colour. It measures almost 3 inches in diameter, and has its surface divided into four boldly projecting discs with considerable convexity, three of which are elaborately carved and the fourth plain. Its ornamentation con-

Fig. 143.—Ornamented Stone Ball found in the Glas Hill, Towie, Aberdeenshire (3 inches in diameter).

sists of double spirals, wavy lines arranged concentrically, interrupted concentric circles and escaping spirals, but the lines are not continuous, and the patterns are not worked out with the regularity and precision so conspicuous in the style of the Christian time when the escaping double spiral formed such a characteristic element of Celtic decoration. In the triangular space between the three ornamented discs is a group of three dots arranged as a triangle.[1]

A ball of fine-grained clay slate (Fig. 144) found at Free-lands, near Glasterlaw, Forfarshire, has six projecting discs of

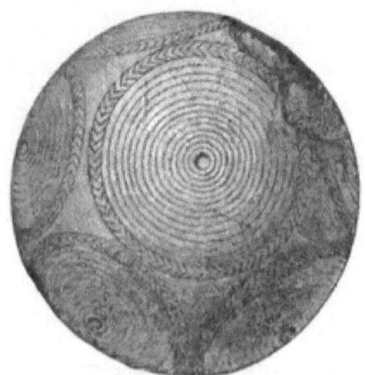

Fig. 144.—Ornamented Stone Ball found at Freelands, Glasterlaw, Forfarshire (3 inches in diameter).

Fig. 145.—Ornamented Stone Ball found at Fordoun, Kincardineshire (2¾ inches in diameter).

slight convexity arranged upon its surface; but the discs are small in proportion to the size of the ball and the interspaces wide. The discs themselves are plain, but the interspaces are partially ornamented. In the space between three contiguous discs is a pattern composed of three triangular figures within each other, formed by the meeting of curved or segmental lines. In the next contiguous space is a double spiral.

A ball of fine-grained dark-coloured sandstone (Fig. 145), found at Fordoun, in Kincardineshire, has its surface divided into seven circular compartments, some of which are simply incised with concentric circles, while in others there is a

[1] This arrangement of triple dots is a very characteristic feature of the illuminated Celtic manuscripts. It appears also on the monuments and metal work of the Christian time. This is the only instance of its occurrence on these balls, and though it may be held to suggest a possible connection, the suggestion is too feeble to imply distinct relationship.

border of chevrony ornament enclosing the concentric circles.

An example in the collection of Sir J. Noel Paton (Fig.

Fig. 146.—Ornamented Stone Ball, in the collection of Sir J. Noel Paton (2¾ inches in diameter).

146) presents a different style of ornament. It is of horn-blendic schist, 2¾ inches in diameter, and has its surface divided into six projecting discs, carved with concentric bands of slight convexity, the bands increasing in width and prominence towards the centre of the disc. The spaces between the discs are ornamented by irregular scoopings of the surface as if with the point of a gouge-like tool—a variety of decoration also seen in the gold object found on Cairnmuir (Fig. 114).

On the top of Craig Beg, near Ballater, previous to 1864, three stone cists were found containing interments which, from the presence of ashes and bones, were assigned to the Pagan custom of cremation. Each cist was also surrounded by a number of boulder-stones arranged in a circle of about 15 feet in diameter. Close to one of these cists a stone ball

(Fig. 147) was found, having its surface divided into six circular discs of slight convexity, and
some of the interspaces between
the discs ornamented with small,
rounded, slightly projecting knobs.

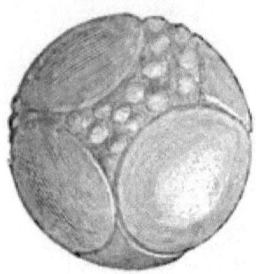

A ball of fine-grained claystone,
in the Perth Museum (Fig. 148),
which is said to have been dredged
up from the Tay, has its surface
divided into four circular discs
which scarcely project beyond the
circular outline of the ball, and im-
pinge upon each other. In one of

Fig. 147.—Ornamented Stone
Ball found at Ballater,
Aberdeenshire (2¾ inches
in diameter).

the discs the ornament consists of projecting knobs, arranged
in rows both ways by the channels between them crossing

Fig. 148.—Ornamented Stone Ball found in the Tay near Perth.

each other at right angles. The knobs rise from a square
base, and are rounded at the summits. This is also the

character of the prickly ornament of the hemispheres of the terminal bulbs of the penannular brooches of silver found at Skaill, to which the ornament on the disc of this stone ball has a distinct resemblance. The treatment of the segmental spaces between the discs is also seen in the example from Freelands, Glasterlaw (Fig. 144), and the simply incised ornament of the remaining discs occurs on two other balls

Fig. 149.—Ornamented Stone Ball found at Inverawe (2⅔ inches diameter).

Fig. 150.—Ornamented Stone Ba found at Loch Lochy (3 inches diameter).

(Figs. 149, 150), which have each but one of their discs ornamented.

An example from the island of Skye (Fig. 151) has its surface covered with small hemispherical protuberances. This variety is akin to another which has the whole surface studded with projections of a pyramidal form. Two balls of this latter variety (Figs. 152, 153) were found in one of the chambers of a curious composite structure, or group of structures, situated close to the shore on the

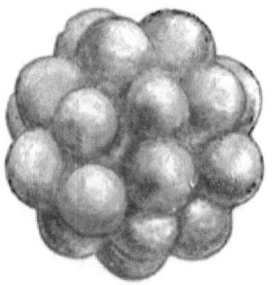

Fig. 151.—Ornamented Stone Ball found in the Isle of Skye (2¼ inches in diameter).

south side of the Bay of Skaill, in the mainland of

Orkney.[1]   One of these (Fig. 152) has the central portion
pierced with a hole.   The perforation is roughly made, and

Figs. 152, 153.—Stone Balls found in an ancient structure at Skaill, Orkney
(3½ inches and 3 inches in diameter).

considerably wider at its external orifices than in the centre,
where it is less than half an inch in diameter.

Another Orkney example (Fig. 154) is allied to these two
by the character of its ornamentation.   One of its ends is
studded with pyramidal projections, the middle portion is
ornamented by a continuous spiral, and the other end is filled
by a peculiar arrangement of segmental curves.

Many of these balls, however, have their discs destitute
of ornament.   But whether decorated or undecorated, they

[1] This structure, which was explored by Mr. William Watt, consisted of
several sub-rectangular chambers with rounded corners, having small cell-like
constructions opening off them.   The chambers were arranged on both sides
of a long winding passage.   Their door-ways had checks for the doors, and
bar-holes behind them.   The largest chamber was about 20 feet square.   From
6 to 8 feet of the height of the walls remained.   They were dry-built, and
converged towards the upper part as if to form beehive roofs.   Hearths of
square form, surrounded by flagstones on edge, were found in the floors.
Many implements of stone and bone were found in the chambers, and a large
accumulation of bones and horns of animals, among which those of the red-
deer and the *Bos primigenius* were abundant.   Among the stone implements
were several polished celts.   The collection is preserved at Skaill House.

usually present the strongly marked typical form, which varies
from the approximately circular with rounded discs, like the

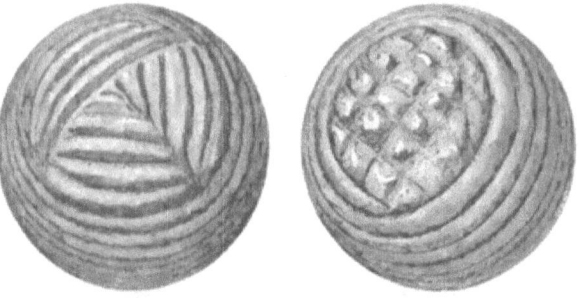

Fig. 154.—Ornamented Stone Ball found at Hillhead, near Kirkwall, Orkney.
Obverse and Reverse (2¾ inches diameter).

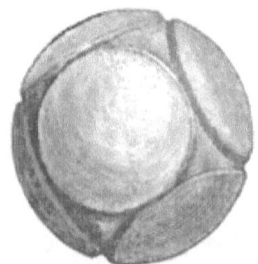

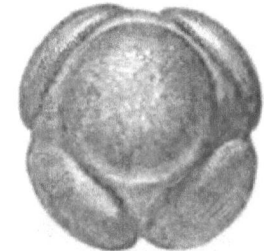

Fig. 155.—Stone Ball found in
Dumfriesshire.

Fig. 156.—Stone Ball found at Dud-
wick, Aberdeenshire.

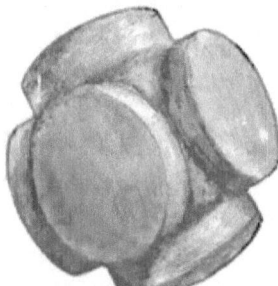

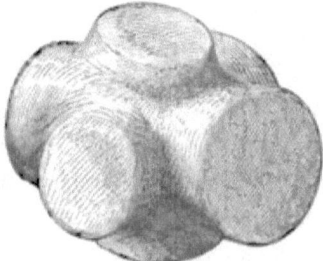

Fig. 157.—Stone Ball found at
Mountblairy, Banffshire.

Fig. 158.—Carved Stone found at Muckle
Geddes, Nairn.

examples shown from Dumfriesshire (Fig. 155), and Dud-
wick, in Aberdeenshire (Fig. 156), to those from Mountblairy,

in Banffshire (Fig. 157), and Muckle Geddes, in Nairnshire (Fig. 158), which take the form of a cylindrical axis with flat-ended cylindrical projections radiating round its circumference.

In all their varieties of form, these objects present certain features which are suggestive of a possible use as weapons. Their ornate character, their specialty of form, which renders them capable of being swung by thongs or bound to the end of a handle, and the fact that one example is pierced by a hole,

Fig. 159.—Unmounted men armed with maces.   From the Bayeux Tapestry.

are indications in this direction. Although there is no con-clusive evidence of the fact, it is at least conceivable that they may have been mounted as mace-heads similar to those metal mace-heads with pyramidal projections which are found occa-sionally among the relics of the Iron Age, and continued in use in the early Middle Ages, and similar, at least in appear-ance, to the mace-heads shown (Fig. 159) in the hands of unmounted men in the Bayeux Tapestry.[1]

[1] Dr. John Alexander Smith has discussed this point fully in his exhaustive notice of these Stone Balls in *Proc. Soc. Antiq. Scot.*, pp. 56-62.

But whatever may have been their special purpose or the precise manner of their use, it is of greater importance for the purposes of our inquiry that we should be able to determine their typical relations and ascertain the area to which they are confined. It is clear that they possess a typical form which has no distinctly definable relations with any other class of stone implements. The type is so peculiar and so strongly marked, that if it exists anywhere out of Scotland we should probably have known of its existence. But, with a single exception, said to have been found in Ireland, there is no record that I can discover of the occurrence of any specimen beyond the bounds of Scotland. Within that area it is widely diffused. There are so many specimens in private hands of whose localities we possess no record, that it is impossible to ascertain with any degree of precision the relative frequency of their occurrence in different districts of the country. But their known range comprehends an area which is but little short of the whole area of Scotland. They are most abundant in the north-eastern districts, but they occur as far north as Caithness and Orkney, as far south as Dumfries, and as far west as Argyle. Whether they belong wholly to the Pagan time or partly to the Christian period, it is clear that the prevailing features of their decoration, though distinctly Celtic in character, are not those of the fully developed style of Celtic ornament which prevailed throughout the early Christian time. Nor does it possess the most striking characteristics of the decoration of these objects in metal, of which so many characteristic examples have now been given. But the zoomorphic ending of the spiral pattern on the bronze

---

Dr. John Evans remarks that "it seems probable that they were intended for use in the chase or in war when attached to a thong which the recesses between the projecting discs seem well adapted to receive." He also states that "these Scottish Stone Balls seem to belong to a recent period, as compared with that to which many other stone antiquities may be assigned."— *Ancient Stone Implements, etc., of Great Britain*, pp. 377-379.

ball from Lanarkshire, and the double and escaping spirals of the Towie, Elgin, and Glasterlaw specimens, are sufficiently distinctive to claim for them a place in the same system of design which produced the peculiar patterns of the Pagan period, and developed from them the more elaborate systems of decoration so widely applied in the early Christian art of Scotland.

In the whole group of objects described in this Lecture we have a series of examples of the art which characterised the Iron Age Paganism of Scotland—the period that lies beyond the Christian time and reaches back until it merges into the Bronze Age culture. The outcome of the whole examination thus appears to be that the early Christian art of Scotland, although it had close relations with that of Ireland, was nevertheless based upon a pre-existing system of Pagan art peculiar to the area of the British Isles. Although remotely connected with certain developments of art that appear obscurely among the Iron Age relics of Central and Southern Europe, this special system of design received its highest development and attained its full maturity in the British Isles alone. There it became a distinctive school of decoration, exhibiting different aspects in England, Scotland, and Ireland, and attaining in each of these areas a separate development marked by a distinct individuality of character. Its manifestations in Scotland are those of a peculiar and highly characteristic style, confining itself to curvilinear forms, combining its simple elements in a manner that is neither rigidly geometric nor fettered by conditions of absolute sym-metry, but producing by the variation and rhythmic recurrence of its peculiar features a series of designs characterised by beauty of form, balance of parts, and harmonious combination. It differs from the art of the Christian time, inasmuch as it pre-sents no intermixture of forms and features that are common to Greek, Roman, or Etruscan art—no interlaced work, no meanders or key-patterns, or fretwork, and no similitude of foliage, or foliageous scrolls. It is zoomorphic, but its zoomorphism is chiefly apparent in the forms of the objects, and seldom exhibited in the designs with which they are decorated. It is more partial to the modelling of solid forms of ornament than to the elaborate enrichment of surface by intricate engraved work, and these solid forms of its surface ornament rarely become zoomorphic. When engraved or chased ornamentation is employed, it is used chiefly to produce broad effects by the contrast between plain spaces in the design and spaces filled with punctulations or chequers of short parallel lines. We find this peculiar style of art employed chiefly in the decoration of metal-work in bronze and gold. The objects so decorated are personal ornaments, arms, harness, and horse-trappings. The technical skill displayed in the fabrication and finish of these objects is great, and the quality of the art displayed in their decoration is high. There is implied in their production a special dexterity in preparing moulds and compounding alloys, in casting, chasing, and engraving, in the polishing and setting of jewels, in the composition and fixing of enamels. But there is further implied an artistic spirit controlling and combining the results of these various processes, giving elegance and beauty of a peculiar cast to the forms of the objects, and increasing the intrinsic elegance and beauty of the form by the harmonious blending of its special varieties of surface decoration, in which forms that are solidly modelled are intermingled with chased or engraved patterns and spaces filled with colour. A style of art characterised by such originality of design and excellence of execution must count for something in the history of a nation's progress, must have its place to fill in the history of art itself, when once we have begun to realise the fact that art was not the exclusive privilege of classic antiquity.

LECTURE IV.

(28TH OCTOBER 1881.)

THE ARCHITECTURE OF THE BROCHS.

IN this Lecture I have to deal with the products of a school of architecture, Celtic in its character, and absolutely peculiar to the Scottish area.

On the small uninhabited island of Mousa, lying off the east coast of the mainland of Shetland, there stands a solitary stone structure, massive in size, peculiar in appearance, and still more peculiar in character. It is a tower of circular form, wide and lofty, but constructed of undressed stones laid upon each other without mortar or other binding material, so that the mass of its uncemented wall coheres simply by its own vertical pressure.

Its situation is peculiar. The island is small, not over a mile in length, and less than half a mile in width, bare, flat, and rocky. The tower is placed on a small promontory on the west side of the island at the point nearest to the mainland. It stands about 20 feet back from the edge of the rocks, which slope irregularly to the tide-mark about 20 feet below. There are slight remains of an intrenchment on the sides which look landward, those facing the rocks and the sea are protected by the natural features of the ground.

The material of which the tower is built is the fissile flag of the island. The stones are flat, sometimes as much as 2 feet in thickness, but mostly much less, and they rather

diminish in size towards the top of the tower. The stones
bear no mark of a tool, and the masonry is not coursed, but
compactly fitted together. The wall goes up with a curve like
that of a lighthouse, and its external appearance (Fig. 160) is

Fig. 160.—Exterior View of the Broch of Mousa, Shetland.

suggestive of great solidity and strength. This suggestion of
solidity, which is due to the bulk of the building rather than
to the character of its masonry, is further intensified by the
absence of external openings, the whole exterior surface being
unbroken by a single aperture except the doorway. It is on
the level of the ground on the S.W. side, and is about 5 feet
3 inches high by 2 feet 11 inches wide, passing straight
through the thickness of the wall, but widening considerably
at a distance of about 7 feet from the outside and rising in
the roof. Entering by this tunnel-like passage through a wall
15 feet 6 inches thick, the visitor finds himself in the interior
of a circular well-like court, open to the sky above, but
completely surrounded by a wall of that thickness and 45 feet
in height. From the inner circumference of this court (as
seen in the ground plan, Fig. 161) there open at various places

other doorways leading into oval chambers constructed in the thickness of the wall nearly on the ground level. These chambers are three in number. One placed to right of the entrance is 16 feet in length, 5 feet 9 inches wide, and 9 feet 9 inches high. Its doorway is small, 3 feet high and 2 feet wide, passing through 4 feet of the thickness of the wall. A second chamber opposite the main entrance is 14 feet long,

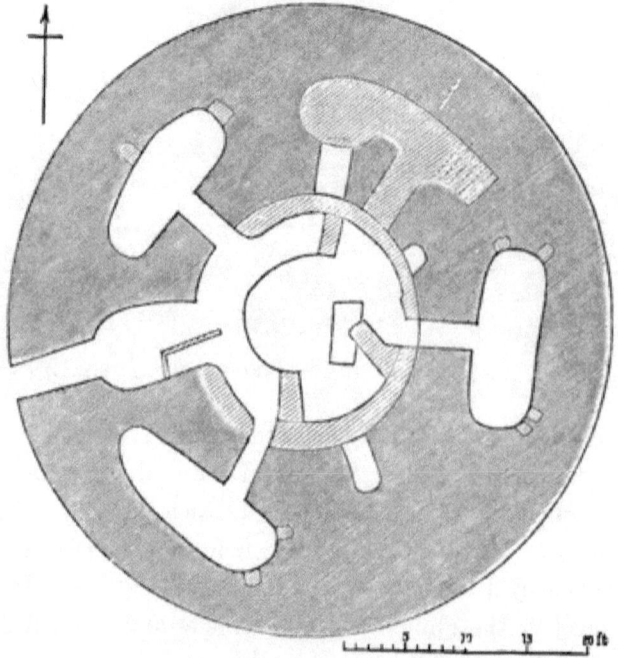

Fig. 161.—Ground Plan of the Broch of Mousa, Shetland.   (From Plan by Sir Henry Dryden.)

6 feet 10 inches wide, and 10 feet 6 inches high. Its doorway is also small, 3 feet 4 inches high and 2 feet 9 inches wide, passing through a thickness of 4½ feet of walling. The third chamber, situated to the left of the main entrance, is 14 feet long, 5 feet 6 inches wide, and 9 feet 6 inches high. Its doorway is 3 feet 2 inches high and 2 feet 3 inches wide,

passing through 4 feet of walling. All these chambers are irregularly oval in form on the ground plan. They are roofed in a peculiar manner. At variable distances from the floor the walls begin to be brought inwards by projecting each stone slightly beyond the face of the stone below it. In this way the distance between the opposite walls is gradually lessened as they rise in height until they come near enough to admit of single stones being laid across the space between wall and wall. This style of converging the walls inwards to obtain support for a roof of single stones is not new to us. We have met with it in the beehive houses of the early Christian monasteries and in the inverted boat-shaped roofs of their churches, built of uncemented stones on a rectangular ground-plan. It is the style of roof which is common to all dry-built structures that are roofed, whether they be of Pagan or of Christian time, because it is the style that is best suited to the material and the manner of construction. The builders of this edifice had no stones long enough to span chambers of six feet wide, and if they had had them long enough they would have been too weak to bear the superincumbent weight of a wall forty feet in height. Therefore they made their chamber-roofs semi-vaulted, while the doors and passages, which were narrow, were simply spanned with strong flat lintels. These chambers on the ground floor are lighted by window-like openings above the doorways, which rise one over the other, and serve not only to admit light and air, but to distribute the weight to be borne by the lintels. In each of the chambers there are small ambry-like recesses in the walls, but no fireplace or chimney. They are small, dimly-lighted, dungeon-like rooms, but neither smaller, worse-lighted, or more dungeon-like than many rooms in the lime-built castles of the nobles of the Feudal ages.

Half-way between the chamber facing the main entrance and the one to the left of it there is a doorway placed at a

height of four feet above the ground level. This doorway,
which is higher and wider than those which lead into the
chambers, is slightly larger than the main entrance itself,
being 5 feet 4 inches high and 3 feet wide. It leads to a stair
constructed like the chambers within the thickness of the wall.
At the foot of the stair there is an oval chamber, from one end
of which the stair rises in a steep slope, but following the curve
of the wall to the top. The steps are single flat stones,

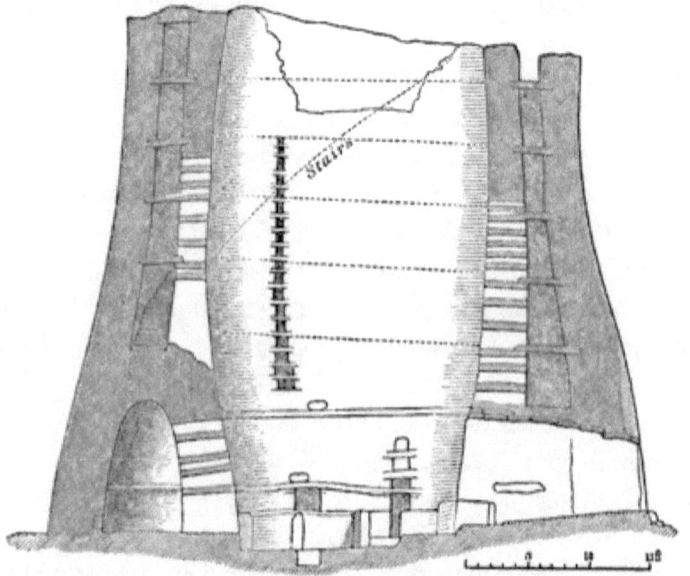

Fig. 162.—Section of the elevation of the Broch of Mousa. (From Plan by
Sir H. Dryden.)

varying in width from ten inches to two feet, undressed, and
laid above each other so that they give a tread of about five
inches and nearly the same of a rise. The upper part of the
tower which is traversed by the stair is differently constructed
from the lower part. To the height of about eleven feet above
the ground level the wall of the tower is carried up solid
except for the vacancy occasioned at intervals in its thickness
by the chambers and their accesses. But above this height

the wall is carried up with a vacancy in its centre (as seen in the section Fig. 162) so as to form a series of circular galleries placed one immediately over another, and crossed successively from the lowest to the highest by the rise of the stair which gives access to them.

These galleries, situated in the heart of the wall, are six in number. Each begins about 3 feet 9 inches in front of the stair, and goes round the whole tower on the level till it comes against the back of the stair, which closes it at that end, so that entrance to the gallery or exit from it can only be obtained by stepping across the space intervening between the end of the gallery floor and the steps of the stair. The floors of the galleries are formed of flat undressed slabs, the end of which reach into the walls on both sides. These slabs are about 6 inches thick, and those whose under surfaces form the roof of the first gallery present their upper surfaces as the floor of the second, and so throughout. None of the galleries exceed 5 feet 6 inches in height or 3 feet 2 inches in width, and some of the upper spaces are now much narrower; but as the position of the upper walls has evidently shifted, the original dimensions of the upper galleries cannot be ascertained. Four of the galleries that now remain (for the tower is incomplete at top) are lighted by four vertical ranges of windows all looking into the interior court. One range of fourteen openings is over the main entrance. Another of eighteen openings is over the entrance to the stairs. The third set has seventeen openings, and the fourth is imperfect, many of the lintels having been broken out. The peculiarities of these windows are—(1) that they are placed close to each other, vertically, with merely the thickness of a lintel between each opening; (2) they are wider than they are high, the greatest width being 2 feet 9 inches, and the greatest height not exceeding a foot; (3) they diminish in size gradually from the lowest to the highest; and (4) they do not range so far upwards as to include the two upper galleries, which are windowless.

Let us now group the main features of this singular building. It is a circular tower, composed of a dry-built wall 15 feet thick, enclosing a court 20 feet in diameter. The wall rises to a height of 45 feet, and has no opening to the outside except the doorway which gives access to the court. Opening from the court are a series of chambers on the ground floor constructed in the thickness of the wall and rudely vaulted with overlapping masonry. Above these are successive ranges of level galleries, also in the thickness of the wall, each going round the tower, and placed so that the roof of the one below always forms the floor of the next above. These galleries are crossed successively by a stair from which access to them is obtained by facing round in the ascent and stepping across the vacant space forming the well of the stair. The three lower galleries only are lighted, and the windows are placed in vertical ranges so close to each other as to be separated only by their upper and lower lintels.

Each of these features, taken by itself, is specially remarkable, and the presence in the one building of such a group of features that are wholly unfamiliar to us invests it with a character that is distinctly peculiar. From this examination of its character, it becomes obvious that although the construction and arrangements of the building are clearly those of a place of strength, it is incapable of association by way of relationship with any variety of castle known in historic times. But a wider survey of the remains of the ancient strongholds of the people who have occupied the land in times of which we have no distinct or detailed historic record will show that it has relationships so close as to amount to an almost actual identity with many similar structures in different parts of Scotland.

For instance, in the small valley of Glenbeg, which runs

nearly parallel with Glenelg, in the west of Inverness-shire, there are two such structures. One is situated on the edge of the meadow which lies in the bottom of the valley. It is greatly destroyed; more than half the circle of the wall is gone, and part of the height of the portion that remains is wanting. The internal diameter of the tower, at the level of the rubbish which encumbers the floor, is 33½ feet, and the thickness of the wall 11 feet. The doorway (Fig. 163), which

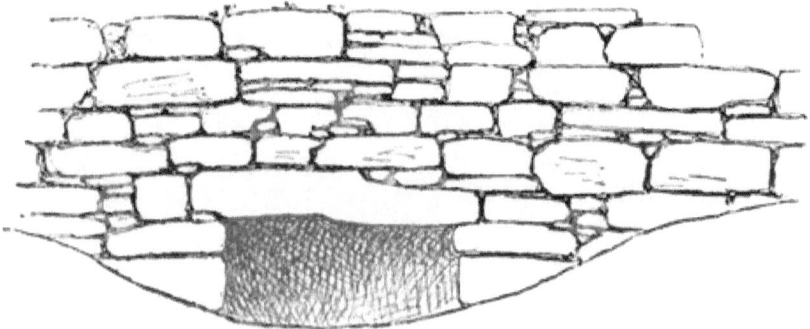

Fig. 163.—View of external aperture of doorway of Broch in Glenbeg. (From a Drawing by J. Romilly Allen.)

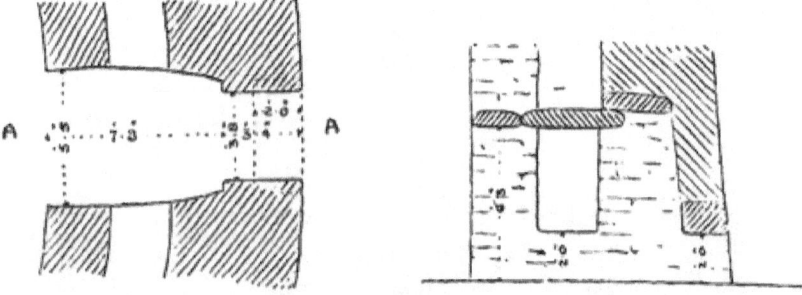

Figs. 164, 165.—Ground plan and section of elevation of doorway and passages through the wall of Broch in Glenbeg. (Drawn by J. Romilly Allen.)

is the only opening to the outside, is 3 feet 5 inches wide at the head, the lower part concealed with rubbish. About 4 feet inside the outer plane of the wall there is a rebate for a door (Fig. 164), with checks in the shape of large slabs set

edgewise in the wall. Within these checks the passage widens
to 5 feet, and the roof rises as shown in the section, Fig.
165. On the south side of the passage there is a guard-
chamber opening from it, and constructed in the thickness of
the wall. Three galleries and part of a fourth remain, but
the stair is gone. The galleries are lighted by vertical ranges
of windows looking to the interior. The greatest height of
wall remaining is not over 30 feet, but 7 feet of its height
were taken by the contractor for the Bernera Barracks in
1722. It must therefore, before that time, have been nearly
as high as Mousa now is.

At the distance of less than a mile up the valley on the

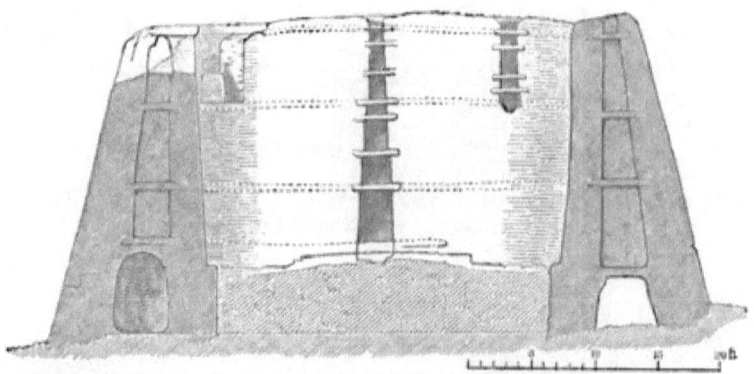

Fig. 166.—Section of the elevation of Broch in Glenbeg, near Glenelg. (From
Plan by Sir H. Dryden.)

same side, and placed on a considerable eminence, is another
ruined structure of the same kind (Fig. 166), but more dilapidated. No part of the height now exceeds 25 feet. The
diameter of the tower internally has been about 30 feet, and
the wall is 12 feet thick. Traces of chambers on the ground
floor are visible, but choked with rubbish. The door and stairs
are gone. Three galleries remain in part. The first is 6 feet
high and 4 feet wide, the second 6 feet high and 3½ feet wide,
the third inaccessible and somewhat smaller.

These structures, so far as their distinctive features remain
unobliterated, present a striking similarity alike in the manner
of their construction and the nature of their arrangements to
those of Mousa. They vary in certain details, as in size, in
thickness of wall, in the presence of a guard-chamber in connection with the passage, but in all the essential features of
plan, construction, and arrangements they are substantially
the same.

Near the head of Loch Duich, a few miles from Glenelg,
is another ruined tower. It stands on the slope of an eminence close under a high crag. The lower part of the structure

Fig. 167.—Ground plan of doorway of Broch at Loch Duich, with its guard
, chamber. (Wall 12 feet thick.)

is entire, but little remains of its height. Its internal diameter
is 31 feet, its thickness of wall 12 feet. The doorway is in
the lower side of the building facing the N.E. It is 3 feet
wide at the outside, and at 4 feet 3 inches within the outer
plane of the wall (Fig. 167) there is a rebate for a door
with checks formed of long slabs 9 inches thick, set edgewise
in the wall. Behind these is a bar-hole on either side for a
long stout bar. The hole, on one side, is long enough for the
bar to lie in it permanently, and on the other only long enough

to receive its end when pulled across behind a door either
constructed of wood or formed of a slab of stone set up
against the checks. On the S.E. side of the entrance passage
(Fig. 168) is a doorway 18 inches wide and 3 feet high, giving

access to an oval guard-
chamber constructed in the
thickness of the wall, 12 feet
long, 6 feet wide, and about
7 feet high, roofed in the
usual manner by overlapping
masonry and flat stones laid

Fig. 168.—Sectional elevation of S.E.
side of entrance passage of the
Broch at Loch Duich, showing
doorway of guard-chamber, and
bar-hole (wall 12 feet thick).

across. There are traces of
other chambers on the ground
floor, and part of a gallery
remains over the entrance,

but all above is gone. The masonry of this tower is more
massive than that of those in Glenbeg, but the general plan
and manner of construction are precisely similar in character.
In point of fact there is so little deviation from the typical
plan of construction among all the examples that are known,
that the detailed descriptions of them are for the most part
repetitions of features that are closely similar. But as we
are dealing with buildings that are in ruins, and, as it
appears, with a class of buildings of which no complete
example is now known to exist, it is important to determine
if possible whether there may be sufficient ground for assigning to the class the general feature of height, of which, in the
majority of cases, no direct evidence now remains.

There is distinct evidence on record that a number of
these massively built towers were of considerable height.
George Low, in 1774, says of the ruined tower or Broch
of Burraness, in the island of Yell, in Shetland, that it
had an inside diameter of 31 feet, a thickness of wall of
10 feet, and a total height of 20 feet. Of the Cullswick

Broch he says that its internal diameter was 26 feet 6 inches, its thickness of wall 18 feet, and the total height remaining 23 feet. Castle Cole (Fig. 169), at the junction of the Blackwater and the Brora, was then 15 feet in height, and part of it still remains of about that height. Dun Dornadilla, in Sutherlandshire (Fig. 170), as described by Mr. Cordiner in 1776,

Fig. 169.—Broch known as Cole's Castle, Sutherlandshire. (From a Sketch by Dr. Arthur Mitchell.)

Fig. 170.—Dun Dornadilla, in Strathmore, Sutherlandshire. (From a Sketch by Dr. Arthur Mitchell.)

and Mr. Pope of Reay, in 1777, had an internal diameter of 27 feet, and the total height then remaining was estimated at 25 to 30 feet, with three galleries and part of the stair. Maitland, in 1757, describes Dun Alisaig, in Ross, as being 30 feet internal diameter, with 12 feet thickness of wall, and three of the galleries remaining, which implies a height of 25 to 30 feet. Dun Carloway, in Lewis, was 40 feet high in the end of last century, and showed the plan of its galleries with their vertical ranges of windows almost as completely as Mousa. Judging from these examples, which still have, or which in recent times have had a considerable portion of their height remaining, and taking into account the quantity of material which envelops the bases of most of those that have been reduced to the condition of mere mounds of ruin, it seems established by evidence that there were many cases in which the total original height could scarcely have been less than that of Mousa, and that height, as well as bulk, was one of the main features of the typical structure.

These examples will suffice to convey a clear idea of the distinctive features of the type of structure with which we are dealing. Its main features of distinction, by which it separates itself from all known types, are (1) that it is a circular tower of dry-built masonry, wide and lofty, and enclosing within it a central area open to the sky ; (2) that all its apertures, except the external opening of the entrance to the central area, look into this enclosed interior court ; and (3) that its chambers, stair, and galleries are contained within the thickness of this enclosing wall.

Having thus obtained a distinct conception of the type, we now proceed to determine its range or area. For this purpose it is necessary to ascertain what structures exist in Scotland, or out of it, possessing these typical features.

On the northern declivity of Cockburn Law, in Berwickshire, there is a natural platform projecting from the shoulder of the hill over the valley of the Whitadder water, about 250 feet above the bed of the stream. On this platform there is an irregularly oval enclosure (Fig. 171), the outlines of which are formed by the remains of two parallel earthworks and an outside ditch. The space thus enclosed is occupied by the remains of various smaller enclosures, some circular and others irregular in form. They are nearly all so ruined that nothing can be made of their details. But the principal structure within the enclosure is still capable of such examination as will suffice to determine its typical relationship with the Brochs of the extreme north. It is circular, consisting of a wall 17 feet thick, enclosing an area of 56 feet in diameter. In the thickness of this wall are two elongated oval-shaped chambers, one of which is 33 feet long and 7 feet wide, the

other 23 feet long and 7 feet wide. In 1793 the roofs were
still on them, and it was then seen that they were covered

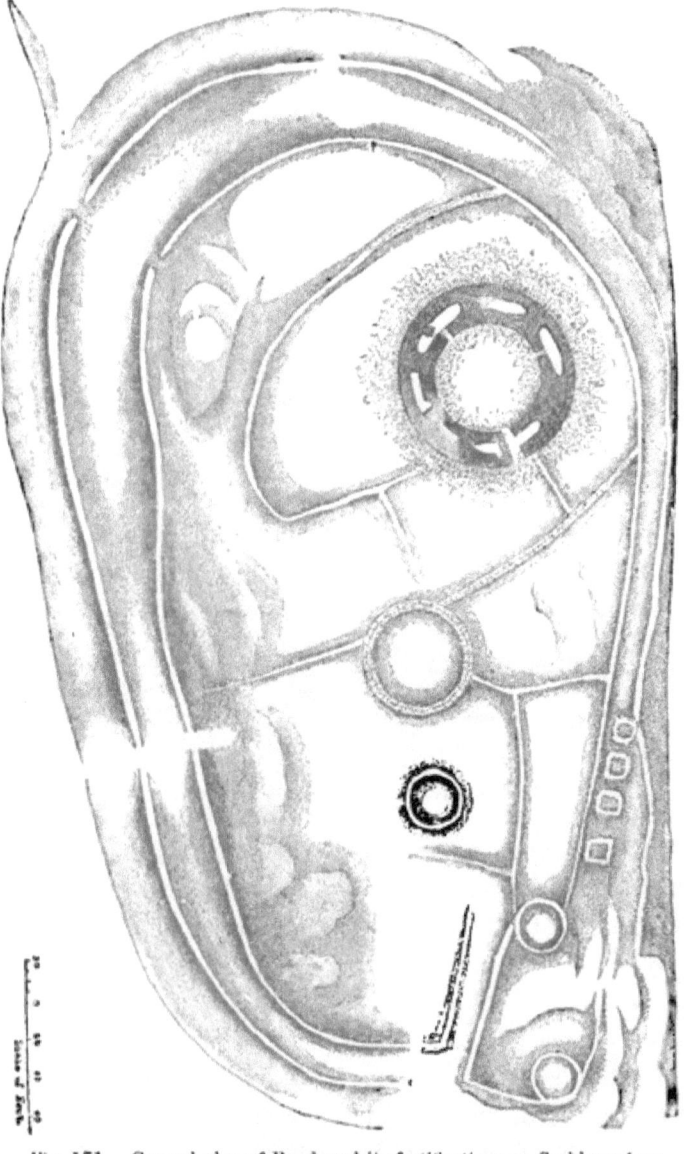

Fig. 171.—General plan of Broch and its fortifications on Cockburn Law,
Berwickshire.

with a rude vaulting of overlapping masonry. Both these
chambers open to the inner area. The only access to this
area from the outside is the main doorway, which passes
straight through the wall, and is flanked by a guard-chamber
constructed in the thickness of the wall on either side. To
the left of the doorway are the remains of the staircase, with
an elongated chamber opposite the foot of the stair. No
remains of galleries exist owing to the absence of the whole
upper part of the structure, but the presence of the stair
implies that they once existed. The masonry is massive in
character (Fig. 172), and the structure is also remarkable for

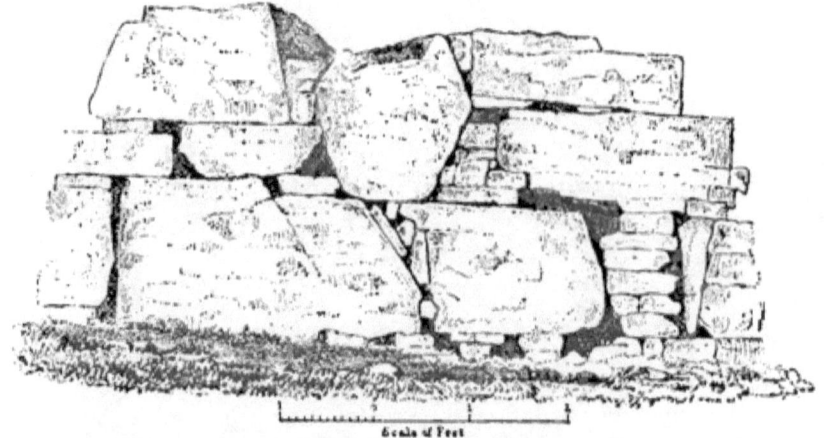

Fig. 172.—Masonry of Broch on Cockburn Law.

its great size, being three times the width of Mousa and twice
that of the Glenelg Brochs. But its features of form and
character, and all the arrangements of its details, so far as
they now exist, are those of the typical Broch structure; and,
taken together, they form a group of features and arrangements
which do not exist in any other type of structure.

On the highest elevation of the Torwood, in the parish of
Dunipace in Stirlingshire, are the remains of a circular structure, excavated in 1864 by Colonel Joseph Dundas. Its

appearance previous to its excavation was that of a conical
hillock situated nearly on the verge of a precipitous crag, and
enclosed on the accessible side by the remains of a double wall
of fortification. After excavation it was found to be the ruin
of a circular tower of uncemented masonry which, by the
gradual dilapidation of its walls, had become a conical hillock
of stones covered with grass and heather, and overgrown by a
clump of large fir-trees. The structure, now cleared from the
superincumbent mass of ruin, is a circular wall 15 feet thick,

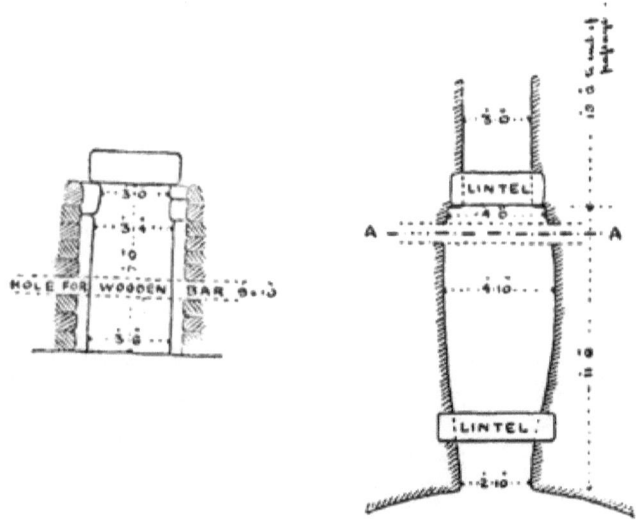

Figs. 173, 174.—Ground plan and section of elevation of doorway in Broch
at Torwood, Stirlingshire. (Drawn by J. Romilly Allen.)

enclosing a central area of 35 feet in diameter. The entrance
doorway has some of the massive lintels still upon it. It is
about 7 feet high and 3 feet wide at the door-checks, behind
which are the usual bar-holes (shown at A A in the ground
plan and section, Figs. 173, 174). To the left of the doorway
is the staircase, as usual in the thickness of the wall. The
height of wall remaining is not sufficient to show any traces of
the galleries, but the presence of the stair implies their former

existence. There are no chambers in the thickness of the wall on the ground floor, but all the other features of the building are those of the typical Broch structure.

On the other side of the valley of the Forth, and farther west, at Coldoch, in Perthshire, a similar mound, covering the ruins of a circular tower of uncemented masonry, was excavated in 1870. The structure consists of a circular wall (as shown on the ground plan, Fig. 175) 17 feet thick, enclosing a central

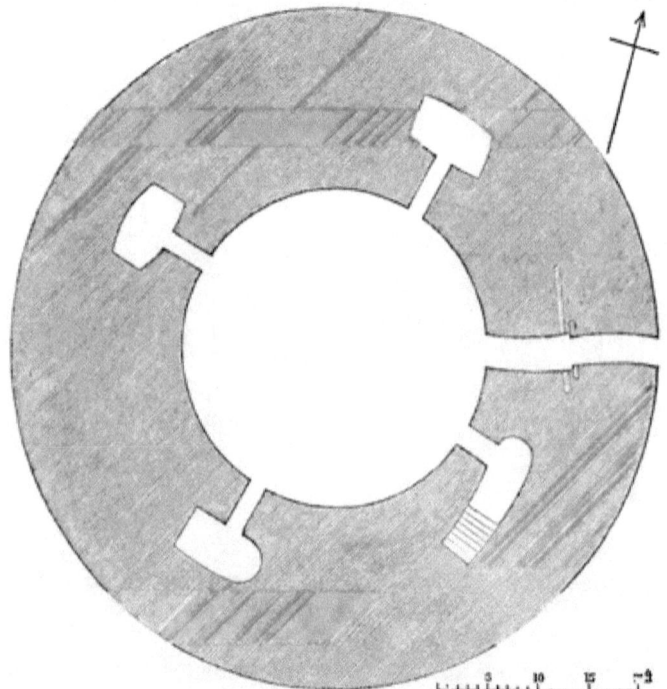

Fig. 175.—Ground plan of the Broch of Coldoch, Perthshire.
(From a Plan by Mr. Ballingall.)

area of 30 feet in diameter. The doorway on the east side passes straight through the wall, and is three feet wide, with checks for the door about half-way through the thickness of the wall, and immediately behind them the usual bar-holes. To the left of the doorway is the staircase. No remains of the upper galleries exist, but the presence of the stair implies that they did exist. Opening from the central area are the entrances to three chambers in the thickness of the wall. They are nearly of a size, 8 feet long, 4 feet wide, and a little over 6 feet high. One still retains its roof, rudely vaulted with overlapping masonry. In this case also the group of features characteristic of the structure and its arrangements is such as can be found only in the typical structure of the Broch.

These three examples are all that are known on the mainland of Scotland south of the Caledonian valley. A few years ago they were mere grass-covered hillocks, indistinguishable from many others that are yet to be seen in various quarters of the same wide district of country. It is impossible to say how many of these unexamined mounds, which exist abundantly in the valleys of the Forth and Teith for instance, may be of similar character. But it is possible to say that where three have been found without being specially looked for, the probability is that more will be found when they are looked for. The present position of our knowledge is that there are three examples south of the Caledonian valley, but if I were to conclude that these three are all that exist in that wide region I should be drawing from my ignorance of the actual facts a conclusion which could only be drawn from complete knowledge obtained by exhaustive investigation.

The case is far otherwise with reference to the district of country that lies to the north of the Caledonian valley and the isles around the northern and western coasts. In such remote and frequently rugged and barren localities the remorseless activity of the agricultural improver has made but little progress in the removal of the ancient landmarks, and Brochs, and sepulchral cairns, stone circles and standing monoliths are still comparatively abundant, though every season diminishes their number. Some years ago I attempted an enumeration of the remains in the northern counties of Scotland that were either certainly known to be Brochs or were inferred to possess that character, judging from external appearances. The list has been published[1] for seven years, and the corrections made upon it during that time have not appreciably affected its total results. These are roughly stated as follows:—in Shetland, there are 75 Brochs; in Orkney, 70; in Caithness, 79; in Sutherland, 60; in Ross-shire, 38; and in Inverness-shire, 47; giving a gross total for the five northern counties of Scotland of 370. Admitting that there must be some instances included in the enumeration which subsequent examination may prove to be remains of a different character, it is equally probable that others will be found which have not been included in the list, and the errors in these opposite directions may be expected nearly to balance each other. But if we suppose that it will be necessary to deduct so large a proportion as 20 per cent, we should still have a gross total of 300 Brochs in the five northern counties. The full significance of such a result is scarcely realised at once. It means that we have here the remains of a period of architectural activity which has no parallel in the early history of our country.

Whatever may be the effect of future discoveries in increasing the number of examples in the district south of the Caledonian valley, it is clear that the principal area of the type lies within the region to the north of that valley, comprehending the five northern counties of Scotland, and including the northern and western Isles. Within that area they are known to exist abundantly, beyond it sparsely. Out of Scotland the type is totally unknown. It is a type possessing features so distinct and peculiar, so numerous and well marked, so pronounced in their absolute individuality, that if it exists anywhere it is capable of being instantly recognised. But no

[1] *Archæologia Scotica*, vol. v. pp. 178-197.

single instance occurs in Ireland, or Wales, or Cornwall. No trace of it is found in England, France, or Scandinavia. It is absolutely confined to Scotland alone.[1] Having thus estab-

[1] The Nuraghi of Sardinia are round towers built of uncemented stones. They are exceedingly numerous in the island, and it has been occasionally asserted that they bear a remarkable resemblance to the Scottish Brochs. It is true that they are like the Brochs externally, because they are round towers, (see Fig. 176), but they possess none of the characteristic features of the

Fig. 176.—Nuraghe of Goni, in Sardinia.

typical Broch structure. They contain vaulted and windowless chambers placed vertically above each other in the centre of the tower. The access to these chambers is by a winding stair, which traverses the thickness of the wall

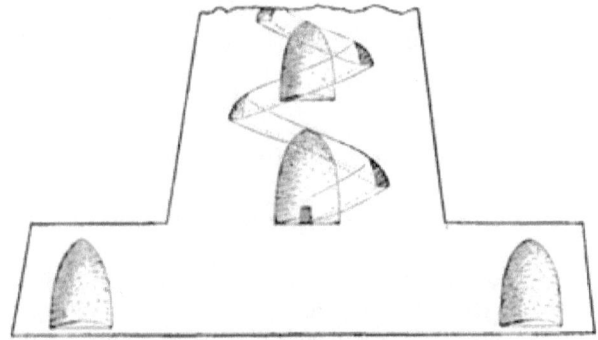

Fig. 177.—Section of Nuraghe, showing form of chambers and spiral stair.
(From Tyndale's *Sardinia*.)

O

lished the essential features of the typical form of the Broch structure and determined the area to which it is exclusively confined, I now proceed to notice a few other examples possessing features which may not have been present or prominent in those previously described.

We have already seen that many of these towers were

Fig. 178.—Broch known as Cole's Castle, in Sutherlandshire. (From a sketch by Dr. Arthur Mitchell.)

built in positions that were naturally strong. One of the most remarkable of these is the Broch of Cole's Castle in Strathbrora, Sutherlandshire (Fig. 178), which has been

completely round the central chambers. Sometimes they have a more complex structure, consisting of a central tower rising from a square basement, with chambers also in the basement, as shown in the accompanying section (Fig. 179). It is thus apparent that the typical Nuraghe differs completely in idea from the typical Broch. Although the external form may be in some cases similar, the essential features of the Broch are not found in any one instance in the Sardinian Nuraghi. No Broch has vaulted chambers disposed vertically over each other in the centre of the tower, and no Nuraghe has its centre open, and its chambers, stairs, and galleries arranged in the ring of walling surrounding the central court and windows looking into it as the Brochs have.

already referred to. It is situated on the top of an isolated
eminence, precipitous on one side, and defended on the side
which is less precipitous by a double fortification of dry-stone
walling. Others whose situations made them capable of being
so defended were protected by ditches and embankments.
The Broch of Snaburgh, in the island of Unst, in Shetland,
which stands on a promontory projecting into the loch, is
protected on the land side by a wet ditch and a rampart of
large stones. The Broch of Burraness, in the same island, is
strengthened on the land side by two deep ditches and high
embankments. The Broch of Cullswick was protected by a
ditch 13 feet wide, and a rampart of earth and stones completely encircling the base of the tower. The Broch of
Burraland, which stood on a promontory in the loch, had a
double rampart and a double wet ditch on the land side, both
well defined. The Broch of Yarhouse, in Caithness, stood on
a low flat promontory projecting into the loch, and was cut
off from the land by a deep ditch from 25 to 30 feet wide,
and had its doorway further protected by a long covered
way. The Broch of Clickamin, at Lerwick (Fig. 179),
although situated on an island in the loch, was fortified by a
wall completely surrounding the island. Within this outer
wall of defence there is an outwork or guard-house, in form a
segment of a circle, 43 feet on its convex face, connected
with the outer wall by a passage. The outwork is 19 feet
wide at the passage through it, slightly narrower at the
ends. The passage is 8 feet high, and about 5 feet in
from the outer face of the work it narrows to 2 feet
11 inches, with checks for a door. Behind these are holes
in the opposite walls for a bar and a slit in the roof of
the passage. Besides these two exterior defences the doorway of the tower itself had checks and a sill for a door
about 10 feet within the outer opening of the entrance passage through the wall of the Broch. This passage is 4 feet

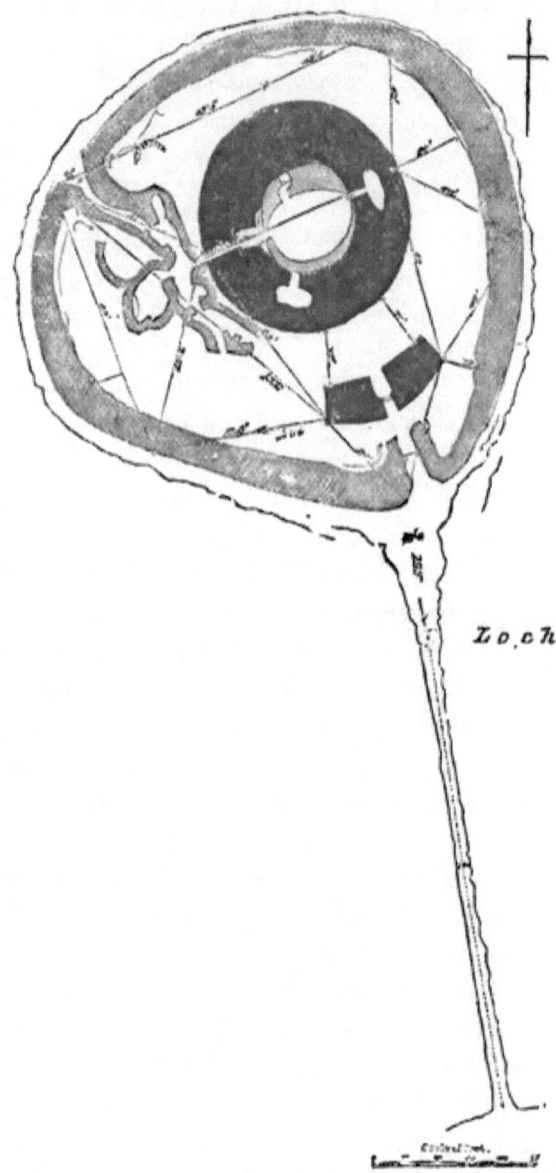

Loch

Fig. 179.—General plan of Broch of Clickamin, near Lerwick, Shetland, showing
the walled island and causeway leading to it. (From a plan by Sir H.
Dryden.)

10 inches high, and the opening between the door-cheeks is 2 feet 11 inches wide at the bottom and 2 feet 6 inches at the top, with bar-holes on either side.

The East Broch of Burray, in Orkney, explored by Mr. Farrer, presented the appearance of a green mound 20 feet high, surrounded by an embankment. The mound when excavated was found to cover the lower portion of a circular tower of uncemented masonry (Fig. 180). The wall of the

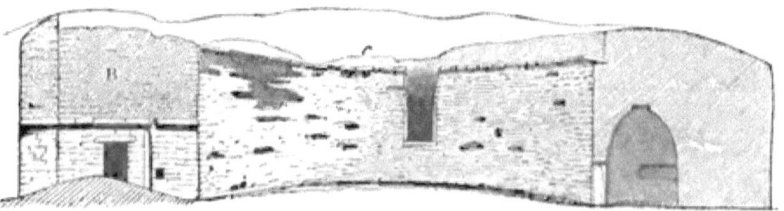

Fig. 180.—Diagrammatic Section of East Broch of Burray.
(From *Archæologia Scotica*, vol. v.)

tower was 15 feet thick, enclosing a central area 36 feet in diameter. The entrance passage as usual went straight through the wall, and had a guard-chamber opening from it on either side. The entrance to one of these is shown in the section and the bar-hole behind it. There were two other chambers constructed in the thickness of the wall opening from the central area, and the entrance to the stair was placed as usual to the left of the doorway, but on a higher level. In all its features it closely resembles all that have been described, but in one feature it differs from them. Close to the doorway, but outside the wall, there is a well with a passage and steps leading down into it. There are other examples which exhibit the same feature.

The Broch of Borrowston, in Shapinsay (Fig. 181), also in Orkney, consisted of a wall 13 feet thick, enclosing a central area 33 feet in diameter. Within the central area of the Broch there was a well 10 feet deep, the lower part dug out of the solid rock, and the upper part faced with dry-built

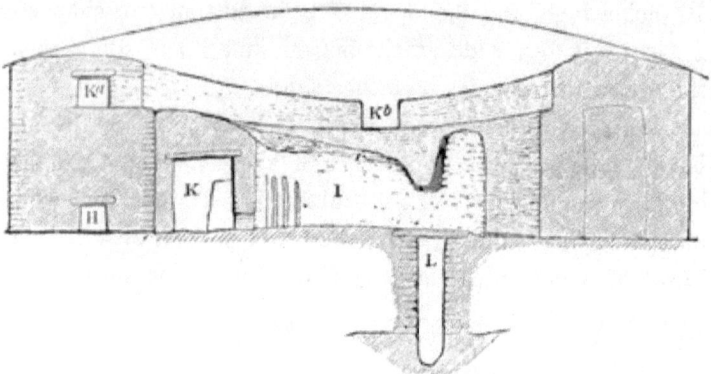

Fig. 181.—Diagrammatic Section of the Broch of Borrowston, showing the well in the area. (From *Archæologia Scotica*, vol. v.)

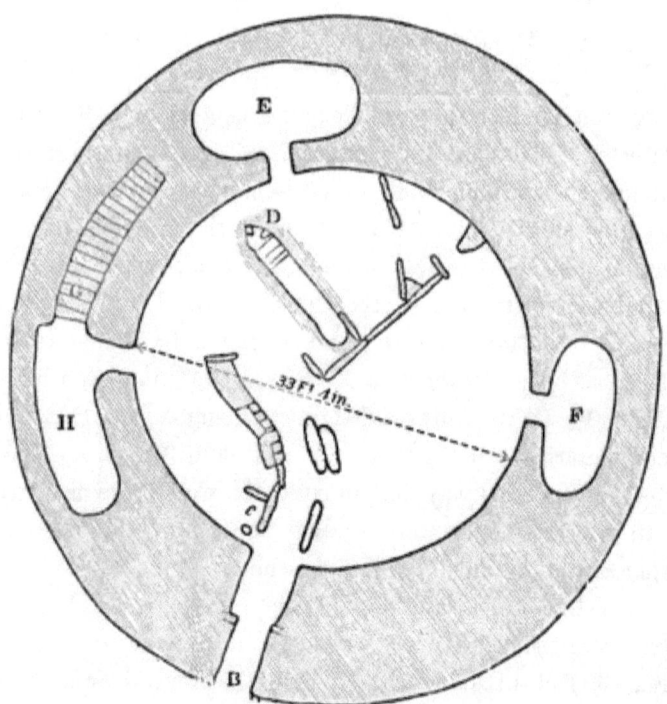

Fig. 182.—Broch at Mause of Harray. (From a Plan by Mr. George Petrie, 1⅛ inch to 1 foot.)

masonry. The Broch of Okstrow, at Birsay in Orkney, which consisted of a wall 12 feet thick, enclosing an area 45 feet in diameter, had a well within the area and a drain from it leading out to the outside of the structure. The Broch near the Manse at Harray (Fig. 182), excavated by Rev. Dr Traill, consisted of a wall 12 feet thick, enclosing an area about 33 feet in diameter. It was surrounded by outbuildings, which were not properly explored. There were no guard-chambers on either side of the passage (B), which shows the checks for the door, at 6 feet within the outer face of the wall. To the left of the main entrance is the usual chamber (II) at the foot of the stair (G), of which 19 steps remain ; and two other oval chambers (E and F), placed at nearly equal distances in the circumference of the wall, complete the resemblance to the general type. Near the middle of the area a subterranean passage terminating in five steps led to a well (D) 9 feet deep excavated in the rock. The subjoined sectional diagram (Fig. 183) shows the construction of the

Fig. 183.—Section of the Well in the Broch at Manse of Harray
(From a plan by Mr. George Petrie.)

well, which still retained water when the excavation of the Broch was made. The Brochs of Skinnet, Harpsdale, and Kettleburn in Caithness, had each a well within the central area. The well of the last-mentioned Broch is still utilised as the existing water supply for the cottars, who live in houses close by constructed of the stones removed from the site of the ancient structure.

The central areas of several Brochs have been provided with drains to convey the surface water outside the building. This same Broch of Kettleburn had a drain which passed out under the foundation of the wall of the tower. It was what is now called a self-cleansing drain, the flat stones forming the water channel being set together in the form of the letter V. Sir Henry Dryden remarks the presence of drains in the Broch of Clickamin. I found a square drain leading from the court of a Broch which I excavated at Brounaben, in the parish of Wick.

The facts that many of these structures were thus provided with drainage, and that they had also secured a water-supply within the enclosed area of the building, are not only significant indications of intelligence and forethought applied to the arrangement of constructional details, but when taken in connection with all the other arrangements of the structure external and internal, they complete a series of characteristics which point definitely to one object as the chief intention of the Broch-structure, viz. security obtained by the simplest of all means—a construction of uncemented stones which could neither be easily forced nor readily reduced.[1]

Reviewing the typical characteristics of the special form

---

[1] That this object was practically attained by these simple means we have evidence in one case from the direct testimony of record. It is related in the *Orkneyinga Saga*, that Erlend, who (about A.D. 1155) carried off the widow of Maddad, Earl of Athol, took her north to Shetland, and took up his residence in Moseyarborg—the Broch of Mousa, described at the commencement of this Lecture. It is said that her son Harald, Earl of Orkney, pursued Erlend, and besieged him in the Borg, "but it was difficult to take it by assault," and the siege failed because "Erlend had made great preparations." This is the only record of the actual use of a Broch as a place of defence, and it bears out the inference drawn from an examination of the nature and arrangements

of structure which has come to be known in recent years by
the local northern name Broch, we see that it is a hollow
circular tower of dry-built masonry, rarely more than 70 or
less than 40 feet in its total diameter, and occasionally at
least 50 feet high. Its circular wall, which may be from
9 to 20 feet thick, is carried up solid for about 10 feet, except
where it is pierced by the entrance, or partially hollowed by
the construction within its thickness of oblong chambers with
rudely-vaulted roofs. Above this height the wall is carried
up with a vacancy of about 3 feet wide between its exterior
and interior portions. At every 5 or 6 feet of its height this
vacancy is crossed by horizontal ranges of slabs inserted as
ties between the outer and inner shells of the wall, so that
their upper surfaces form a floor to the space above and their
under surfaces become a roof to the space below. These spaces
thus form horizontal galleries about 6 feet high and 3 feet
wide, separated from each other vertically by the slabs of
their floors and roofs. They run completely round the tower
except that they are crossed successively by the stair which
gives access to them. They are lighted by ranges of pecu-
liarly-constructed windows placed vertically over each other,
and all looking into the central area enclosed by the wall of
the tower. This area or court varies from 20 to 45 feet in
diameter. At various points of its interior circumference
are · placed the openings which give access to the chambers
on the ground floor within the wall, and to the stair which

of the structure, that it was difficult to take by assault, and equally difficult
to reduce by siege, if the defenders were provided with supplies. It is also
stated in the Saga of Egil Skalagrimson, that about two centuries and a
half before this time (or somewhere about A.D. 900), Bjorn Brynjulfson,
fleeing from Norway with Thora, Roald's daughter, because her father
would not consent to their marriage, was shipwrecked on the island of
Mousa, landed his cargo and lived in the Borg during the winter, cele-
brating his marriage in it, and afterwards sailed for Iceland.—The *Orkneyinga Saga* (Edinburgh, 1873), p. cxi. and chap. 92.

ascends to the galleries. The only aperture on the outside of
the tower is the doorway formed by the external opening of
the tunnel-like passage through the wall which gives access
to the central court. It is always on the ground level, square-
headed, usually with slightly inclined sides,[1] 5 to 6 feet high,
and rarely more than 3 feet wide, passing straight through
the thickness of the wall, and thus varying from 9 to 18 feet

---

[1] Having mislaid my measurements of the doorways of Caithness Brochs,
I am unable to give examples from that county. But I am favoured, by
the Rev. Dr. J. M. Joass of Golspie, with the following measurements of the
doorways of Sutherlandshire Brochs :—

| | Height of Doorway. | | Breadth of Doorway. | | | |
| | | | Above. | | Below. | |
	Ft.	In.	Ft.	In.	Ft.	In.
Broch of Carnliath—						
Door in Outworks . . .	5	9	2	10	3	9
Door in Broch Wall—						
Outer Opening . .	6	6	2	5	2	9
In middle of Passage . .	6	0	2	7	3	0
Inner Opening . .	6	6	3	0	3	5
Broch of Kintrolla—						
Door in Broch Wall—						
Outer Opening . .	7	0	3	0	3	6
In middle of Passage . .	5	5	2	3	2	8
Inner Opening . .	4	11	1	9	2	9
Broch of Backies—						
Door in Broch Wall—						
(2 feet of rubbish in passage,						
height above that 4 feet.)						
Outer Opening . . .			2	11	3	3
In middle of Passage . . .			2	1	2	6
Inner Opening . . .			2	9	3	8

I learn from Mr. W. G. T. Watt that the doorway of the Broch of Burwick, near Stromness, in Orkney, which is 5 feet 2 inches in height, measures
3 feet 1 inch in width at the top, and 3 feet 5 inches at the bottom. From
these examples and the measurements of the doorways of Shetland brochs by
Sir Henry Dryden, it may be held as demonstrated that the characteristic
feature of inclined instead of perpendicular door-jambs, which was constant
in the constructions of the early Christian time, was also characteristic of
the Brochs.

in length. Some 4 feet or thereby within the outer end of the passage there is a rebate of the masonry faced with strong slabs inserted edgewise in the wall, and forming checks for a door, behind which are the bar-holes, and behind them the opening of a guard-chamber built in the thickness of the wall.

On further consideration of this remarkable group of excessively peculiar features, it becomes evident that they all point more or less obviously to the presence of a double intention in the minds of the constructors of the Brochs. The design of the whole structure and the arrangements of all its separate parts exhibit a careful and laborious adaptation of means and material to the two main objects of shelter and defence. The clever constructive idea of turning the house outside in as it were, placing its rooms within its walls, and turning all their windows towards the interior of the edifice, implies boldness of conception and fertility of resource. The height of the wall, which effectually secured the inmates against projectiles, also removed its essentially weak upper part beyond reach of assault, while the pressure of its mass knit the masonry of the lower part firmly together, and its thickness made it difficult to force an entrance by digging through it—if such a wall could be approached for this purpose when the whole of its upper materials were deadly missiles ready to the hands of the defenders. The door, securely fastened by its great bar, is too strong to be carried by a rush. Placed four feet or more within the passage, it can only be reached by one man at a time, and the narrowness of the passage prevents the use of long levers. In all probability the door itself is a slab of stone, and impervious to fire. But even if it is forced, and entrance gained to the interior court, the enemy finds himself as it were in the bottom of a well 30 to 40 feet in diameter with walls 50 feet high, pierced on all sides by vertical ranges of windows, or loopholes, commanding every foot of the space below, and rising to the number of twenty or more, immediately over the door which gives access to the galleries. In short, the concentration of effort towards the two main objects of space for shelter and complete security was never more strikingly exhibited, and no more admirable adaptation of materials so simple and common as undressed and uncemented stone for this double purpose has ever been discovered or suggested. Perhaps there is no characteristic of the typical structure more remarkable than the extreme constancy of its essential features. The uniformity of plan and construction is so unvarying among all the known examples that there exists no means of tracing the development of the form through a series of primitive or immature stages. In this respect there is a striking analogy between the Brochs and the Round Towers of Ireland. The Irish Towers also appear fully developed, and exhibit a general uniformity of plan and construction which is quite as remarkable in its manifestations among them as it is among the Brochs.[1] Their origin is assignable to peculiar circum-stances in the history of the ecclesiastical communities, and chiefly to their constant liability to sudden danger of plunder and murder by roving bands of marauding Norsemen. This specialty of purpose accounts for, and harmonises with, their

[1] It is to be observed that the type of Round Tower peculiar to Scotland, and known by the name Broch, differs totally, and in all its essential fea-tures, from the tall, slender, round Towers of Ecclesiastical construction in Scotland and Ireland. The Brochs are dry-built, the Ecclesiastical Round Towers are lime-built. No hewn stone is used in the construction of a Broch ; the doors and windows of the Ecclesiastical Round Towers are often of hewn stone, and sometimes ornamented with sculptures. The Brochs have their chambers, stairs, and galleries in the thickness of the wall enclosing the central area ; the lime-built Round Towers possess none of these features. The Brochs have their doorways always on the ground and their windows opening to the interior area ; the Ecclesiastical Round Towers have their windows open-ing in the exterior wall, and their doors placed at a considerable height above the ground. There is thus no point of similarity between the two types of structure except their external roundness.

specialty of form ; and their remarkable uniformity of plan is the natural result of the special fitness of the typical form for its special intention—the provision of a secure refuge from dangers which, though of frequent occurrence, were of transient duration.

In Scotland the area which is chiefly occupied by the Brochs was peculiarly exposed to similar occurrences. Over the whole of the northern and western districts there ebbed and flowed continuously for centuries a species of irregular intermittent warfare, consisting chiefly of plundering forays by bands of foreign marauders. And as the special association of the Round Towers of Ireland with the ecclesiastical sites of the country supplies the clue to their special purpose, the Brochs of Scotland have also their special association from which their special purpose may also be fairly deduced. Although they are often placed in situations of natural strength, yet, as a rule, they mark the area of the best land in the districts in which they are situated. This is specially true of their local distribution in Caithness, while in Sutherland we see them thickly planted in the fertile straths, and following the courses of the rivers to distances of twenty-five or thirty miles inland. They are therefore the defensive strongholds of a population located upon the arable lands, and not in the mountain fastnesses of the country ; and their peculiar nature as exceptionally secure places of refuge for non-combatants and cattle, and for storage of produce, explains the fitness of their association with the arable soil of the area in which they are most abundantly present. Against such oft-recurring but transient dangers to the cultivators and to the produce of their soil there could be no more effective system of defence provided than a multitude of *safes*, which should be burglar-proof, and big enough to contain the families, goods, and cattle of their proprietors.[1]

[1] In some Archæological Notes contributed to the *Academy* of March 25,

If it be thus suggested by the relations of the Brochs to the arable lands of the districts in which they are situated, that they belonged to the possessors and cultivators of the soil, the affinities of the typical structure itself go far to show that in its character and origin it is distinctively Celtic. None of its essential features have been observed in any construction outside of the Celtic area. And within that area no building with a stair and an arrangement of galleries similar to that of a Broch has been met with out of Scotland. But the circular wall, with chambers in its thickness, which may be regarded as the germ from which the Broch structure has grown, is a characteristic feature of Celtic construction. We have met with it in the walls of the cashels surrounding the ecclesi-

1882, on the Terra d'Otranto in the South of Italy, M. Lenormant mentions a peculiar usage still kept up by the inhabitants of the provinces of Bari and Lecce of constructing in their fields structures of uncemented stones called *truddhu*, which exactly reproduce on a smaller scale the type, arrangements, and mode of building characteristic of the Nuraghi of Sardinia, the Sesi of the island of Pantellaria, and the Talayots of the Balearic Islands. Like the Nuraghe, the Truddhu is a massive conical tower of uncemented stones with a central circular chamber rudely vaulted by the overlapping of the successive courses of its masonry. A low door gives access to the chamber. Sometimes a second chamber is constructed over the first, and approached by a narrow flight of steps winding along the side of the tower. These steps are present even when there is no second chamber, and forming a spiral round the outside of the tower, they give access to the paved platform on the top of the structure. The Truddhu serves as a shelter in bad weather and as a dwelling-place by night in the agricultural season, as the peasant proprietors often live in the towns and travel to and fro in bands for fear of brigands. Sometimes this structure is changed into a permanent home, and the village of Alberto-Bello consists wholly of houses of this form. Thousands of these constructions stud the plains. Some are being built, others are in all stages of dilapidation and decay. Although it is almost impossible to distinguish those that are ancient from those that were made but yesterday, M. Lenormant is of opinion that the origin of the custom must be referred to prehistoric times. A similar custom of constructing stone-built towers of refuge also prevails in the Caucasus, and Mr. Freshfield speaks of having as many as sixty of these structures in view at one time.

astical settlements of Christian times. It is common in Irish
Cloghauns and Scottish
beehive houses, and is
so persistently Celtic
that it appears also in
Wales and Cornwall.
The ground plan of the
most perfect of a group of
beehive huts at Bodinar,
in Cornwall (Fig. 184),
exhibits an arrangement
of oval chambers in the
thickness of its wall
precisely similar to the

Fig. 184.—Ground plan of Structure at
Bodinar, Cornwall.

arrangement which prevails in the Brochs. The long narrow
gallery (the essential feature of the earth-houses of Scotland,
Ireland, and Cornwall) is also a form of construction which
is specially characteristic of the Celtic area. The typical
Broch structure thus presents a combination of features and
forms of construction[1] which are found existing separately in
other constructions of Celtic character and origin, although
the typical combination which distinguishes the Broch structure from all others is confined to Scotland alone.

In the previous course of Lectures it was shown that as
a nation we are the possessors of the remains of a school of
art exemplified in a series of monumental types which are so
truly unique that no other nation possesses a single example.

[1] The ideal Broch is composed of a series of galleries like those of the earth-
houses, superimposed upon a basement with a ground plan like that of the
structure at Bodinar, and connected by a stair. Although the stone forts of
Ireland occasionally exhibit chambers within the thickness of their walls and
have double stairs placed against the interior face of the wall to give access to
the wall-head, they never have galleries superimposed on each other, and stairs
in the thickness of the wall.

It has now been demonstrated that we are also the possessors of the remains of a school of architecture which is as truly unique and even more pronounced in its features of absolute individuality. I do not claim for it any higher merit than that it has designed a typical form of structure possessed of almost perfect fitness for the purposes for which it was intended. It has no special beauty of form, nor is there evident in any of its parts the least attempt at ornamentation or decorative construction. But, judged by its proper standard—the measure of its fitness for its special purpose—its peculiar characteristics fulfil the most exacting requirements of architectural criticism. The fact that this peculiar type of structure exists only in one area must necessarily have some significance in relation to the history of architecture; but the fact that their remains may still be counted by hundreds must also have great significance in relation to the unwritten history of Scotland, for it is obvious that the presence within its area of this vast series of massive structures, so closely alike in their general features, and so admirably contrived in their special arrangements, implies a wide-spread concentration of thought and energy towards a common object which is found only in communities that have attained to a comparatively high condition of general culture and social organisation.

LECTURE V.

(31st October 1881.)

THE BROCHS AND THEIR CONTENTS.

In 1852 the late Mr. A. H. Rhind of Sibster, the founder of the Rhind Lectureship, made a systematic investigation of an ancient structure at Kettleburn, near Wick, in Caithness. It was a work of great magnitude, employing a number of men for upwards of three months.[1] It is easy for us, with more extended knowledge of this class of buildings, to recognise the features of the structure as those of a Broch, although it was not so considered by Mr. Rhind.

The external appearance of the ruin was that of a mound somewhat more than 120 feet in diameter, and 10 feet high. It stood in a cultivated field; the plough had regularly passed over it for a quarter of a century, and a cottage had been built out of one of its sides. Though thus diminished and dilapidated, there remained enough of its structure underneath the surface to show clearly what were its general features.

When fully cleared from the ruin of its upper portion, the lower part of the building showed a circular construction (*b b* in the accompanying plan, Fig. 185), consisting of a wall

---

[1] An account of the excavation, with plans and drawings, was given by Mr. Rhind in the *Archæological Journal*, vol. x. p. 212; and also in the first volume of the *Proceedings of the Society of Antiquaries of Scotland*, vol. i. p. 265.

P

15 feet thick, surrounding a central area of 30 feet diameter. The doorway (*c*) passing straight through the wall, was flanked by a guard-chamber (*t*) on either side. Remains of two oblong chambers (*r*, *i*) constructed in the thickness of

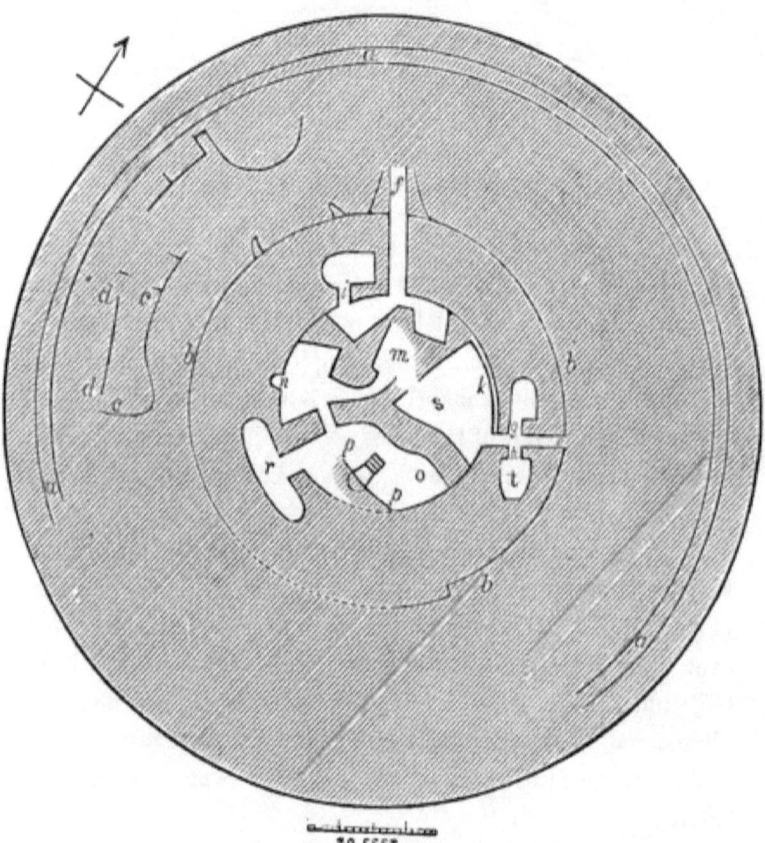

Fig. 185.—Ground plan of Broch of Kettleburn, near Wick, Caithness.
(From a Plan by Mr. A. H. Rhind.)

the wall were also found some distance apart. The roofs of all the chambers were gone, but the lintels remained on the passages leading into them. There was a well with steps leading down to it in the central area. It was 9 feet deep, and being covered for the support of a partition wall (*p p*) which passed over it, was full of good spring water when discovered. The area enclosed within the circular wall of the Broch was subdivided into irregularly-shaped spaces (*m*, *s*, *o*) by walls built across it in various directions, and abutting on the main wall. I shall have more to say of such irregular constructions within and around these towers when we come to deal with them in other cases, which show that they are secondary constructions, built out of and upon the fallen materials of the primary edifice. The area outside the tower for a distance of 25 feet from its external wall was covered by the ruins of similar irregular constructions (*c d*), and the whole was surrounded at that distance from the central tower by a wall (*a*) 3 feet thick, of whose height little more than the foundations remained.

The objects found during the excavation of the buildings are preserved in the Museum. They were not very numerous, but they formed the first collection made by the systematic excavation of a Broch, and thus were possessed of inestimable value and interest. In point of fact, the gift of this collection to the National Museum gave a new character to the collection of Scottish antiquities, and a new direction to the science of Scottish Archæology. The Museum had previously been enriched by multitudes of donations of objects illustrating the unwritten history of the country, but they were mostly objects whose associations and relations were matters of inference and speculation. This group of objects, on the other hand, was one of which it could be said—(1) that they were related to each other by their common association with a single inhabited site; (2) that they all had relations with a certain typical form of structure; (3) that very various characteristics of form, material, art, and industry were shown to be thus inter-associated; (4) that the condition and culture of the occupants of the structure are truly disclosed by the study of this group of relics, in so far as the objects of which it is composed are capable of affording such indications ; and (5) that the special knowledge thus acquired from the study of a group of relics derived from one structure is also an important contribution to our general knowledge of the class to which it belongs.

The group of objects recovered from the ruins of the Broch consisted—(1) of manufactured articles used in connection with the daily life of the inmates ; and (2) of objects not manufactured, which were plainly the refuse of their food.

The manufactured articles included objects fabricated in stone and bone, bronze and iron. The stone objects were principally querns or stones of the old small hand-mills for grinding grain ; stone pounders or oblong naturally rounded pebbles of various sizes, having their ends worn down by use ; flat circular discs of thin slaty stone, varying from 3 or 4 to 10 or 12 inches diameter, which might have served such purposes as are still occasionally served by similar articles in country dairies and kitchens ; oval-shaped boulders of sandstone, having roughly-formed oval or cup shaped cavities in their upper surfaces, which may have held a dab of tallow, with a wick of tow or moss, and thus served as lamps (Fig. 186); other hollowed cup-shaped or bowl - shaped stones, more regularly formed externally and internally, some of which

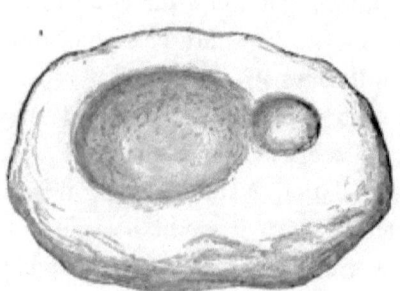

Fig 186.—Lamp of Sandstone from Broch of Kettleburn.

were furnished with handles, and were therefore obviously domestic dishes ; seven stone whorls for the spindle ; several whetstones and various other articles of indeterminate purpose.

Among the articles fashioned in bone were pins and bodkins, made out of the long bones of various animals; rounded knobs like buttons, cut out of the outer table of the jaw-bone of the whale, and retaining part of the loop of iron inserted into them; and two long-handled combs (Fig. 187) of the same

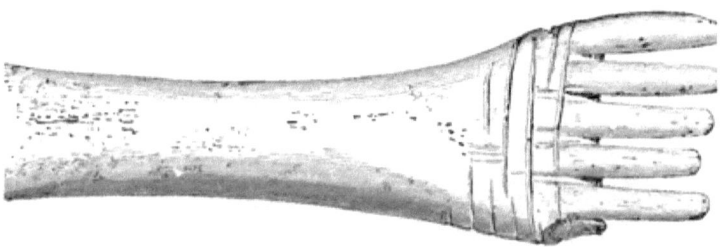

Fig. 187.—Long-handled Comb of Bone, from Broch of Kettleburn.

material, furnished with stout teeth, about an inch in length, at the end of the handle. These peculiar implements are so frequently found in Brochs that no considerable group of Broch relics is without them. They are of great interest; but their purpose has to be inferred from considerations of their form, associations, and marks of use. It is sufficiently obvious from their form, that as *long-handled* combs they are quite distinct in character from the ordinary double-edged combs for the hair, which are also common in Brochs.

The objects in bronze found in the Broch of Kettleburn were a small bronze pin and a pair of bronze tweezers of large size (Figs. 188, 189), $4\frac{1}{2}$ inches in length by $1\frac{3}{4}$ inch in breadth, elegantly formed and ornamented in a style that is suggestive of the peculiarly bold and effective ornamentation of the metal-work of the early Celtic period, described in a former Lecture. They are $4\frac{3}{4}$ inches in length and $1\frac{3}{4}$

inches in width. Their special purpose is unknown;[1] but they are still strong and serviceable for any purpose for which such implements may have been employed. They possess

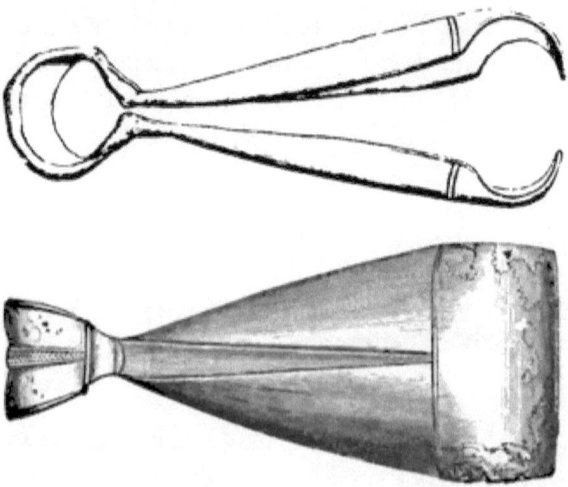

Figs. 188, 189.—Front and side views of Bronze Tweezers from Broch of Kettle-burn (4½ inches in length).

a peculiar interest as being the only pair of tweezers known to have been found in Scotland.

The objects of iron were mostly in such a fragmentary condition and so greatly oxidised that little more could be said of them than that they were portions of implements of iron.

[1] Bronze tweezers are not uncommon accompaniments of female inter-ments of the Bronze Age in Denmark, and it has been suggested that they were used as sewing implements when the material to be sewed was skin and the thread a thong. This supposition is strengthened by the fact that small awls of bronze are occasionally found with them, and it is obvious that the end of a thong hardened in the fire, and pushed partially through the holes bored by an awl, could be readily seized by such a pair of tweezers and so dragged tight. But the tweezers found in the Kettleburn Broch do not belong to the Bronze Age. Their ornamentation is that of the Iron Age, and they were found in association with objects of iron.

The fragments of pottery were abundant. They were coarse in texture and unglazed. They mostly represented globular vessels with everted rims and bulging sides.

The unmanufactured objects consisted chiefly of bones and shells, which were so abundant that they were evidently the remains of a long accumulation of the refuse of the food of a considerable number of individuals who had neither fared scantily nor without variety. Their diet had included beef and venison, pork and veal, mutton and lamb, fish and shell-fish, with an occasional fowl. The animal remains were determined by Mr. Quekett, who notes that the bones and teeth of a small horse, larger, however, than the Shetland pony, occurred in great numbers; there were also remains of a horse of much greater size. The other animals were red-deer and roe-buck, the ox, sheep of small size, goats, and swine. Many remains of dogs were found, some indicating a variety larger than a pointer, others being smaller. There were also bones of the whale and seal, and some remains of a bird of the size of the heron or swan. The fish-bones were not determined. The shell-fish were principally the peri-winkle, the whelk, and the limpet. A few human bones were found intermixed with the relics, but there is no record of their precise associations, and other examples will show that the mounds covering these ruined Brochs were frequently selected as burying-places in subsequent ages. The occur-rence of the bones of the dog and the horse, the seal and the whale among the food refuse of a community, does not neces-sarily imply that the animals were eaten. But there is reason to believe that tastes differed in this respect at different times. The horse was eaten among the northern nations of Europe till within the historic period. The whale appears down to the sixteenth century among the provision made for rich and royal tables in Scottish and English records. The seal was salted with the ashes of burnt sea-

ware, and eaten in the Hebrides in the beginning of the last
century. While, therefore, it may be a fair inference from
the occurrence of many bones of these animals in the food
refuse of this Broch that its occupants used the flesh of such
beasts as a common article of diet, it is obviously an equally
fair admission that they are no more to be regarded as
savages on that account than the people of historic times
who were partial to the same kind of food. In point of fact,
so far as the evidence goes, there is no reason for attributing
to them an exceptionally low condition of culture or civilisation. We have seen that the type of defensive dwelling with
which we find them associated is one which possesses remarkable features of constructive merit and originality of design.
Their diet was not less varied in kind and quality of nutri-
ment than that of modern times. They possessed iron and
bronze, and their manufactured implements show that they
were neither destitute of technical skill nor deficient in
artistic taste.

The Broch of Kintradwell, three miles north of Brora,
excavated by Rev. Dr. J. M. Joass,[1] was situated on a natural
terrace close to the edge of the declivity which marks the
old sea-margin of the east coast of Sutherlandshire. Previous
to its excavation it was a rounded grass-covered knoll.
Within this mound, formed of the debris of the structure,
the basement of the broch was found entire to the height
of about 14 feet. The circular wall, 18 feet in thickness,
enclosed a central space 31 feet in diameter. The doorway
was 7 feet high, with inclined instead of perpendicular sides,
so that the width was 3½ feet at the bottom and 3 feet
at the top. The entrance passage went straight through the
wall, and was provided with checks for two doors, the first at

---

[1] See a paper by Rev. Dr. J. M. Joass, in *Archæologia Scotica*, vol. v.
p. 95, entitled "The Brochs of Cinn Trolla, Cairn Liath, and Craig Carril, in
Sutherland," etc., with plans and drawings.

6 feet within the outer face of the wall, and the second 8 feet farther in. These checks were formed by wall-fast slabs whose edges projected, the wall being also slightly set back at their inner faces, and a corresponding slab on edge projected a few inches above the floor across the passage-way to check the bottom of the door. Between the two doors a guard-chamber opens on the right of the passage. The sill of its doorway is 2 feet above the floor, the opening 4 feet high by 2 feet wide, and the passage into the chamber 4½ feet in length. The guard-room itself is circular in form on the ground-plan, 7 feet in diameter, and 11 feet high, and roofed in the usual way by overlapping stones (Fig. 190). The

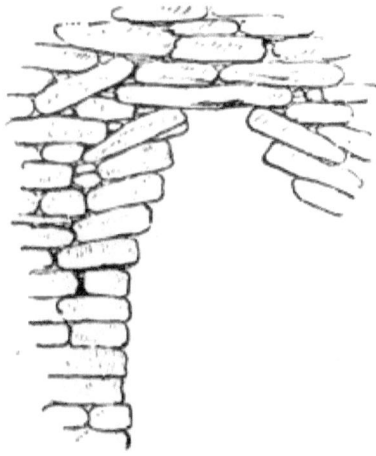

Fig. 190.—Section of Chamber in Broch of Kintradwell, showing rude vaulting of roof. (From a Drawing by Rev. Dr. Joass.)

whole length of the passage leading through the wall into the central area is 18 feet, and the lintels covering it are 8 inches apart. This feature is frequently seen, and as there is often a vacant space which may have formed an apartment over the lintels of the passage, the openings left between them may have had a special purpose in connection with the defence of the doorway. To the left of the main entrance

was an oval-shaped chamber 11 feet long and 10 feet high,
constructed in the thickness of the wall ; and, still farther to
the left, were the remains of the staircase, also constructed in
the interior of the wall, with an oblong chamber at the stairfoot. Thirteen steps of the stair remained, but the galleries
above were gone. In one side of the area was a well 7 feet
deep, with steps leading down to a point 3 feet from the
bottom. A stone cup (Fig. 191), presumably the common

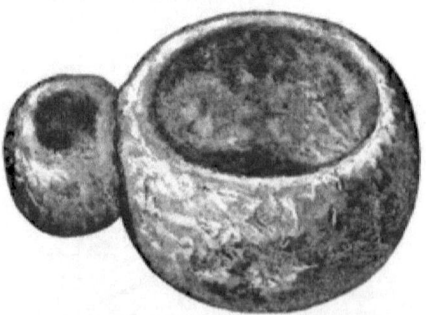

Fig. 191.—Stone cup from the Broch of Kintradwell (5 inches diameter).

drinking-cup of the establishment, lay near the steps of the
well.   In its constructive features and arrangements this
Broch is similar to all the others that have been described.
But it also presents some features which have not hitherto
been noticed, because they have either been wanting or only
obscurely presented in previous examples. The inner wall of
the court or central area was faced by a roughly-built wall
about a foot in thickness, rising to a height of about 8 feet,
and there terminating and forming a scarcement projecting
from the main wall. This inner shell or scarcement, although
bonded with the main wall at the door-corners, was not so
throughout. It was evidently an addition to the original
wall built against its inner face all round, at some time
subsequent to the construction of the main wall.[1]   We

[1] " As to the scarcement or facing wall, about 1 foot thick and 8 feet high,
of such frequent occurrence in the Brochs, it has been suggested that it may

shall meet with this feature in other examples, and in circumstances which will clearly demonstrate its secondary
character.

Again, on the outside of the tower, to a distance of 60
feet from its base, the ground was covered with the foundations of irregularly-built constructions, with passages and
doorways communicating with an access leading up to the
main entrance to the tower. These outbuildings were much
less massive, much more irregular, and much less carefully
constructed than the main building. They were chiefly
clustered about the entrance to the tower, and a little to the
north-west of the principal group of them was a shallow open
cavity lined with flat stones set on edge, and containing the
fragments of a human skeleton and an iron dagger-blade. In
one of the outbuildings also there were found a human skeleton
and an iron spear-head. Portions of eight other human
skeletons were found in and about the ruins, mostly at a
depth of from 2 to 2½ feet under the turf which covered the
mound, but not in such circumstances as would necessarily
imply that they belonged to the period of the occupation of
the Broch.[1]

The relics found in this Broch included a variety of
manufactured objects in stone and bone, bronze and iron. The

have formed the resting-ledge for a conical wooden roof covering the (lower
part of the) central area. Others have supposed that it formed the support
of a narrow roof, sloping downwards like that of a shed or series of lean-to
booths surrounding the wall. It may be noted that it seems rarely of such
massive structure as the wall proper with which it appears to be bonded only
at the door-corners. This, with the fact that it was found covering what was
almost certainly an original doorway to a wall-chamber at Clickamin, suggests the possibility of the scarcement being sometimes, if not generally, a
secondary structure."—Rev. J. M. Joass, LL.D., in *Archæologia Scotica*, vol.
v. p. 112.

[1] It is rather suggested by the frequency with which such remains have
been met with in other cases, that burials were occasionally made in these
mounds long after they had become grass-grown hillocks.

stone objects formed a very considerable and striking group. Among them there were upwards of fifty querns or hand-mill stones, and an immense quantity of oblong naturally-shaped stones from 3 or 4 to 15 or 18 inches in length, water-worn originally, but also wasted at the ends by use as hammer-stones or pounders. A number of the largest of these were found set in the ground in rows both inside and outside of the tower. There were also a large number of stone mortars, irregularly-rounded blocks, with wide-mouthed rounded cavi-ties, worn smooth by use. Most of the other stone articles were small. They consisted of the drinking-cup already mentioned (Fig. 121) as a bowl-shaped vessel, neatly made, with a handle at one side; a thin smoothly-polished disc of quartzose sandstone, about 2½ inches diameter, similar to others of mica schist, and other materials that have been found in Brochs and Crannogs, but of undetermined use; a small black whetstone or burnisher, smoothed and polished by use; a small flattish ovoid pebble of quartzite (Fig. 192),

Fig. 192.—Oval pebble of quartzite marked by use as a point-sharpener, from the Broch of Kintradwell (3¼ inches in length).

having indentations produced apparently by point-sharpening on its opposite sides; a quantity of fragments of rings or bracelets of lignite probably obtained from the Brora beds, and a considerable number of spindle-whorls of various forms and sizes. The bone implements were mostly of the nature of handles made of deer-horn, and spatulæ, which Dr. Joass has suggested may probably have been potter's tools. No implements or ornaments of bronze were found, but the presence of the metal was determined by the finding of three fragments of well-made crucibles with adhering portions of the melted metal. The iron objects were a spear-head, a dagger-blade, a knife-blade, a socketed chisel, and several fragments of implements of indeterminate character. The only other object of metal discovered was a small and thick ring of lead a little more than an inch in diameter. The fragments of pottery found were for the most part portions of coarsely-made vessels, all unglazed and unornamented. The refuse of the food of the inmates was present in considerable quantity. The land animals represented among these remains were the reindeer, the red-deer, the roe, the ox, the sheep, the goat, the pig, the fox, the wild-cat, and either the wolf or a very large dog. The marine animals were the whale, the grampus, the porpoise, the dog-fish, and the cod and haddock, while the remains of such edible shell-fish as the oyster, the mussel, the cockle, the periwinkle, and the limpet were very abundant.

The Broch of Carn-liath, in Dunrobin Park, also excavated by Rev. Dr. Joass, consisted of a wall 18 feet thick, enclosing a central area of 30 feet in diameter. The doorway was 7 feet high and 3 feet wide. As usual, it goes straight through the wall; and at a distance of 8 feet within the outer face of the wall there are checks for a door, and a guard-chamber opens on the right side of the passage immediately within them. This Broch differs from that last described in having no chambers in the thickness of the wall, and it also presents the unusual feature of having two underground chambers faced with slabs, underneath the level of the central area. The only opening from the court into the thickness of the wall is the entrance to the stair, of which 25 steps remain, but the galleries are gone. Around the outside of the tower are the foundations of irregularly-formed constructions, of which it is now difficult to determine the character with certainty. The objects found in the excavation of this Broch consisted of about a dozen querns, three large stone mortars, a considerable quantity of hammer-stones or pestles, a large number of rings of shale or lignite—many in process of manufacture, two stone cups, scooped out of steatite, and a large ladle-

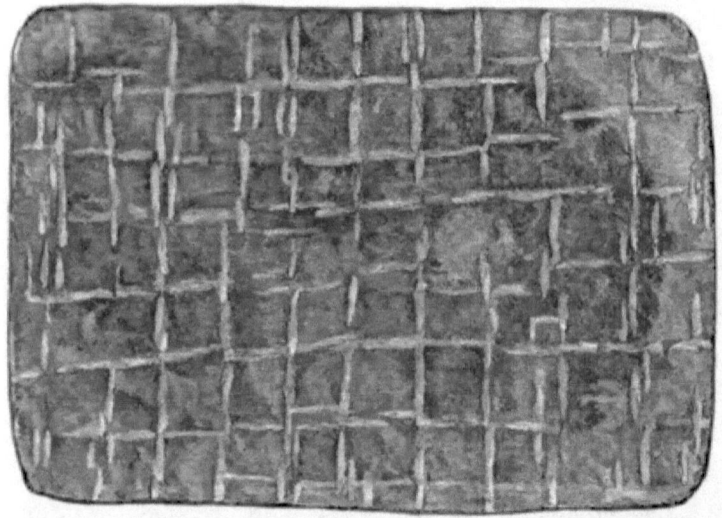

Fig. 193.—Hammer-marked Plate of Brass found in the Broch of Carn-liath (11¼ by 7¼ inches).

like dish of the same material, a stone sinker rounded, oblong, conical at top and flat at bottom, and the top perforated by a hole for a cord, and another sinker with a longitudinal groove and circular depressions on either side. Of bone objects, there were two long-handled combs, and a piece of whalebone like a club, 14 inches long. Among the objects in metal, the most interesting were two plates of brass, each a little more than ¼-inch in thickness, the one (Fig. 193) oblong, rectangular, 11

inches in length, and 7½ inches in breadth; the other nearly
semicircular, and about 7½ inches in radius.   Both were found
near the floor of the interior area of the Broch.   They are
hammer-marked with blows of the pin end of the hammer in
lines across the surface.   Dr. Joass remarks of them that this
perhaps was one of the forms in which the metal was
imported into the northern districts of Scotland for home
manufacture.   That they are brass and not bronze is certified
by the analysis made of the one now in the Museum by Dr.
Stevenson Macadam.   The composition was found to be 82
parts of copper to 16 of zinc, with one part of tin, and a trace
of lead.   This fact is important, because while the alloy of
copper and tin, which constitutes bronze, has been in use from
an indefinitely remote prehistoric period, the alloy of copper
and zinc, which constitutes brass, is not found earlier than
the period of the Roman Empire.   A silver fibula of peculiar
form was also found in this Broch.[1]   The form is not Celtic,
but belongs to a type which is widely distributed over Central
and Southern Europe, and is commonly associated with objects
of a late Roman character.   The only article in iron found in
this Broch was a dirk-like blade greatly corroded.   The
pottery was abundant, but coarse and fragmentary, and destitute of ornamentation.

In 1866 and 1867 I excavated the Broch of Yarhouse, situated in the south end of the loch of the same name, about six
miles south of Wick, in Caithness.   The ground plan of the
structure is shown in Fig. 194.   Its appearance before excavation was that of a conical grass-covered mound, 200 paces in
circumference, and 18 to 20 feet high.   It stood on a low
flat triangular projection of the shore of the loch, and was cut
off from the land by a ditch now silted up, and varying from
25 to 30 feet wide.   In the upper part of the mound we

---

[1] It belongs to the class of fibulæ which are often described as bow shaped
and cruciform, and is represented in *Archæologia Scotica*, vol. v. plate 16.

found portions of two human skeletons, at a depth of from 2½ to 3 feet under the turf; and at different places on the sides

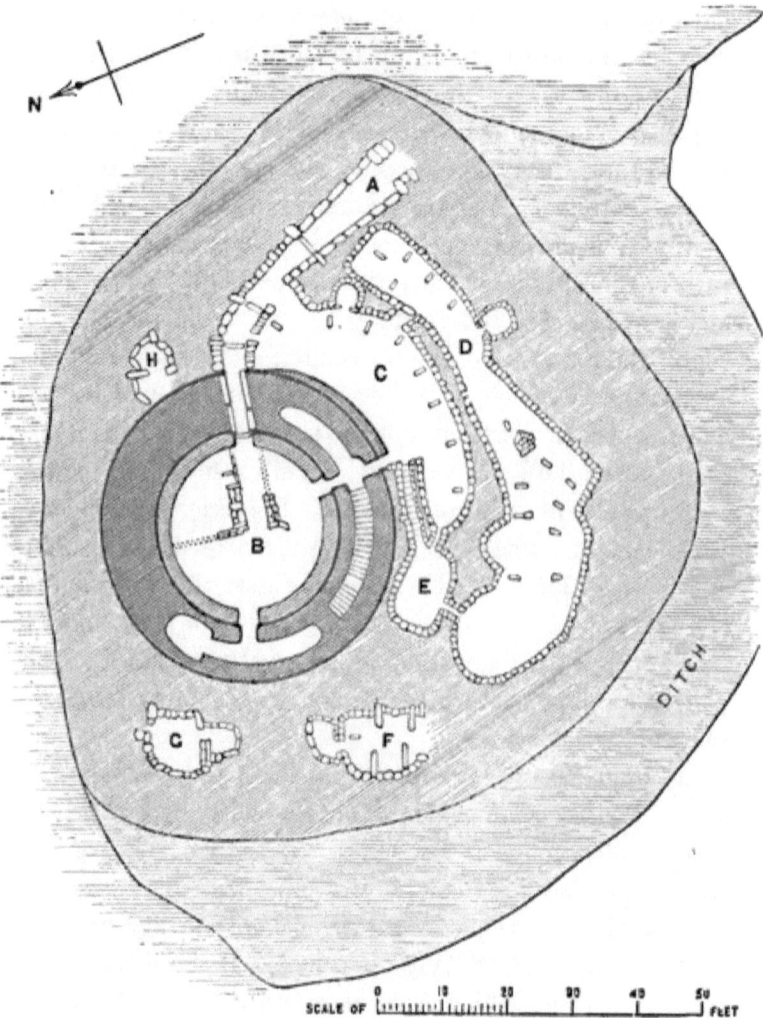

Fig. 194.—Ground plan of the Broch of Yarhouse, Caithness, with its Secondary Constructions, on a peninsula in the Loch of Yarhouse, cut off from the land by a ditch.

of the mound, lower down, the remains of three other skeletons were met with. Near one of those first found was a flat circular brooch of brass (Fig. 195), of about 2½ inches diameter.

Fig. 195.—Circular Brooch of Brass, found with a burial in the mound covering the ruins of the Broch (2½ inches diameter).

It was rudely inscribed with letters which appear to be a blundering attempt at the formula ISVS NAZAR [ENVS], a common and popular talismanic inscription on the brooches of the thirteenth and fourteenth centuries. These skeletons were not enclosed in cists, but simply embedded in the earth and stones of the mound. They were not deep enough to have any determinable relation with the structure of the Broch below. They were all incomplete and the bones in disorder, though this might perhaps be accounted for by the movement of the loose material of the slope of the mound in the course of ages. The inference appeared to be that they were casual interments made in the mound long after it had become a grassy knoll. This was also the conclusion to which Dr. Joass came with respect to the burials in the mound at Kintradwell. It is easy to see how such a practice might have arisen in remoter districts, where burial-grounds

Q

connected with ecclesiastical sites were distant and roads were few. In point of fact, there is evidence which seems to connect the custom with the later Paganism of these northern parts. Mr. Petrie found a small cemetery of stone cists, containing interments after cremation, overlying the ruined Broch of Okstrow, in Orkney. In this case, the mound which covered the ruins must have been chosen as a place of heathen sepulture because it was a mound. A grave containing two oval bowl-shaped brooches, and therefore belonging to the heathen Viking time, was found in the upper part of a mound covering the ruins of a Broch at Castletown, in Caithness. I found a single burial in a stone-lined grave laid close to the doorway of the Broch of Brounaben, not far from Yarhouse ; and burials were found in the mounds covering the ruins of the Brochs of Thrumster and Dunbeath, in Caithness. It is therefore probable that in all such cases the interments that are found immediately below the surface of these mounds belong to a time when the Broch had been so long in ruins that it appeared to those so using it as a natural grassy knoll.

When excavated, the Broch of Yarhouse consisted of a circular wall, 12 to 13 feet thick, enclosing a central area, 30 feet in diameter. The height of the wall remaining was about 15 feet. The doorway which passes straight through the wall is about 6 feet high and $2\frac{1}{2}$ wide, slightly narrower at top than at bottom, and well built with long flat slabs, some of which were 8 feet in length. The opening of the doorway into the interior area and recess above it are shown in Fig. 196. There were no guard-chambers or barholes, and the checks for the door were quite on the inner side of the wall. But this Broch stood on what was practically an island, cut off from the land by a ditch 25 to 30 feet wide, and the access to the doorway was carefully protected by the outworks to be subsequently described. Opening from the

interior area to the left of the doorway was the entrance to
the stair (Fig. 197), which also gave access to an oblong
chamber at the stairfoot. The stair itself was 3 feet wide,
and 16 steps up there was a landing, with a light hole or
window looking into the interior of the Broch. Above the
entrance to the stair there were also three windows, placed

Fig. 196.—Interior aperture of Doorway in Broch of Yarhouse.
(From a Photograph.)

vertically over each other—all that remained of a vertical
range of windows, such as we have seen in the case of Mousa,
Dun Carloway, and the Glenelg Brochs. On the side of the
area opposite to the doorway was an oblong chamber in the
thickness of the wall, roofed in the usual manner by overlapping stones. In this Broch, as at Kintradwell, there was

an interior wall, of inferior masonry, built against the main wall, and partially bonded into it at the door openings. This inner wall was 2½ feet thick, and rose to a height of 8 feet, where the wall-head formed a level scarcement all round the

Fig. 197.—Entrance to the stair and window-like openings over it, in the Broch of Yarhouse. (From a Photograph.)

interior. Partition walls (shown at B in ground plan, Fig. 194) ran half way across the area from both sides of the doorway, and that on the right of the entrance bent at a right angle towards the Broch wall. These partitions were partly built, and partly formed of long slabs set on end. They rose to about 8 feet—the same height as the scarcement. The partitions and the inner wall forming the scarcement were founded on an accumulation of rubbish largely mixed with ashes and food refuse, which covered the original floor of the Broch to the depth of 12 to 14 inches. They were therefore clearly secondary constructions, made to adapt the Broch to the purposes of a secondary occupation. Outside the Broch wall are two long irregularly-shaped enclosures, and several smaller cells. The outer enclosure (D in plan, Fig. 194) is 100 feet in length, and varies in width from 6 to 20 feet. The length of the inner enclosure (C) is 70 feet, and its width about 12 feet. They have each a little cell, provided with door checks opening off them. In some places their walls remained entire to the height of 10 feet, without showing any sign of overlapping for a roof. Both these large oblong enclosures had irregular rows of long slabs set on end in their floors, as if to divide them into cattle stalls. A long covered way (A) leading to the entrance of the Broch traversed the N.E. end of these enclosures. It varied from about 3 feet wide at the door of the Broch to about 5 feet wide at the outer end, and had checks for doors at four different places in its length. The secondary character of all these exterior constructions was obvious from the fact that underneath their foundations there was a considerable depth of stones overlying the original soil, and mingled with ashes and food refuse. It was also evident that various occupations of the interior of the Broch had taken place from time to time, when the original floor had become covered with rubbish to a considerable depth. Partition walls were met with at three different levels, dividing the internal area on three different plans; the last being a partial partition, utilising only one side of the area, at a time when the original floor had become covered with 8 feet of stones and rubbish. The relics obtained in the course of the excavation were few in

number compared with the size and apparent importance of
the structure. No querns were found, but about a dozen
grain rubbers and stones hollowed like mortars, large numbers
of stone pestles, pounders, or hammer-stones, abraded at the
ends by use; several whetstones (Figs. 198, 199), a large

Figs. 198, 199.—Whetstones from Broch of Yarhouse
(3 inches in length).

number of thin circular discs of slaty sandstone, from $2\frac{1}{2}$
inches up to 14 or 15 inches in diameter, many stone balls
$2\frac{1}{2}$ to 3 inches diameter, a small rounded pebble of quartz,
with a hole through it, a number of spindle-whorls of
stone, and one of burnt clay. The objects in metal were
a ring of bronze, half an inch in diameter, an armlet of
bronze (Fig. 200), made of a wire $\frac{1}{16}$-inch in diameter, square
for half its length, and twisted so that the corners form a
spiral pattern, the other half being the plain round wire. A
few fragments of iron knives, and some indeterminate objects
of small size, greatly corroded, were all the remains of iron
implements that were found. The pottery was very abundant,
but the fragments were in general small. Some were coarse
and thick, others thin and fine; all unglazed, and entirely
without ornament, except that some pieces showed a slightly
everted lip. The animal remains included those of the reindeer (Figs. 201, 202) and red-deer, the horse, the ox, the sheep,

the pig, the dog, and some undetermined birds and fish. Although the site is a long way from the sea, there was a

Fig. 200.—Bronze Armlet from the Broch of Yarhouse (2¼ inches diameter).

considerable accumulation of the common shore shells, chiefly periwinkles and limpets. The occurrence of the remains of the reindeer among the refuse of the food of the occupants of the Brochs of the North of Scotland is a fact of much interest in

Figs. 201, 202.—Portions of Horns of Reindeer found in the Broch of Yarhouse, Caithness.

various ways. It establishes the correctness of the statement made incidentally in the *Orkneyinga Saga*,[1] when, in record-

[1] The *Orkneyinga Saga* (Edinburgh, 1873), p. 182. See also Dr. J. A. Smith's Notice of "Remains of the Reindeer in Scotland," in the *Proceedings of the Soc. Antiq. Scot.*, vol. viii. p. 186.

ing the movements of Harald and Rognvald, Earls of Orkney, in the year 1158, the writer says that "every summer the Earls were wont to go over to Caithness, and up into the forests to hunt the red deer or the reindeer." It also shows that in Scotland at least the association of reindeer remains with those of prehistoric man does not of itself or necessarily indicate extreme antiquity.

The Broch of Old Stirkoke, which I watched during its removal by the farmer for drains and top-dressing, was a grass-covered mound 120 paces in circumference, 12 feet high, and nearly 40 feet diameter across its level summit. The wall of the Broch was 13 feet thick and the enclosed area 30 feet diameter. A square drain ran under the floor. The objects casually recovered from the rubbish were a bone bodkin 8 inches long, a polished bone needle 3 inches in length, a thin polished disc of mica schist $2\frac{1}{2}$ inches diameter similar to other objects of the same character (of which the intention is not obvious) found in Brochs and Crannogs, a stone lamp, a few spindle-whorls, two whetstones, hammer-stones, thin circular discs of slaty stone, a fragment of bronze and a portion of the hilt end of an iron sword with a very broad double-edged blade.

The Broch of Bowermadden, also removed by the farmer, had a well in the area with steps leading down to it. It was impossible to obtain with any degree of precision the general dimensions of the structure, but so far as I could ascertain it differed in no feature of importance from the others which have been described. The objects found in it were a number of stone balls similar to those found in the Broch of Yarhouse, a stone mortar, a small oval vessel of red sandstone (Fig. 203), a number of spindle-whorls, and several stone vessels of large size which I did not see. The farmer said that the largest one was 3 feet deep, and that as they were always in his way he smashed them up and saved only

a few of the smaller ones to be utilised as hen troughs, etc.
A bead of vitreous paste enamelled with a yellow spiral ornament (Fig. 204), a very
pretty small comb of bone
(Fig. 205), with an open semicircular handle, and a bronze
pin having an open circular
head with ribbed ornamen-
tation on the upper part of
the circle (Fig. 206), were
also found. A few frag-
ments of iron implements

Fig. 203.—Vessel of Red Sandstone
(6 inches in length).

Fig. 204.—Bead of Vitreous Paste
(actual size).

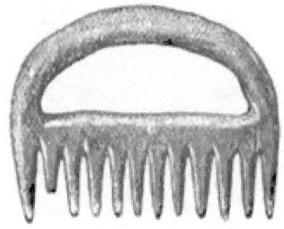

Fig. 205.—Small Comb of Bone
(actual size).

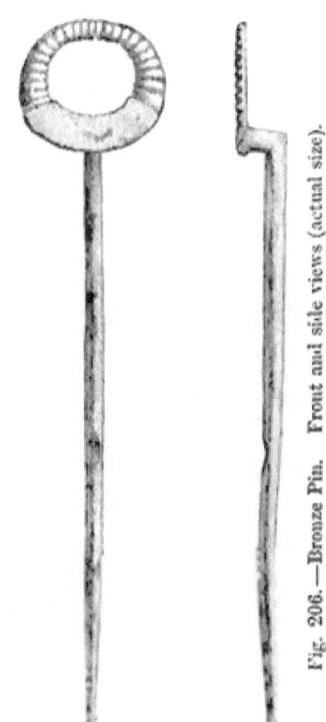

Fig. 206.—Bronze Pin. Front and side views (actual size).

occurred, but they were greatly corroded and indetermin-
able.

The Broch of Dunbeath, situated in the angle formed by the confluence of the Burn of Houstry with the Water of Dunbeath, which was excavated by Mr. Thomson Sinclair, jun., of Dunbeath, had larger and loftier chambers in the thickness of its wall than any of the others. One of these measured 12 feet 6 inches by 6 feet 6 inches, and 13 feet high. Among the relics found in this Broch were an iron spear-head 5 inches in length, a whetstone, and some bone implements. A quantity of charred grain, bere, and oats was found on the floor.

These examples will suffice to convey a general idea of the nature and contents of the Brochs of Sutherland and Caithness, and to show how closely they resemble one another alike in the style of their construction, the nature of their arrangements, and the general character of their contained relics. I now proceed to notice briefly a few of those which have been excavated in Shetland and Orkney. They all exhibit the same typical structure, with variations in their details which need not be minutely specified. It is necessary, however, to examine the groups of relics which have been obtained from them in order to complete the general view of the evidence from which we arrive at conclusions as to the nature and quality of the culture and civilisation of their occupants.

The Broch of Levenwick in the parish of Dunrossness, Shetland, excavated by Mr. Gilbert Goudie in 1869 and 1871 (Fig. 207), had an internal diameter of 29½ to 30 feet, the wall varying in thickness from 12 to 16 feet, while the greatest height of wall remaining was 15 feet. It presented the unusual feature of a "scarcement" or secondary wall, about 6 feet high and 6 feet wide, built against the face of the interior wall. From this secondary construction there were five buttress-like projections from 2½ to 4½ feet in length, placed at regular distances from each other, and extending into the en-

closed area. At one side of the area opposite the shortest of
the projecting walls was a fireplace (*d*), consisting of three
flags placed on edge. The entrance passage (*b c f*) led straight
through the wall of the Broch and through the secondary
wall in its interior, widening to the outer part of the secondary wall. There were two of the lintels of the passage

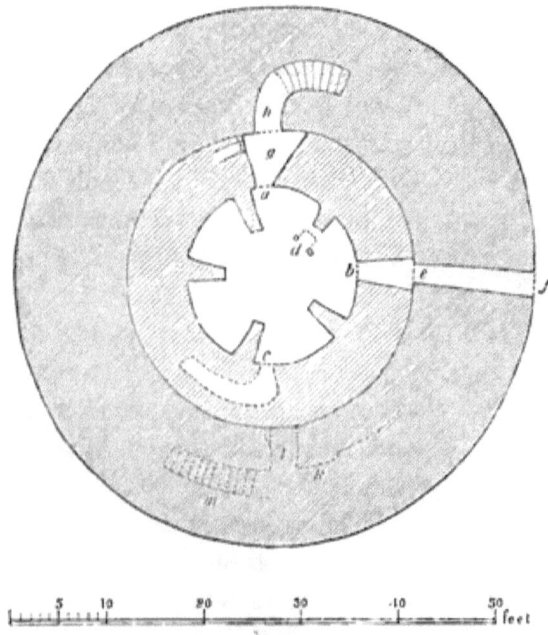

Fig. 207.—Ground plan of the Broch of Levenwick, Shetland.
(From a plan by Mr. Gilbert Goudie.)

remaining, but the outer part of the original entrance way
was much dilapidated. On this account perhaps the checks
for the door were not visible and there is no appearance of
guard-chambers. Contrary to the usual experience also, the
stair ascends from an opening to the right of the main
entrance in the middle of the east side of the building (at *h* on
the plan), and ascending to a height of 8 or 10 feet, enters a
level gallery which apparently went half way round the

building to the west side (at *m* on the plan), where there is
another flight of 15 steps remaining. At the point where
this second flight of steps starts from the gallery, there is a
window opening to the interior area. This arrangement of
the stair differs from that of Mousa. At the Broch of Yarhouse in Caithness what remained of the
stair was similarly divided into two
flights, though the distance between them
was less than at Levenwick. The objects
found in this Broch were few, consisting
of quern-stones, pounders, and roughly-
hollowed stones. It is chiefly interesting
on account of the variation exhibited in
its structural details.

In one of the Brochs in the parish
of Harray, in Orkney, excavated by Mr.

Fig. 208.—Bronze Knob   Farrer, a number of stone lamps, circular
found in Broch of   discs, and perforated stones were found,
Harray (3½ inches in
length).   and along with them the bronze object
here figured (Fig. 208).[1]

The East Broch of Burray, also explored by Mr. Farrer,
yielded a number of stone vessels of various sizes, a lamp of
stone, a thin circular disc of mica schist, polished, like those
found in the Brochs of Old Stirkoke and Kintradwell, small
bead-like objects made of bone, a bone cup made of one of
the vertebral joints of a small whale (Fig. 209), a number of
bone pins from 1½ to 3½ inches long, four long-handled combs of
bone, two broken portions of double-edged combs of the same

[1] Six of these bronze objects were found at Lisnacragher Bay, Parish of
Braid, County Antrim, in 1868, along with a sword-sheath of bronze decorated
in that peculiar style of Celtic Art of which examples have been given in
Lecture III. They seem to have been mountings of the ends of spear-shafts,
and two of them still retained part of the wood of the shaft.—*Proc. Soc. Antiq.
Lond.*, 1868, Second Series, vol. iv. p. 256.

material, a bronze pin with a flat circular head (Fig. 210),
and an iron chisel and knife-blade. Besides the ordinary
unglazed pottery of native
manufacture there was
found in this Broch a fragment of the red lustrous
ware commonly called
Samian. This ware, which
is found abundantly on
the sites of Roman settlements, as at Inveresk for
instance, is always one
of the most characteristic
indications of Roman in-
fluence, and its presence
necessarily betokens some
degree of contact with the
effects of Roman civilisa-
tion. In this Broch also a quantity of charred bere or barley

Fig. 209.—Cup made from Vertebra of
Whale from Broch of Burray (4½
inches high).

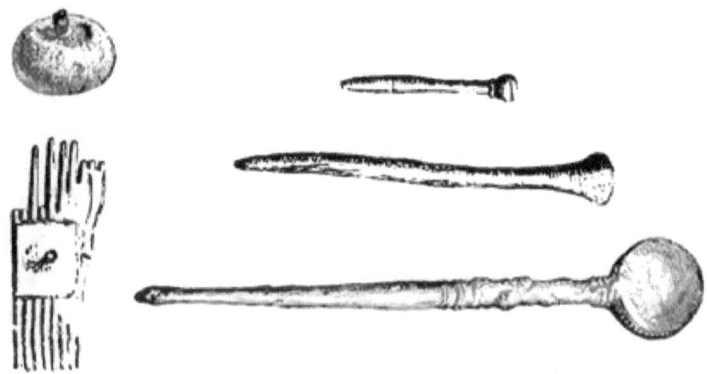

Fig. 210.—Bone Button with iron shank, Fragment of Comb and Pins of Bone
and Bronze from Broch of Burray (actual size).

lay on the floor, and the most remarkable feature of the collection of food refuse from its rubbish was the presence among the bones of the ordinary domestic animals, of great numbers of the horns of the red-deer, many of which belonged to animals of considerable size. There are now no red-deer in Orkney, but there is no Broch which does not contain their remains abundantly.

At Burwick, near Stromness, in Orkney, a Broch situated on a rugged promontory rising to a considerable height above the sea has been recently explored by Mr. W. G. T. Watt. The external appearance of the ruin previous to its excavation was that of a circular mound about 15 to 20 feet in height occupying the whole width of the promontory and sloping to the crag on both sides. On the landward side, about 50 feet from the exterior margin of the base of the mound, there is a deep and wide ditch across the neck of the promontory isolating the part on which the tower stands from the mainland. The ditch is 160 feet long and about 40 feet wide, and is faced on the inner side by a well-built wall 9 feet high, 6 feet thick at the bottom, and sloping to from 3 to 4 feet at the top. The Broch itself consists of the usual circular wall, averaging from 12 to 13 feet in thickness. No part of the wall now exceeds 16 feet in height. The entrance to the interior area of the Broch is 5 feet 2 inches high, 3 feet 5 inches wide at the bottom and 3 feet 1 inch at the top. The passage through the wall is paved in the bottom and diminishes slightly in width and height until at the distance of 9 feet 9 inches inwards, where there are checks for a door, the opening of the doorway is only 4 feet 6 inches high and 2 feet 11 inches wide. Inside this doorway the passage widens by 12 inches on either side, and on the right side there is a guard-chamber entering by a doorway 3 feet 5 inches high and 2 feet wide, lighted by an opening above the lintel of about 1 foot square. The chamber seems to have been about 12 feet long and has been roofed in the usual manner by overlapping stones. The interior area was occupied by secondary constructions founded at a height of 3 feet above the original floor-level upon a bed of stones and rubbish which had accumulated to that depth upon the original floor previous to the time of this secondary occupation. The area within the Broch wall, which had been originally 24 feet in diameter, was diminished to 16 feet in diameter by a roughly-constructed circular wall or "scarcement" built against the inner wall of the Broch, rising to the height of about 6 feet. Unlike many of these "scarcements," it presents great inequality in thickness, varying from about 7 feet on one side of the area to about 2½ on the other. The area is further intersected in various directions by several partition walls of the same inferior character of masonry. The space outside the Broch wall, intervening between it and the ditch, is also occupied by secondary constructions, and an underground passage has been traced for about 50 feet towards the ditch.

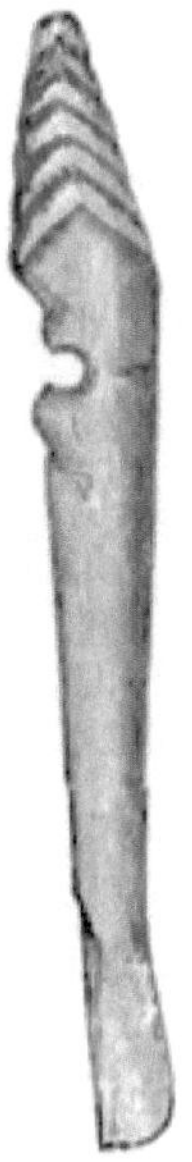

The articles found during the excavation consisted of a number of stone pounders or hammer-stones, wasted at the ends by use, round flat stone discs of various sizes roughly chipped to shape, broken mortars or vessels of various sizes roughly hollowed in naturally-shaped boulders of sandstone (one being apparently a stone mould for an iron *crusie*), a considerable number of bone implements of various kinds, among which are several bone pins, one of which (Fig. 211) is flat at the point, has an ornamented head, and has been furnished with a loop for suspension at the side; a polished bone handle in which an instrument, apparently of iron, has been inserted; two spindle-whorls,

Fig. 211.—Polished Bone Pin from Broch of Burwick. (Actual size.)

one of bone and the other of stone; portions of deer-horns cut into slips and pierced by peg-holes; two long-handled combs made of deer-horn, one of which is here figured (Fig.

Fig. 212.—Long-Handled Bone Comb from the Broch of Burwick
(4½ inches in length).

212); one double-edged comb of bone, and one single-edged comb with round back (Fig. 213), both formed in several pieces,

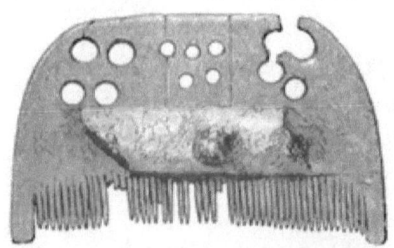

Fig. 213.—Round-backed, single-edged Comb
from Broch of Burwick.

neatly joined and held together by transverse slips of bone fastened with rivets. The only iron object found was a portion of a cylindrical rod. The pottery was coarse, thick, unglazed, and unornamented, except one piece of dark-coloured ware resembling the black ware made in Roman kilns in several parts of England. The animal remains were chiefly those of the ox, the sheep or goat, the horse, the swine, and the red-deer.

The Broch of Okstrow, in Birsay, excavated by Mr. Leask of Boardhouse, yielded a number of the commoner implements of stone, such as hammer-stones and rough circular discs, a well-made cup of sandstone, 3½ inches in diameter (Fig. 214), its cavity still bearing the marks of the pointed tool by which it was fashioned; a thin flat disc of compact slaty stone, 3¼ inches diameter, smoothly polished on both sides, and ground flat on the edges like those from the Brochs of Burray, Old Stirkoke, and Kintradwell;

Fig. 214.—Cup of Sandstone from Broch of Okstrow (3½ inches in diameter).

three lamps of sandstone, one of which seems an unskilful imitation of the form of a Roman lamp (Fig. 215); while the

Figs. 215, 216.—Lamps from the Broch of Okstrow.

others (Fig. 216) are similar to the lamp from Kettleburn. Among the other objects found were two of the long-handled combs of bone, a flat piece of bone resembling a weaver's rubbing implement for smoothing or calendering the web after it is woven, and several spindle-whorls of stone and bone; a bone ring, 2 inches diameter, perforated with small holes, and a tableman made of an ox tooth. The objects in metal were a bronze pin, 4¾ inches in length (Fig. 217), ornamented with engraved lines, and having a small ring, ¾ inch in diameter, inserted in a loop at the head of the pin; a small penannular brooch of bronze of Celtic form (Fig. 218), with flattened and slightly expanded ends terminating in the semblance of

Fig. 217.—Bronze Pin from Broch of Okstrow (4¾ inches in length).

animals' heads ; and a mounting of bronze, 3 inches in length (Fig. 219), chased on the upper surface, and having perforated

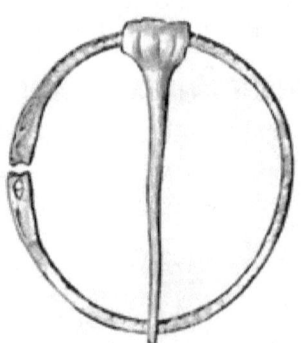

Fig. 218.—Penannular Brooch of Bronze from Broch of Okstrow (1½ inch in diameter).

prolongations, as if for fastening it to some other object. Besides the usual fragments of plain unglazed pottery of native manufacture, there were in this Broch again several pieces of the red lustrous ware commonly called Samian. These pieces indicate two vessels— one a bowl of about 6 inches diameter ; the other a shallow straight-sided vessel of considerable size. Both had been broken and mended by the insertion of soft metal clamps in holes drilled close to the sides of the fracture.

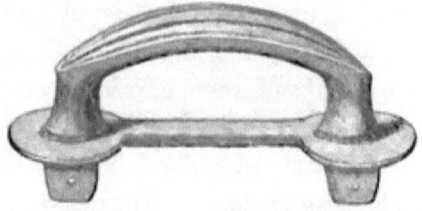

Fig. 219.—Mounting of Bronze from Broch of Okstrow (3 inches in length).

The Broch of Lingrow at the head of the Bay of Scapa, near Kirkwall, explored by the late Mr. George Petrie, had little of its height remaining, but was specially remarkable for the number and extent of the outbuildings clustered round its base.   These were not all explored, but so far as they were laid bare they are shown on the plan (Fig. 220).   The articles found were—a large number of querns, a stone lamp, a num-

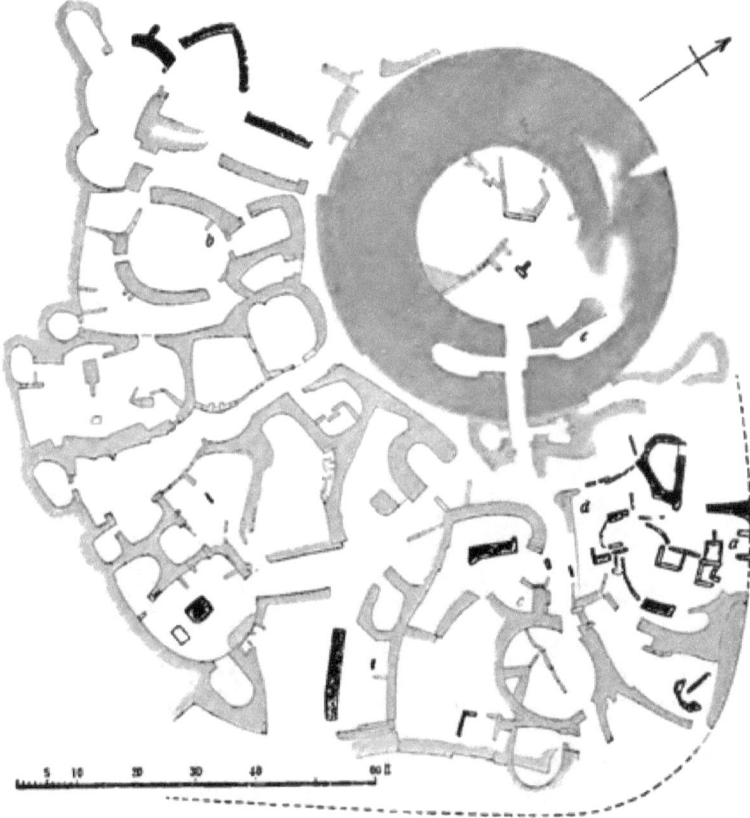

Fig. 220.—Ground Plan of the Broch of Lingrow, Orkney, with its Secondary Constructions.   (From a Plan by Mr. George Petrie and Sir H. Dryden.)

ber of quartz pebbles indented on their flat sides by use as point-sharpeners (Fig. 221), like those from the Broch of Kintradwell, a large number of implements in red-deer horn, one of which is shown (Fig. 222), bone pins and needles, and long-handled combs, spindle-whorls of stone, some fragments

of bronze, a clay mould (Fig. 223) for casting bronze pins with open circular heads bearing the same ornamentation, and precisely of the same form as the pin from Bower-madden (Fig. 203), in Caithness; playing dice of bone, and a very large quantity of pottery ornamented in various patterns, but all unglazed, and of the coarse black paste charac-teristic of native manufacture. In different parts of the outbuildings

Fig. 221.—Pebble of Quartzite marked by use as a point-sharpener, from Broch of Lingrow (2½ inches in length).

there were found four silver Roman coins—denarii of the Empire. Mr. Petrie did not live to draw up a detailed account

Fig. 222.—Implement of Deer-horn from Broch of Lingrow (4¼ inches in length).

of the excavation, and his notes do not indicate the reigns to which the coins severally belonged.[1] But the occurrence in

---

[1] I am indebted to Mr. James W. Cursiter, Kirkwall, for the extracts from the *Orcadian* newspaper in which the finding of these coins was recorded. A denarius of the reign of Antoninus (Pius ?), is noted in the issue of Nov. 26, 1870. On Dec. 10, one of Antoninus, and one of Vespasian, having a sow on the reverse. On Jan. 21, 1871, one of Hadrian, with Clementina on the reverse, and a female figure holding a patera in the extended right hand, and a spear in the left. A jotting by Mr. Petrie on the rough plan of the Broch also mentions " two coins of Crispina and bone dice found here."

this Broch of imperial coins, and in others of the red lustrous ware of late Roman or Gallo-Roman origin are indications of the occupation of the Brochs subsequently to the Roman conquest of the southern part of Britain.

The Broch that has yielded the largest and most interesting collection of objects is that of Burrian in the island of North Ronaldsay, excavated by Dr. William Traill of Woodwick, the proprietor of the island. The structure was essentially similar to those that have been previously described. The wall of the tower was 15 feet thick at the base, enclosing an area of 30 feet in diameter. The greatest height of the wall remaining was 10 feet. The doorway was on the south-east side facing the sea. It was 3 feet 3 inches wide at the outer

Fig. 223.—Clay Mould for casting Bronze Pins, from Broch of Lingrow (actual size).

face of the wall, and had checks for a door consisting of two slabs projecting on either side of the passage so as to narrow the aperture to 2 feet 10 inches. Within the door-checks the passage widened to 4 feet 3 inches. There was but one chamber in the thickness of the wall on the north-east side of the tower. It measured 9 feet 9 inches by 5 feet 9 inches on the floor, and was about 5 feet high, the roof having fallen in. The entrance from the interior court to the chamber was 3 feet 3 inches high, and 2 feet 2 inches wide. The objects found in the course of the excavations consisted of a large number of hammer-stones or oblong water-worn pebbles wasted at the ends by use, a number of querns and grain-rubbers, sinkstones, pieces of black vesicular lava, roughly pear-shaped, with holes bored through their smaller ends, and circular discs of thin slaty stone of various sizes. Among the objects made of bone, which were exceptionally numerous, were an implement of bone $5\frac{1}{2}$ inches in length (Fig. 224), made from the radius or wing-bone of a

Fig. 224.—Bone Implement from Broch of Burrian ($5\frac{1}{2}$ inches in length).

bird by cutting it obliquely across at one end, and grinding the section smooth; ninety pins of bone varying in size from $4\frac{3}{4}$ inches to somewhat less than $1\frac{1}{4}$ inch in length, many of which have ornamental heads of the character shown in Fig. 225, while others of larger size are of the forms shown

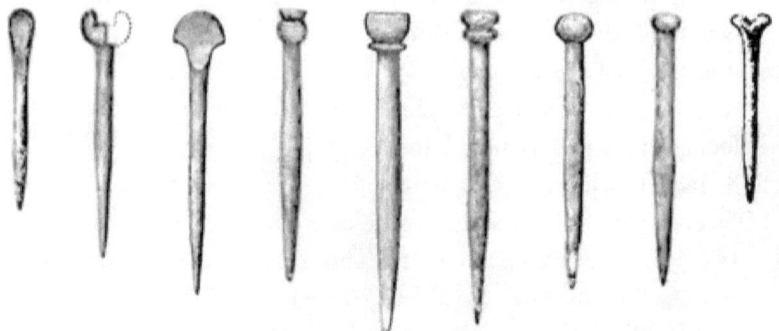

Fig. 225.—Bone Pins, with ornamental heads, from Broch of Burrian (actual size).

in Fig. 226, a large number are crutch-headed like Fig. 227, while one neatly-made pin with a rounded body (Fig. 228) is cleverly ornamented by its head being carved in the similitude of two horses' heads looking opposite ways, and another coarsely-made pin without a head (Fig. 229) is marked with

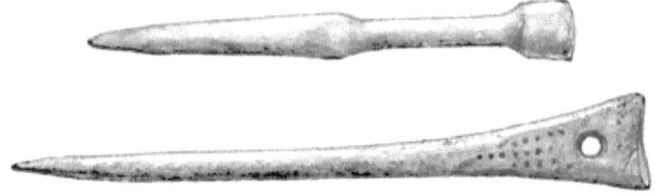

Fig. 226.—Bone Pins from Broch of Burrian (actual size).

transverse scorings. Besides the pins there are three needles of bone with elongated eyes, one broken, the others (Figs.

Fig. 227.—Crutch-headed Bone Pin from Broch of Burrian (actual size).

Figs. 228, 229.—Bone Pin with ornamental head, and pin with transverse markings, from Broch of Burrian (actual size).

230, 231) 2¼ and 1¾ inches in length respectively. There are also a number of pegs of bone, roughly finished, varying

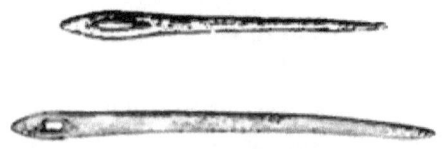

Figs. 230, 231.— Bone Needles from Broch of Burrian (actual size).

in length from 3 inches to 1½ inch, and from nearly ¼ inch

to about ⅛ inch diameter. These have evidently been used in pegging slips of bone or wood, and several slips of bone, about 3½ inches in length, convex on one side and flat on the other, occur among the relics, two of them having the pegs still in the holes. There are also a large number of shaped pieces of bone and deer-horn which might have served as the handles of small implements—hafts of knives, and suchlike. Among the smaller objects of bone there are several button-like articles, one apparently the half of a square-shaped stud or button of ivory with a small hole for the shank discoloured by oxide of iron, and two others made from short sections of the shank-bone of a sheep. One of these has the iron shank still in the hole. Akin to these in the manner of their formation are several playing dice, manufactured from sheep shank-bones. They are simple sections of the shank-bone 1⅔ inch in length, with one or more of the sides rubbed smooth and marked with the customary numbers in the shape of dots

Fig. 232.—One of a set of Dice made from a sheep shank-bone found in the Broch of Burrian (actual size).

and circles. The one here figured (Fig. 232) is ground smooth on one side, on which there are six points ; on the convexity of the bone there are five points ; on the naturally flattened side of the bone (which is broken) there are no markings to be seen at the ends, but the centre portion shows one marking. The second example has only one side of the bone remaining, which shows four points. The surface of the bone has scaled off the third example, and obliterated the numbers.[1] Among the miscellaneous articles of bone to which no definite use can be assigned, although they are obviously tools or im-

[1] Dice of this form have not been otherwise found in Scotland. They are occasionally found in Viking graves in Norway.

plements intended for special purposes, there is one (Fig. 233), strongly made of a roughly cut bone, having a rounded point

Fig. 233.—Tool of Bone found in the Broch of Burrian (actual size).

with two grooves cut in it so as to have prominent parallel ridges between and on either side of them. Among the objects of personal use are sixteen combs, most of them more or less broken, but several still in a fair state of preservation. One is round-backed and single-edged (Fig. 234), measuring 3 inches by 2 inches, the back pierced with three triplets of small holes, and ornamented with a profusion of dots and circle markings. It is formed of five thin slips of bone laid together lengthwise, and held in their places by two slips laid transversely across them on opposite sides, and fastened · by four iron rivets. The teeth of the comb have been very regularly cut by a fine saw, and the saw-marks on the under edges of the transverse slips show that the cutting of the teeth was performed after the pieces of the comb were fastened together. The rest of the combs are all double-edged. One

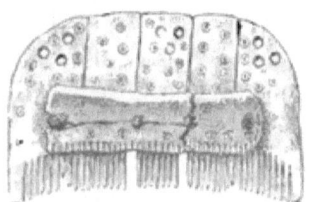

Fig. 234.—Round-backed Comb of Bone from Broch of Burrian (half actual size).

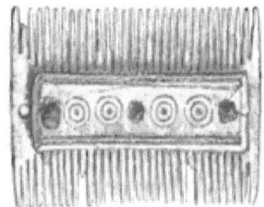

Fig. 235.—Double-edged Comb of Bone from Broch of Burrian (half actual size).

measuring $2\frac{3}{4}$ inches by 2 inches (Fig. 235), is formed of four slips of bone inserted between two transverse slips, and held together by three rivets of iron. The transverse slips are ornamented by a single line incised along each border, and by four sets of two concentric circles with central dots ranged at equal distances along the centre of the slips. The teeth are widely but regularly cut, narrowing towards the points, and those towards the sides of the comb shorter than those in the middle. Another comb of the same character (Fig. 236) measures 5½ inches in length, by 2 inches in breadth.

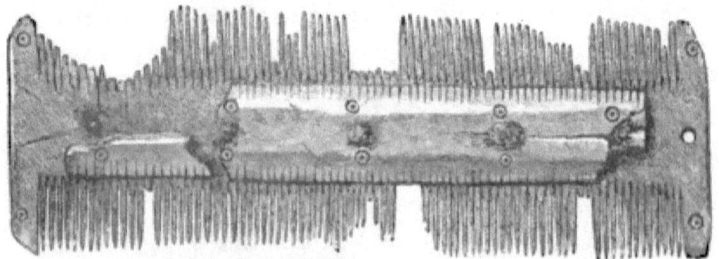

Fig. 236.—Double-edged Comb of Bone from Broch of Burrian (5½ inches in length).

This is the largest comb obtained from a Broch. It is formed of six slips of bone enclosed between two transverse slips fastened by five rivets of iron. Above and below each rivet is an ornamented dot and circle marking. A similar marking is placed in the centre of each of the broad terminal teeth at either end of the comb. The transverse slips are much marked by the saw. The teeth are well cut and regular in length and thickness; they show strongly the marks of wear by use, chiefly towards their bases, where minute transverse lines are worn deeply into the corners of the teeth, almost completely encircling them. Besides these combs for the hair, there were found no fewer than eighteen of the long-handled combs, which are of such frequent occurrence among the relics recovered from Brochs. That shown in Fig. 233 appears to be of deer-horn, but they are mostly made from portions of the outer table of the jaw-bone of the whale. They vary in length from

3 inches to 5½ inches. They also vary considerably in the

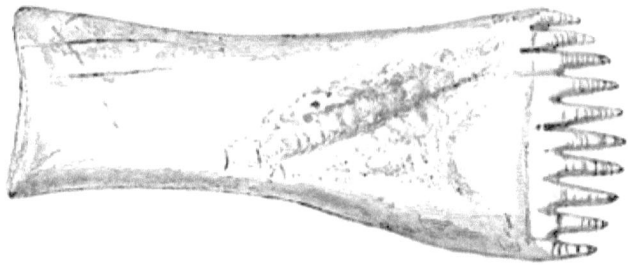

Fig. 237.—Long-handled Comb from the Broch of Burrian, Orkney (4¾ inches in length).

size and form of the teeth, some, like Fig. 238, having teeth that are short and pointed, and rounded in section, while the

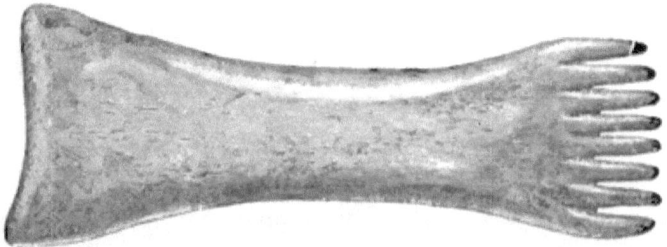

Fig. 238.—Long-handled Comb from the Broch of Burrian (4¼ inches in length).

teeth of others, like those in Fig. 239, are longer, less pointed, and more rectangular in section. It has been already stated

Fig. 239.—Long-handled Comb from the Broch of Burrian (4 inches in length).

that sixteen combs of the ordinary single and double-edged

forms which are characteristic of the comb used for the hair were found in this Broch. It is therefore probable that these eighteen long-handled combs were intended for some other purpose. They are not only unfitted by their clumsiness for this special and personal use, but the strength of the teeth, their coarseness, and the manner in which they are marked by the use to which they have been put are suggestive of implements for some manufacturing process rather than objects of the toilet. Another circumstance of their association is of some importance in the inquiry as to the nature of their special purpose. There is only one other implement which occurs with equal frequency in collections made from Brochs. In this same Broch, which yielded sixteen combs for the hair and eighteen of the long-handled implements, there were upwards of thirty spindle-whorls for spinning with the distaff and spindle. As this implies the existence of a very considerable manufacture of thread, and as the presence of the industry of weaving is also suggested by the occurrence of a number of smoothing or calendering imple-ments of bone (Fig. 240), which had seen much service, it is

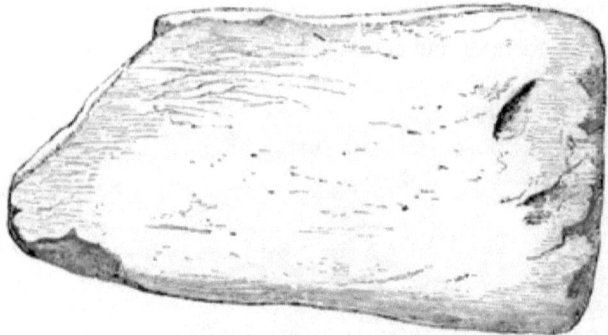

Fig. 240.—One of a number of Smoothing Implements of Bone from the Broch of Burrian (6½ inches in length).

probable that these eighteen long-handled implements may have had some connection with the process of making cloth from the thread spun by the spindle-whorls. The evidence as to the special use of the implement is derived (1) from the specialty of its form—it is long-handled; and (2) from the marks of wear upon its teeth, which are more distinct towards the apices of the teeth than towards their bases. These marks are such as would result from combing fibres in the preparation of lint or even of wool for spinning; but for this use the implement is not well suited by its form, and the marks on the teeth are often such deeply-cut transverse lines, as would rather imply the contact and friction of threads. And it is the fact that a comb of this special form, long-handled, and having a few stout teeth on the end of the handle, was used in the operation of weaving when the warp was fixed upright, as it always was in the older form of loom. The purpose for which the comb was used was the driving of the weft home as each successive thread was passed through the upright sheds of the warp by the shuttle. Such weaving-combs were used by the Egyptians,[1] the Greeks, and the Romans,[2] and they continued in use throughout Europe even

---

[1] An Egyptian weaving-comb of wood from the tombs at Thebes is in the Museum. Its teeth are differently formed, but the principle of its use is evidently the same. Rich figures a long-handled weaving-comb from a tomb in Thebes, which is now in the British Museum.

[2] Ovid (*Met.* vi. 55) gives a minute description of the process of weaving as follows—

> "Tela jugo vincta est ; stamen secernit arundo
> Inseritur medium radiis subtemen acutis
> Quod digiti expediunt, atque inter stamina ductum
> Percusso feriunt insecti pectine dentes."

Also (*Fasti*, iii. 820) he says that Pallas was the inventress of weaving, and adds—

> "Illa etiam stantes radio percurrere telas
> Erudit ; et rarum pectine denset opus."

Juvenal (*Sat.* ix. 30) makes Nævolus complain that he gets cloth from a Gaulish weaver greasy and badly woven—"Et male percussas textoris pectine Galli ;" while Virgil (*Æn.* vii. 14) represents Circe as—

> "Arguto tenues percurrens pectine telas ;"

in late mediæval times. In some varieties of carpet-weaving, in which alone the upright mode of working is now retained, the weft is driven home by a similar instrument made of iron. The Hindoo weaver of the present day retains the form of the implement used by his remote ancestors, although the materials of which it is made are now wood and iron. One such implement (Fig. 241) is in the National Museum.

Fig. 241.—Weaving-comb of Wood and Iron used in India (13 inches in length).

Although its teeth are of iron, a close examination suffices to show the marks of use, and in the iron comb as well as in those of bone, it is towards the apices and not towards the bases of the teeth that the transverse striations appear.[1]

and again in the *Georgicon* says—

> " Interea longum cantu solata laborem
> Arguto conjunx percurrit pectine telas. "

These descriptions specify the precise operations necessary for closing or driving home the weft, if the instrument employed were a comb held in the weaver's hand. Alexander Neckham, in his work *De Naturis Rerum* (written in the twelfth century, and recently printed in the series of Chronicles by the Master of the Rolls), has a chapter (cap. clxxi., De Textore) on weaving, in which, after describing the insertion of the weft by means of the shuttle, he says—

> " Inde textrix telam stantem percurret pectine,"

thus using the same words to describe the same operation.

[1] Dr. Malcolm Monro Mackenzie, Civil Surgeon, Dharwar, Bombay, states that in the jails in Bombay, where the work of the convicts is chiefly weaving, the implement used for beating in the weft is a hand-comb generally of wood, with iron teeth like that represented above in Fig. 241. The late Mr. Whytock, carpet manufacturer, when applied to for information as to the nature of the implement used in carpet-weaving, stated that " In the manufacture of the Persian or Axminster carpet, made in one piece and worked in

The collection of relics from this Broch contains a greater number of objects than has been found in any other, and it is also remarkable as presenting some varieties of objects which have not been found in any other. These are—(1) an oblong pebble of sandstone (Fig. 242), with an incised figure

Fig. 242.—Stone with Incised Figures of Crossed Triangles, from Broch of Burrian (6 inches in length).

on each of its flatter sides resembling the talismanic device of the Middle Ages known as Solomon's seal; (2) the metatarsal bone of a small ox, bearing on one side the peculiar symbol of the sculptured monuments resembling a crescent, crossed

an upright loom, the instrument used for beating down the weft or pile was about 4 inches broad, with iron teeth resembling those of a horse-comb, fastened into a short handle." He was kind enough to supply a sketch from memory of the instrument as formerly used in the factory at Lasswade. The sketch showed an implement in shape somewhat like the short flat hand-brush used by painters in whitewashing, or a good deal like the Indian loom comb (figured above), only a little broader in proportion to its length. The nature and use of these long-handled combs formed the subject of two papers in the *Proceedings of the Society of Antiquaries of Scotland*, vol. ix. pp. 118, 548.

by a V-shaped rod or sceptre (as shown in Fig. 243);
(3) a small iron bell; and (4) a slab of sandstone with a

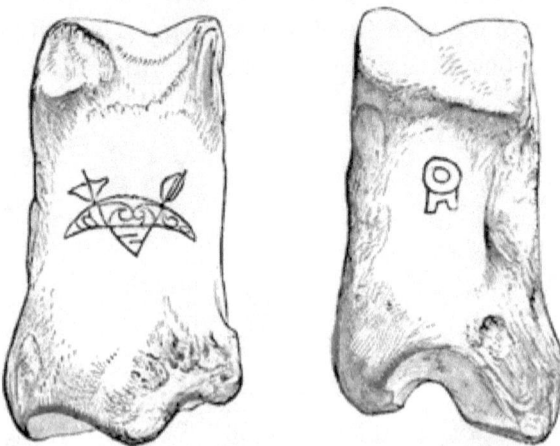

Fig. 243.—Metatarsal Bone of Ox (front and back views), with incised symbols,
from Broch of Burrian (actual size).

cross of Celtic form, a fish, and an Ogham inscription. The
bell and the monumental slab have been already described,
and need not be further alluded to.[1] The stone with the
geometric figure of Solomon's seal lay within a cist-like construction half filled with red ashes, which was in a paved
floor that overlay the original floor, and was separated from
it by a layer of from 1 to 2 feet of ashes and rubbish. The
cross-bearing slab was found at a point near the side of the
Broch, where the wall was so low that though the slab lay
not much above the floor of the tower it was also not far
below the surface of the mound. It cannot therefore be said
of any of these objects that they were certainly associated
with the earlier occupation of the Broch, and as they differ
in character from all the objects usually found in such structures, their exceptional occurrence here can have no bearing

[1] *Scotland in Early Christian Times; The Rhind Lectures* for 1879, p.
175; and Second Series for 1880, p. 211.

on the discussion of the general questions of the character and relations of the group of relics usually found in Brochs.

That character and these relations are now distinctly established. The general character of the relics obtained by the systematic excavation of these northern Brochs is not that of a primitive group, but of a group which is the product of an advanced stage of culture, civilisation, and social organisation. The inference deducible from the character of the relics is the same as that which has been deduced from the type of the structure, and when the whole of the facts are thus marshalled and their significance is calmly considered, it becomes plain that there is even less ground for ascribing a low condition of culture, of civilisation, or of social organisation to the people who constructed and occupied these massive towers, than there is for ascribing such a condition to the builders of the beehive huts and dry-built churches of Christian times. Reviewing the various aspects of the life of the occupants of Brochs, as these have been successively disclosed, we see them planting their defensive habitations thickly over the area of the best arable land, fringing the coasts, and studding the straths with a form of structure perfectly unique in character and conception, and for purposes of defence and passive resistance as admirably devised as anything yet invented. We see that this system of gigantic and laboriously constructed strongholds has been devised and universally adopted with the plain intention of providing for the security of the tillers and the produce of the soil. We find their occupants cultivating grain, keeping flocks and herds, and hunting the forests and fishing the sea for their sustenance. We find them practising arts and industries implying intelligence and technical skill, and apparently also involving commercial relations with distant sources of the raw materials. The probability is that they manufactured all the weapons and implements they used, and we find them using swords, spears, knives, axes, and chisels of

S

iron, and pincers, rings, bracelets, pins, and other articles of
bronze or brass. We know that they made their own ornaments in these metals, because the clay moulds, the crucibles,
and the cakes of rough metal have been found in different
Brochs. Gold has not been found in any well-authenticated
instance, but silver and lead are not wanting. They utilised
the bones and horns of animals in the fabrication of such
things as pins, needles, and bodkins, buttons, combs, spindle-
whorls, and various other implements, ornaments, and furnishings of everyday life and industry. They also used stone
when it suited their purpose. They made beads and bracelets
of jet or lignite, and they had other beads of variously-
coloured vitreous pastes, enamelled on the surface with spiral
lines and other devices. They also made beads and discs of
highly-polished stone, such as serpentine, marble, and mica
schist, with imbedded garnets. From the commoner varieties
of stone they made millstones or querns, mortars, pestles,
pounders and hammer-stones, whetstones and point-sharpeners,
bowls, cups with and without handles, lamps, and culinary
vessels of various kinds, net-weights, sinkers, and spindle-
whorls. They made pottery, plain and ornamented of various
kinds, chiefly round-bottomed globular vessels with bulging
sides and everted rims. The women practised the arts of
spinning and weaving, and probably also made the pottery
and ground the grain, while the men made the weapons and
tools of metal, and the ornaments and implements of bone
and stone, did the hunting and fishing, and the warfare when
needful, and erected the great structures which made the
industrious quietude of domestic life possible to them.

That the people thus occupying these peculiar strongholds
were the people of the soil, and not strangers effecting a
lodgement in a hostile territory, is obviously suggested both
by the character and relations of the typical structure, and
by the character and relations of the relics of their domestic
life. It has been demonstrated in the previous Lecture that

while the typical structure, taken in the totality of its characteristics, stands absolutely alone and quite apart from all other types of construction, ancient or modern, its essential features are those which are characteristic of early Celtic constructions. It is circular, it is dry-built, its doorways have inclined instead of perpendicular sides, the roofs of its chambers are formed of beehive vaulting of overlapping stones, and its galleries are comparable to a series of earth-houses placed one over the other. It has now been shown that the relics of the life of the occupants of the Brochs constitute a group of objects differing widely from those which characterise the Scandinavian occupancy of the north and west of Scotland. No group of objects in its general *facies*, entirely comparable to the group which is characteristic of the Brochs, exists on the continent of Europe or anywhere out of Scotland. But when the typical forms of the Broch group of relics are compared with those of other groups existing in Scotland, it becomes at once apparent that they are forms which are characteristic of the Celtic area and of post-Roman times. This unique series of objects from a unique type of structure illustrates a peculiar phase of the early Celtic or Iron Age culture and civilisation of our country which until recently was absolutely unknown. And as we find the investigation on which we have embarked continuously disclosing series after series of similarly unique types, it becomes increasingly apparent that its final result can be nothing less than the establishment of the fact that Scotland has an archæology—in other words, that the un-written story of her early systems of culture and civilisation is dispersed among the *disjecta membra* of her scattered remains, and is only to be disclosed by the systematic collection and study of all existing materials illustrative of her native industry and native art, with their associated indications of social organisation and potential culture.

LECTURE VI.

(NOVEMBER 2, 1881.)

LAKE-DWELLINGS, HILL-FORTS, AND EARTH-HOUSES.

A BROCH like that of Clickamin (see the Frontispiece), situated upon an island in a loch, accessible by a causeway from
the island to the shore is practically a lake-dwelling. But
there are many defensive structures occupying similar positions which are not Brochs, although they are often constructed of stone. Most of them are now in such a ruinous
condition that it is impossible to say what may have been
the precise nature of their form and architectural construction.

In the Loch of Hogsetter, in the island of Whalsay, in
Shetland, there is a small island containing a defensive
structure of dry-built masonry (Fig. 244) which is plainly not
a Broch.[1] The structure occupies the greater part of the
available surface of the island, and its form has evidently
been determined by the form of the island. It consists of a
dry-built wall of stones with a minimum thickness of 3 to
4 feet, enclosing an oblong oval of about 70 feet by 75 feet.
A causeway, 33 yards in length, has been constructed to give
access to the island from the shore, and on the side next the
causeway the enclosing wall is amplified so as to admit of
the construction of a doorway, flanked on each side by a

---

[1] Described in Low's *Tour in Orkney and Shetland*, 1774 (Kirkwall, 1879),
p. 177; and by Dr. Arthur Mitchell in the *Proceedings of the Society of
Antiquaries of Scotland*, vol. xv. p. 304.

chamber, as seen in the detached work protecting the entrance to the island of Clickamin. This part of the con-

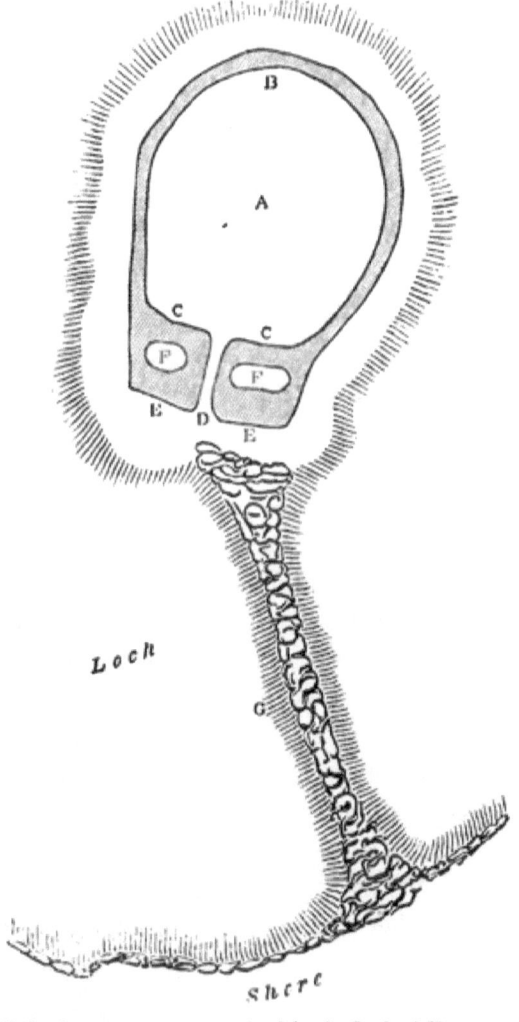

Fig. 244.—Defensive structure on an island in the Loch of Hogsetter, Whalsay, Shetland. (From a Sketch Plan by Dr. Arthur Mitchell.)

struction is solidly built, and the chambers, which are placed to right and left of the entrance passage, occupy the interior

of a somewhat rectangular expansion of the wall, measuring
about 20 feet by 12 feet, and now only about 8 feet high.
When Low visited Whalsay in 1774, this part of the construction was 15 feet high, and the chambers and their
entrances were quite entire. They were beehive roofed, the
entrances going straight through the back wall from the
enclosed area. The main entrance, which was $2\frac{1}{2}$ feet wide
and $4\frac{1}{2}$ feet high, was covered by the masonry which joined
the two sides of the construction over its lintels, and at about
two-thirds of its length inwards there were checks for a door
and the usual bar-holes on either side. Dr. Mitchell states
that above the two lower chambers there appear to have
been other two forming a second tier, but as Low did not
observe them, and no trace of a stair or other access to the
upper level now remains, it seems possible that they may
have been chambers of construction, or merely vacancies left
to lighten the weight on the roofs of the chambers below.
Apart from the peculiarity of its chambers, which are unlike
the guard-chambers of the Brochs in having their entrances
opening to the enclosed space and not directly opening
into the passage, this structure has more affinities with the
stone cashels than with the Brochs. Like them it adapts its
form to the space in which it is situated, and like them it
consists of a simple rampart with cells in the thickness of
the wall. The wall is low, and of no great strength, and like
the wall of a cashel is merely meant to add to the defen-
sibility of a naturally defensive position. The special
peculiarities of this defensive construction are, that it is a
dry-built structure which is not a Broch but a cashel, and
that it is situated on an island in a loch and rendered
accessible by a causeway. The island is of natural formation, and has been thus utilised, because of its suitability
for defensive purposes.

Such instances of the adaptation of natural islands in

lochs as places of strength by constructing defensive buildings of stone upon them are not uncommon, although it rarely happens that the form and characteristics of the buildings themselves are so clearly traceable. But there is another variety of defensive construction which is more frequently found in similar positions. It possesses the additional peculiarity of being either wholly or partially constructed of wood.

The Lake-Dwellings in Scotland, which are either wholly or partially constructed of wood, and which on that account are known as Crannogs, are very numerous, but so few of them have yet been systematically explored that it is impossible to determine with any degree of certainty the special characteristics of their typical form and structural arrangements. Indeed, it is questionable whether this knowledge may be in any measure attainable by investigation of their existing remains. Constructed of perishable material, which, as long as it survived the ravages of time, was capable of being adapted to many and various purposes of general utility, the parts of the Crannogs that stood above the water were almost certain to be gradually destroyed. But whatever may have been the special form of the superstructure of the Lake-Dwelling when it was built of timber instead of stone, the typical Crannog, taken as a whole, differs from the stone-built strengths that are placed in lakes not only in the substitution of timber in place of stone as the material of its construction, but also in being constructed usually on an island that is itself an artificial construction. The Crannog is therefore a Lake-Dwelling, actually built up from the lake-bottom. Of the structure which stood above the water, and gave shelter and habitable houseroom to the inmates, there is usually no trace whatever. Occasionally the remains of a pavement of timber or of flagstones, or the site of a hearth with its accumulations of ashes and food refuse marks the level of the floor, and sometimes a succession of such indications at different levels may betoken successive occupations. But the story of the Crannog as told by the casual relics imbedded in and around its submerged foundations is clearly intelligible, although it reveals nothing of the precise form and arrangements of the habitable part of the structure.

In the Loch of Dowalton, situated in the centre of the peninsula, bounded on the west by the Bay of Luce, and on the east by the Bay of Wigton, in Wigtonshire, a group of Crannogs was investigated by Earl Percy (then Lord Lovaine) in 1863, and subsequently examined by Sir William Maxwell of Monreith, and the late Dr. John Stuart, then Secretary of the Society of Antiquaries of Scotland. One of these, situated on the south side of the loch and near the west end, presented the appearance of a mass of stones and soil surrounded by numerous rows of piles formed of young oak-trees. On the north-east side of the island a number of beams of oak mortised together like hurdles were visible, and below them layers of round logs laid horizontally. A few vertical piles were observed, which, in some cases, had cross-beams mortised into them. Below the layers of logs were masses of brushwood and fern. The only sign of occupation noticed was the site of a hearth, with an accumulation of ashes, burnt wood, and bones of animals. In the adjacent refuse-heap a small fragment of bronze was discovered, and close by the island a bronze basin was found. Near the eastern margin of the loch was a group of three Crannogs. The largest of these was about 23 yards in diameter. It was surrounded by many rows of piles, some of which had their ends cut square across with a hatchet. The surface of the Crannog was covered with stones resting on a mass of brushwood, fern, and heather, intermingled with stones and earth. The whole mass was penetrated and kept together by piles driven through it into the bottom of the loch. On the south side were the remains of a massive construction of planks of roughly-squared oak, 5 feet long, 2 feet wide, and 2 inches thick, laid side by side in layers crossing each other transversely, and pinned together. The general framework of this platform-like structure was of massive beams mortised together, the mortises measuring about 10 inches by 8 inches. On the north-east side, and underneath part of the timber construction, a canoe was found, 21 feet in length and 3 feet 10 inches wide at the stern. The canoe was of oak, hollowed out of a single tree, and the stern was closed by a board sliding in a groove cut in both sides, and secured by a thicker piece 3 inches in height pegged down over it. A washboard projecting slightly over the edge and pegged into the upper margin of the canoe, ran all round the sides. There were two thole-pins inserted in square holes on each side, and one of the thwarts remained in position. A portion of a shoe formed of stamped leather (Fig. 245) was discovered

Fig. 245.—Portion of a Shoe of stamped leather (length, 7 inches).

among the mass of material thrown out in excavating the canoe. One hearth was discovered. It was simply a paved space, showing marks of fire and an accumulation of ashes and food refuse. The bones were those of the common domestic animals, the ox, the pig, and sheep. Among the relics found on the Crannog were a bronze penannular brooch with knobbed ends, the knobs somewhat quadrangular in form, two iron hammers, and four whetstones.

Another Crannog, nearly circular, and 13 yards in diameter, lay a little to the southward. Its construction was in every respect similar to that last described, and it was surrounded by an immense number of piles, extending in rows for 20 yards outside the circumference of a solid construction of brushwood and logs, covered by earth and stones. One canoe was found on its margin, 24 feet long and 4 feet 2 inches wide in the middle; and another was found between

Fig. 246.　Saucepan of Roman form found in Dowalton Loch
(height, 5½ inches).

it and the shore of the loch, 18½ feet long and 2 feet 7 inches wide. Among the refuse of the occupancy of the Crannog, consisting chiefly of bones of domestic animals, were found a broken bead of glass, and portions of two amulets of glass, one ornamented with a yellow streak and the other with streaks of blue and white.

Between this Crannog and the shore a bronze saucepan (Fig. 246), of the form usually associated with remains of the

Roman period,[1] was found in the mud of the loch. It is an elegant and well-finished vessel of bronze, tinned inside, and measuring 8 inches in diameter across the mouth and 5½ inches deep. The flattened handle springing from the upper edge is 7 inches in length. The bottom of the vessel is furnished exteriorly with five projecting concentric rings. In front, opposite to the handle, is an ornamental ring, swung by a loop projecting from beneath the upper margin of the rim, and encircling a well-modelled figure of a human face in relief. On the handle is the stamp of the maker, CIPI POLIBI F.[2]

About 60 yards from this last Crannog was a smaller one, presenting no essential points of difference, and nearer the south-east shore of the loch was a group of six, still smaller and less distinct in outline, but all apparently similar in construction.

The other objects found in association with these Crannogs or in the loch-bottom in their immediate neighbourhood, were a number of beads of variegated glass or vitreous paste, one of which (Fig. 247) has a lining of bronze in the perforation; one amber bead; a small bronze ring; a clay crucible; several whetstones; five querns;

Fig. 247.—Bead of glass with lining of bronze (length, 1 inch).

---

[1] This special form of saucepan with curved sides and flat bottom, concentrically moulded on the outside, is found in most collections of antiquities obtained from sites of Roman occupation. In the Museo Borbonico, at Naples, there are about 200 examples, mostly of this type.

[2] His full designation apparently was Publius Cipius Polibus. His saucepans are widely distributed. Two found in a nest of five dug up at Castle Howard, in Yorkshire, bore his stamp, the one having P·CIPI·POLIB, and the other P·CIPI·POLVIBI. In the Museum at Zurich there is a handle of a saucepan with the stamp CIPI·POLIBI, and one found in Lower Saxony has P·CIPI·POLIBI.

a bronze dish (Fig. 248), about 12 inches in diameter and 3 inches deep, hammered out of the solid, and having a flat rim

Fig. 248.—Bronze Basin found in the Loch of Dowalton (height, 3 inches).

1 inch in breadth, turned over, and slightly bent downwards; another dish similarly made, but without the flattened rim, 12 inches diameter and 4 inches deep; and a third (Fig. 249)

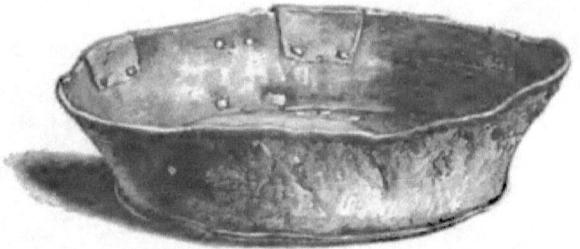

Fig. 249.—Basin of thin bronze found in the Loch of Dowalton (height, 4 inches).

of thinner metal, flat-bottomed with sloping sides, 10 inches diameter and 4 inches deep, the bottom and sides patched in several places by pieces fastened on with flat-headed double-toed rivets exactly like the modern paper-fasteners; a large bronze ring attached to the upper part of a caldron of thin bronze; a portion of a tube of cast bronze of unknown use; a wooden paddle; and a number of fragments of articles of iron complete the list.

In the Black Loch, in the parish of Inch, Wigtonshire, an

island explored in 1872 by Mr. C. E. Dalrymple was found
to have been a Crannog formed upon a shoal in the lake.
In the centre of the island there was a circular mound,
45 feet in diameter, and rising to about 5 feet above the
level of the loch and 3½ feet above the general surface of the
island. At a depth of about 5 feet in the centre of the mound
there was a flooring of trunks of trees, chiefly oak and alder,
crossing each other at right angles. This log flooring covered
a circular space of about 50 feet in diameter. At different
levels above it and over the whole of its area there were
found many fireplaces or hearths, formed of two long narrow
slabs set on edge and parallel to each other with a paved
space between, and filled and surrounded by ashes and bones
of animals broken and split. In one of these accumulations
of ashes and food refuse there were found a fragment of
bronze and a portion of an iron knife; and in another a
broken armlet of glass. A broken double-edged bone comb,
ornamented with dots and circles, and a portion of a stone
disc with a bevelled edge, were also found. The island
seemed to have been surrounded with piles, and a small
canoe, dug out of a single tree, was discovered in the loch,
near the narrow channel which separates the island from the
shore.

The general character of the group of relics obtained from
these structures is that of the Iron Age, with indications of a
period subsequent to the Roman conquest. The same character and the same indications are presented by the group of
relics obtained from the Crannogs of Ayrshire, which have
been so carefully investigated by Dr. Munro.[1] The Lochlee

---

[1] Since these Lectures were delivered an exhaustive treatise on *The Lake-
Dwellings of Scotland*, by Dr. Robert Munro, of Kilmarnock, has been issued
In this copiously illustrated work Dr. Munro has described the Crannogs in
Ayrshire recently excavated under his personal superintendence, and system-
atised the whole subject in a manner that leaves nothing to be desired.

Crannog, near Tarbolton, yielded a very large collection of objects in the various materials of stone, bone, wood, bronze or brass, iron, glass, and jet or cannel coal. But with the single exception of a polished stone celt, the types of the Stone and Bronze Ages are entirely absent from the group. The same thing is true of the collections obtained from the Crannog at Lochspouts near Maybole, and the Buston Crannog near Kilmaurs. But in these Crannog collections there are certain groups of objects which are closely akin to those found in Brochs. These are the hammer-stones, oblong water-worn pebbles wasted at the ends by use, spindle-whorls and querns, the round polished discs of stone, the peculiarly-shaped bone pins, needles, and borers, the double-edged bone combs, the deer-horn implements, the bronze brooches, rings, and pins, and the spiral finger-rings. There are also certain objects in these collections which present features of form and ornamentation clearly of the early Celtic types, such as a bridle-bit from Lochlee (of the same form as that shown in Fig. 101), a block of ash-wood from the same Crannog with Celtic patterns cut in both sides, and a bronze mounting from Lochspouts, which is characteristically Celtic in style. On the other hand, there are certain objects which, like the harp-shaped fibulæ and the lustrous red ware (commonly called Samian), are indicative of post-Roman times. The bulk of the relics from the Crannogs being thus of Iron Age types with indications of post-Roman time, and with a striking general affinity to the group of relics obtained from the Brochs, the place of these Lake-Dwellings in the general series may be considered as sufficiently established.[1]

---

[1] That the use of such strongholds in the lochs of Scotland and Ireland continued in historic times is abundantly attested. In the *Register of the Privy Council of Scotland*, under the date of 14th April 1608, one of the articles proposed to Angus M'Concill, of Dunnyvaig, and Hector M'Clayne, of Dowart, for reducing them and their clans to obedience is :—"That the

There is no class of ancient remains within our country of which we have less precise knowledge than the Hill-Forts. The reason of this is not their rarity, because they form perhaps the most numerous and widely-distributed class of ancient structures now existing. But the ordinary methods of obtaining precise knowledge of their form, structure, and contents have not been applied to them, and the ordinary agencies of destruction, incident to a high condition of social and agricultural progress, have long been busy amongst them.

They differ essentially from all other constructions, because they are adaptations of naturally elevated sites for defensive purposes. The natural site is the defensive position, and the fort itself derives its form and in many cases also its character of construction from the form and nature of the eminence or promontory on which it is built. It would, therefore, be contrary to the nature of the circumstances to expect that they should exhibit any such uniformity of plan or structure as is so conspicuous in the case of the Brochs. Yet it is clear, from the little we do know of them, that there are certain groups possessing certain features of construction in common which differ from other groups possessing other features of construction in common; and it is evident that if a sufficient body of available materials existed on record regarding the different members of these groups

haill houssis of defence, strongholdis, and cranokis in the Yllis perteining to thame and their forsaidis sall be delyverit to His Majestie." Three-legged pots of brass, and ewers of the forms in use from the thirteenth to the sixteenth century and later, have been found in several of the Scottish Crannog sites. The *Irish Annals* contain frequent notices of the taking of Crannogs. For instance :—"A.D. 1436. The Crannog of Loch Laoghaire was taken by the sons of Brian O'Neill. On their arrival they set about constructing vessels to land on the Crannog in which the sons of Brian Oge then were ; on which the latter came to the resolution of giving up the Crannog to O'Neill and made peace with him."—*Annals of the Four Masters.*

their typical characteristics might be readily deduced. But before this can be done with that precision and certainty which are requisite for scientific work, it is necessary (1) that a series of plans and sections to scale of a sufficient number of examples from each of the various groups should be obtained; (2) that a series of observations as to the methods of construction employed in different circumstances and situations should be made; and (3) that a series of examinations of the enclosed areas and surrounding ground should be undertaken, with the view of ascertaining the character of the relics that are associated with the structures. In the meantime it is only possible to indicate some of their general characteristics as exhibited by a few of the better known examples.

They naturally divide themselves into two great classes by their construction—(1) those that are earth-works; and (2) those that are constructed of stone.

In most cases the earth-works are so low and slight that they could not have been of much service unless crowned with palisades. They are usually on sites that are more susceptible of cultivation than the hill-tops which are the common positions of the stone-works, and hence they have suffered more generally from agricultural operations than the forts of stone. They are usually irregularly circular or oval in plan, consisting of a varying number of low embankments drawn round the summit of a natural eminence. The only one of which a scale-plan has been made is a very character-istic example (Fig. 250), on the Midhill Head, on the estate of Borthwick Hall, Midlothian.[1] The space enclosed by the embankments is 410 feet in length from east to west, and 284 feet in breadth from north to south. The embank-

---

[1] *Proc. Soc. Antiq. Scot.*, vol. xiv. p. 254. The Society is indebted to the liberality of the proprietor, D. J. Maclie, Esq., for the plan of this character-istic earth-work, surveyed and described by Mr. W. Galloway, architect.

ments are four in number, occupying a space round the
enclosure, varying from 130 feet to about 80 feet in breadth.
They are nowhere more than from 4 to 5 feet in height.
There are two entrances to the enclosed space at the ends of
the oval, and a third on the south side. This example represents in a general way the class of earthworks of most

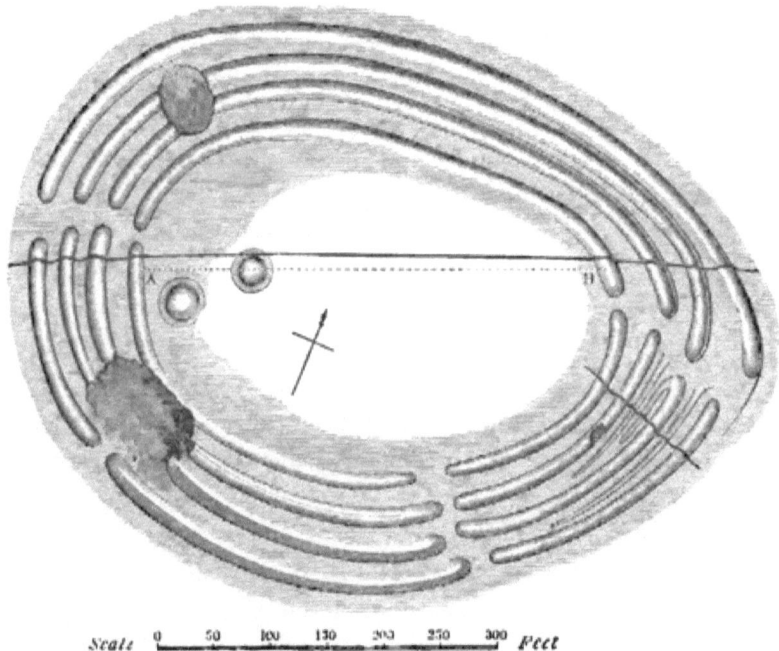

Scale 0   50   100   130   200   250   300 Feet

Fig. 250.—Ground plan of Earthwork on Midhill Head, Midlothian.

frequent occurrence, consisting of a series of circumvallations
enclosing the highest part of an eminence of no great
elevation.

The Hill-Forts which are constructed of stone sometimes
consist of a single wall drawn round the brow of a hill, and
enclosing the more or less level area which forms its summit.
One of this description at Garrywhoine, in Caithness, is an

T

oval enclosure about 200 paces long by 65 in breadth. The foundation of the wall is about 14 feet thick, and in some places 3 or 4 feet of its height remains. In the thickness of the wall on the east side the remains of two chambers are visible. There were two entrances to the area of the fort, one at the north end and the other at the south end of the hill. The entrance at the north end has three of the great corner-stones of the gateway still in position. They are single stones or flat boulders about 5 feet high, set on end, having their broad faces in line with the exterior and interior faces of the wall, and the ends in the line of the entrance which is 7 feet wide. Only one of the stones similarly placed remains at the south entrance. The dilapidation of this remarkable example of a stone cashel was due to the construction of a mill-dam in the valley below, the stones having been rolled down the hill to form the embankment. I notice it because it is the only Hill-Fort I have seen which still retains the stone-pillars of its gateway, and because the story of its demolition illustrates the fate of many of the most perfect and interesting remains of our country's antiquity.

A more complex variety consists of two, three, or more walls drawn concentrically round the upper part of a conical hill, at short distances apart, as in the case of the example known as the White Caterthun in the parish of Menmuir, Forfarshire. The area enclosed is a long oval about 450 by 200 feet. The enclosing wall has been of enormous size. Its remains have spread themselves over a width in some places of nearly 100 feet, and they now form a somewhat rounded embankment of from 4 to 6 feet high, encompassing the summit of the hill. About 150 feet lower down on the slope of the hill is another wall, equally ruined, and below it are the remains of a third. Beyond this there is an enclosure of an oblong form and of less massive construction,

abutting against one side of the outer wall of the fort.[1] A
fort of smaller size, but presenting somewhat similar features
of construction, crowns the spur of Ben Ledi which overlooks
the ford at Coilantogle, a little below the outlet of Loch
Vennachar.   The hill is precipitous on one side, and the walls
do not encircle it completely, but the external faces of three
encircling walls are in some places visible for a considerable
distance round the less precipitous part of the hill.   Abutting
on the outer wall, on the side which is most accessible, is an
oval enclosure less massively constructed, as at Caterthun.

There is another variety of these Hill-Forts which has
attracted more attention on account of the singularity of the
phenomena which they present.   These are the Vitrified
Forts, so called because in their walls there is always more or
less of the scorified or vitrified appearance which is the result
of the action of fire upon masses of loose stones.   Although
there has been perhaps more written about these singular
structures than about any other class of antiquities, there is
really little known of their special phenomena, and less of
their real character.[2]   In point of fact the real knowledge

[1] Such constructions are frequently found in similar juxtaposition to the
walls of these forts, and rightly or wrongly they have been regarded as
cattle-folds.

[2] For this reason we are unable to compare the vitrified forts of Scotland
with the scorified and vitrified ramparts which have been occasionally remarked as occurring in other countries of Europe.   I know no example in
England, but a considerable number have been noticed in France (*Mémoires
de la Soc. Antiq. de France*, vol. xxxviii. p. 83), one of which, at Peran in
Brittany, has only the upper part of the walls vitrified, a circumstance which
has also been noticed with respect to several of the Scottish forts.   From the
fact of a Roman roofing tile having been found firmly attached to the melted
stones of the vitrified part of the wall of this fort, it is inferred that the
period of the vitrifaction was subsequent to the Roman conquest.   Scorified
ramparts in Bohemia have been described by Dr. Jul. E. Fodisch in the
Proc. Soc. Antiq. Scot., vol. viii. p. 155.   It has been frequently stated that
they do not occur in Ireland, but Dr. Petrie has noted four in Londonderry
and one in Cavan (Stokes's *Life of Dr. Petrie*, p. 223).|

relating to the form, measurements, and composition of the structures and the observation of the phenomena they present has been entirely overlooked in fruitless discussions as to the modes in which the vitrifaction of the walls has been produced, and the reasons which may be conjecturally assigned for it. The result is that to this day, so far as I am aware, there is not a single scale-plan with sections, of a single one of them. When such plans and sectional drawings are available in sufficient numbers, we shall be able to say that the materials exist for the commencement of a systematic investigation of the nature and typical relations of the structures.

The fort on Knockfarril, which overlooks the valley of Strathpeffer, in Ross-shire, encloses an oval area of about 120 paces in length by about 40 in breadth. It was first described by Mr. John Williams in 1777.[1] Sections were then made through it from side to side, and Mr. Williams states that on the north side he found the ruins of the wall 12 feet high, although he came to the conclusion that this was a section of the width of the wall which had fallen flat outwards. With regard to the phenomena of vitrifaction, he states that the whole wall has been run together into one solid mass, but in another place he states that at the outskirts of the ruins and at the bottom of the hill there was a great quantity of large stones which had not been touched by fire, and from this he concluded that there had been some kind of stone buildings going round on the outside of the vitrified walls. It is to be observed that when he speaks of the whole wall being run together into one solid mass, he is not stating a fact, which he has observed, but a conclusion which he has formed from a partial examination.

[1] *Account of some remarkable Ancient Ruins recently discovered in the Highlands. In a series of Letters by John Williams, mineral engineer.* Edinburgh, 1777.

" I am of opinion," he says, "and it appears by the ruins that the whole of the surrounding wall on Knockfarril has been run together by vitrifaction much better than the most of the kind I have seen." He states also that immediately on the inside of the surrounding walls there were ruins of buildings in which the vitrifaction was much less complete, and these he imagined to have been a range of habitations reared under the shelter of the outer wall.

Craig Phadrig, near Inverness, when examined by Williams, presented the peculiarity of two vitrified walls, the remains of which could be traced quite round the inclosed area, while the remains of a third were visible at the entrance at the east end. The outer wall was founded on the rock, about 6 or 8 paces distant from the inner wall. Its greatest height did not then exceed 4 or 5 feet, but he found large masses of it adhering to the rock where it was first run. The area enclosed was from 80 to 90 paces long by about 30 broad.

The fort at Finhaven, near Aberlemno, in Forfarshire, is an irregular oblong with rounded corners, about 150 paces in length by about 36 in breadth. The walls are greatly dilapidated, and but a small part of their height is now visible. They appear to have been about 10 feet in thickness, and in some places there is still 4 or 5 feet of the height remaining. The vitrifaction is very unequal, and many parts of the wall scarcely show the action of fire, while in others the melted matter has run down among the interstices of the stones.

Dun Mac Uisneachan, in Loch Etive, was described by Dr. Macculloch in 1824, and more recently by Dr. R. Angus Smith, who made extensive investigations of the area of the fort in 1873-4.[1] It occupies the top of an oblong hill which is either

---

[1] *Proc. Soc. Antiq. Scot.*, vol. ix. p. 396, vol. x. p. 70, vol. xi. p. 298, and vol. xii. p. 13.

very steep or actually precipitous on all sides. The area enclosed is about 250 yards long by 50 yards broad. It is encompassed on the verge of the hill by a wall which is still in some places from 5 to 6 feet high. The points made out by the investigation are thus stated by Dr. Angus Smith— (1) the weaker parts of the dun or defensible position were walled, the outer wall or part of wall being vitrified; (2) the wall of the western part is double; the outer being vitrified, the inner built in layers of flat stone, 9 feet being the distance from surface to surface; (3) the walls were built without mortar as in all these forts ; (4) vitrified portions of walling were found overlying portions built in the ordinary manner and unvitrified. This I regard as the most interesting and important point ascertained by Dr. Angus Smith's investigations regarding the construction of the so-called Vitrified Forts. It shows distinctly that the wall of a Vitrified Fort is not always, and in every part, a vitrified wall; and it suggests that instead of taking this for granted, in every case in which signs of vitrifaction are observed, the inquiry ought to be directed to the determination of the extent of such partial vitrifaction, wherever it is found to have been partial. Another interesting result of his researches was the discovery of the remains of dwellings within the area of the fort. They were rectangular constructions, having dry-built walls about 2 feet thick. A large refuse-heap of bones of the common domestic animals was found near them. Some querns, a portion of an iron sword, an iron ring about 2 inches diameter, and a convex plate of bronze $1\frac{1}{4}$ inch diameter, ornamented with concentric circles, the hollows of which were filled with red and the centre with yellow enamel, were found in the course of the excavations. The character of this relic, with its red and yellow enamels, is closely allied to that of the similarly enamelled bronzes which have been already described, some of which have been found in constructions of a very peculiar type which have yet to be noticed.

The latest examination of Vitrified Forts is contained in a paper by Dr. Edward Hamilton,[1] in which he gives detailed descriptions of two such structures in Arisaig, one of which is situated on a promontory in Loch na Nuagh. It is an irregular oval occupying the whole summit of the promontory, and measuring about 100 feet in length by about 50 feet in breadth. The enclosing wall varies from 6 feet in thickness and 7 feet in height to about 5 feet in thickness and 3 feet in height. In this case also the wall was not vitrified down to the foundation. Underneath the vitrified portion there was a depth of 3 feet of walling formed of water-worn boulders quite unvitrified. The internal part of the upper or vitrified portion of the wall was also unvitrified. From these appearances Dr. Hamilton concludes that the vitrifaction was the result of fire applied to the upper part of the wall externally.

From a consideration of these examples it is evident that the Vitrified Forts do not differ in any essential point of their character from the forts that are not vitrified—if vitrifaction be not a feature in the method of their construction. The results of former investigations have not produced evidence sufficient to carry the conclusion that the vitrifaction was accomplished at the time of their construction, or that it was a method of construction. The determination of this question lies at the end of an exhaustive investigation, and can only be obtained from evidence furnished by the phenomena of the structures themselves.

There is one fort in Scotland, at Burghead, in Morayshire, which presents the peculiar feature of being partially constructed of logs of oak alternating with layers of stones. The peculiarity of its dry-built stone rampart is thus described by Dr. Macdonald:—"To strengthen it, beams of

[1] *Archæological Journal*, vol. xxxvii. p. 227.

solid oak (still measuring from 6 to 12 feet in length) take
here and there the place of stones, and similar beams inserted
end-ways pass into the mass behind." [1]   We only know the
Vitrified Forts from their greatly dilapidated ruins, and it is a
legitimate object of investigation whether any of them may
yet present evidence of having been constructed with logs
and stones in the manner exemplified at Burghead.   This
method of construction is characteristic of the Celtic or Gaulish forts of France.   The rampart of Murcens, on the river
Lot, is constructed like that of Burghead, of unhewn and
uncemented stones.   In its mass, at regular intervals, there
have been laid courses of oak logs disposed longitudinally
and transversely as "binders" and "headers."   The spaces
between the logs are filled with stones, and where they
cross each other the transverse logs are fastened to the
longitudinal rows by massive iron nails.   There are two rows
of logs laid parallel to the face of the wall and a little apart
within its thickness, and these are crossed at every 3 or
4 feet by logs lying transversely and extending the whole
thickness of the wall, so that their opposite ends appear
in its exterior and interior faces.   This is repeated at every
3 or 4 feet of the height of the wall.   The same method of
construction, with a greater proportion of timber to the mass
of the wall, appears in the fort of Impernal, also on the
river Lot. [2]   It is obvious that by the application of fire to
ramparts constructed on this principle, a partially scorified
and partially vitrified appearance would be given to
their ruins. [3]   In the early annals the burning of fortified

---

[1] *Proc. Soc. Antiq. Scot.*, vol. iv. p. 350.   A section and elevation of the
rampart showing the oak-beams in position are given in Plate IX. of the
same volume.

[2] Memoire sur les ouvrages de fortification des Oppidum Gaulois de
Murcens, d'Uxellodunum et d'Impernal situes dans le department du Lot.
Congrès Archeologique de France, xli. session.   Paris, 1875, p. 427.

[3] The late Mr. Ramsay, Director of the Geological Survey, records a cir-

places appears as the common method of reducing them, and the legendary prophecy of the coming of Birnam Wood to Dunsinnane possessed a peculiarly fateful meaning if its walls were built not of stones alone but of stones and logs.

The Hill-Fort of Dunsinnane (a section of which is shown in Fig. 251) is an oval circumvallation crowning the summit of

Fig. 251.—Section of Hill-Fort of Dunsinnane, showing underground chambers within its area. (Not to scale.)

a conical hill, some 800 feet in height. The rampart is now chiefly composed of earth intermixed with boulders, and is in some places about 20 feet wide at the base, rising to a height of from 6 to 8 feet. Fragments of vitrified matter, cementing masses of small stones together, are found in the rampart. The space enclosed is about 150 yards long by 70 yards wide and almost level. Towards its south-east side

cumstance which has an obvious bearing on the question of the possibility of such vitrifaction. Near Barnsley, in Yorkshire, the country affords no good material for road-metal, the sandstones made from the debris of granitic gneiss pounding up rapidly under cart-wheels. "To obviate this defect the follow-ing process is adopted :—The stone being quarried in small slabs and frag-ments is built in a pile about 30 feet square and 12 or 14 feet high, somewhat loosely ; and while the building is in progress brushwood is mingled with the stones, but not in any great quantity. Two thin layers of coal about 3 inches thick, at equal distances, are interstratified with the sandstones, and a third layer is strewn over the top. At the bottom, facing the prevalent wind, an opening about 2 feet high is left, something like the mouth of an oven. Into this brushwood and a little coal is put and lighted. The fire slowly spreads through the whole pile and continues burning for about six weeks. After cooling, the stack is pulled down, and the stones are found to be vitrified. I examined them carefully. Slabs originally flat had become bent and contorted, and stones originally separate glazed together in the process of vitrifaction."—*Proc. Soc. Antiq. Scot.*, vol. viii. p. 150.

were two underground chambers 20 feet in length, from 6 to 8 feet in width, and 5 to 6 feet high. The chambers communicated with each other, near their extremities, by two passages low and narrow, not much exceeding 2 feet in width and 3 feet high. The floors of the chambers were paved with rough slabs. The walls were built with undressed stones, which at the height of 2 to 3 feet above the floor began to converge until the roof was spanned by flagstones laid across. The floors were covered with ashes and refuse, consisting chiefly of the bones of horses and cattle, and horns of deer. A quern was found by the side of one of the passages, and in another were parts of three human skeletons. Near the entrance to the circumvallation a bronze spiral finger-ring, described as of exquisite workmanship and formed like a serpent, was found.[1]

Dunsinnane is the only Scottish hill-fort associated with underground chambers. But there is a class of underground structures of peculiar form which is common in Scotland, though unconnected with any variety of defensive structure. They are mostly situated in arable land now under cultivation, and have usually been discovered by the plough coming in contact with the stones of the roof.

One was so discovered at Broomhouse in the parish of Edrom, Berwickshire. It had been known before and most of the roofing stones removed, but on this occasion it came under the observation of Mr. Milne-Home, who communicated an account of it to the Society of Antiquaries.[2] It is to such casual circumstances that we owe the materials of our science. The structure presents the form (shown in the ground plan, Fig. 252) of a long narrow gallery, entering by a low and narrow aperture nearly on a level with the surface, widening and deepening from the entrance inwards, turning

---

[1] *Proc. Soc. Antiq. Scot.*, vol. ii. p. 95, and vol. ix. p. 379.

[2] *Ibid.*, vol. viii. p. 20.

first sharply to the left and then to the right, and terminating in a closed and rounded end. The opening (A) faced nearly to the south-east. The whole length of the gallery, measured along the central line of the floor, was 30 feet, its width at the entrance 2 feet, and at the widest part 6 feet. Only three of the roofing stones (B, C, D) remained in position. The

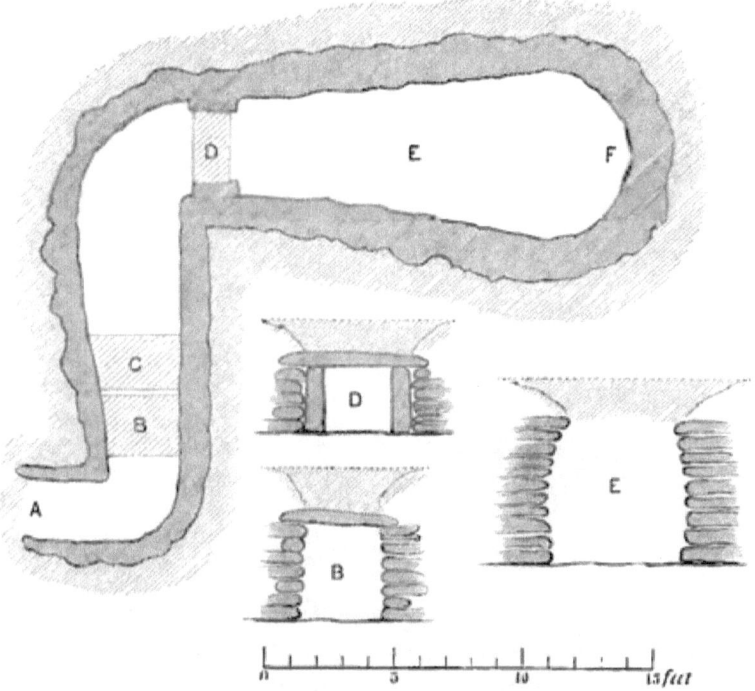

Fig. 252.—Ground plan and sections of Earth-house at Broomhouse, parish of Edrom, Berwickshire.

vertical height of the walls at the widest part of the structure was 5 feet, and under the roofing stone (B) next the entrance only 3 feet. It seemed as if the floor had been paved with natural water-worn stones, but this point was not clearly ascertained. At the second bend (D) there are checks for a door, consisting of two oblong stones set on end and still carrying a massive lintel. The side walls, from the entrance inwards to this inner door, are vertical. In the wider part of the structure (E) beyond the inner door they are brought towards each other by the stones overlapping inwardly, so that the roof might be covered by single slabs laid across. Nothing was found within it but fragments of bones of animals, among which the roe-deer was the only one that could be certainly determined.

At Migvie, in Aberdeenshire, an underground structure (Fig. 253) was discovered in 1862.[1] It was situated in the

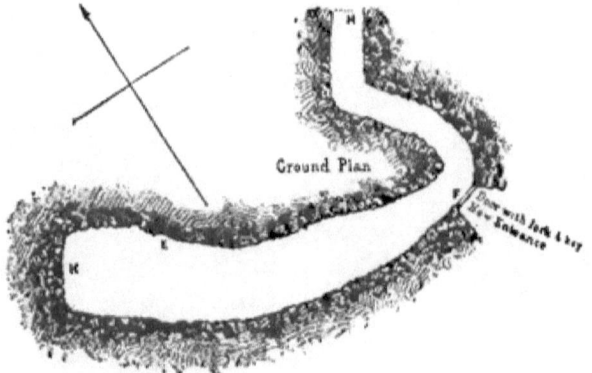

Ground Plan

Fig. 253.—Ground plan of Earth-house at Migvie, Aberdeenshire.
(From a plan by Mr. Jervise.)

summit of a gravel hillock, and was in form a long, low, and narrow gallery, entering by an aperture nearly on the level of the original surface, turning first sharply to the left and then to the right, widening and deepening from the entrance inwards and terminating in a squarish end slightly rounded at the corners. The whole length of the gallery measured along the curvature was 41 feet, the width at the entrance 2 feet, and at the widest part about 5 feet. Nine stones covering the portion next the entrance remained in position, the height of the gallery under them increasing from about

2½ feet at the aperture to 4½ feet at the place where the covering ceased. The vertical height of the walls beyond this seemed to have been at least 5 feet. The side-walls were built with rough boulder stones laid pretty regularly. When the interior was cleared out the only objects found were a bronze ring, several rude stone-vessels like roughly-formed cups, large quantities of ashes and charred wood, and corroded fragments of iron implements.

The similarity of these two structures is no less striking than the excessive peculiarity of their distinctive features. These features are—(1) their position under ground ; (2) the

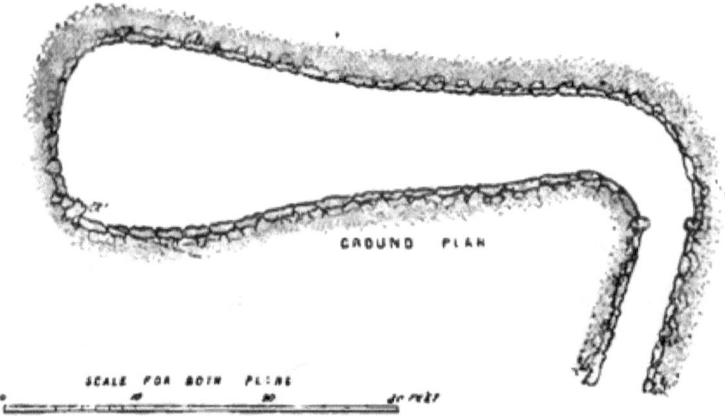

Fig. 254.—Ground plan of Earth-house at Buchaam, in Strathdon.

contracted entrance ; (3) the form of the chamber—a long, low, narrow, and curved gallery gradually widening inwards ; and (4) the construction of the chamber—with convergent side-walls supporting a heavily-lintelled roof.

Closely analogous to these in its main features is the underground structure (Fig. 254) at Buchaam, in Strathdon.[1] It is a long narrow gallery entering by a small aperture in the narrow end nearly on a level with the original surface of the ground, gradually widening and increasing in height inwards,

[1] Described by Dr. Arthur Mitchell, *Proc. Soc. Antiq. Scot.*, vol. iv. p. 436.

and terminating abruptly in a slightly-rounded end. It differs in one respect from the two previously described, inasmuch as though it is curved it has not the double curvature which is the special feature of their form. It curves sharply to the left, but the curvature is not repeated in the opposite direction. It is 58 feet in length following the curve along the middle line of the floor. Its width at the entrance is 3 feet 6 inches, and it gradually widens until it attains a maximum breadth of 9 feet 3 inches. The height increases from about 5 feet near the entrance to about 7 feet at the farther end. The roofing stones were mostly in position and were of great size, some being 7 to 8 feet in length, 3 feet in width, 18 inches in thickness, and weighing more than a ton. The walls rise perpendicularly for 2 or 3 feet and then incline inwards with a curve, so that where the width of the chamber at the floor is 9 feet 3 inches, it is contracted to 7 feet 9 inches at 4 feet above the floor and at the roof to 5 feet. The walls are well built, the lower courses of large cubical stones, undressed, and at the distance of about 12 feet inwards from the entrance there are checks for a door formed of two oblong stones set edgeways in the wall and projecting a few inches from its interior surface. The whole floor of the chamber was paved, and a drain, 10 inches square, well built with a good roof, sides, and bottom, and having a peculiar box-like opening or sink in the inside of the chamber, was found leading from its south-east corner. The chamber when opened was nearly filled with earth and rubbish, and at the bottom there was a layer of fine blue clay 20 inches in depth, which had been carried through the walls by percolation of water from the clay bank outside. In or below this clay which covered the paved floor were found the following relics of human occupation—an iron ring, and an object in iron which looked like the shoe of a wooden spade, some staves of a small wooden cog, a wooden comb, some fragments of pottery of coarse workmanship, a portion of a quern or handmill for grinding grain, fragments of deer's horns, and bones of the sheep and common domestic fowls. At one corner of the inner end of the chamber the ashes of a fire remained, and immediately above them there was a well-built smoke-hole.

A similar structure (Fig. 255) at Culsh, in the parish of Tarland in the same county, differs from this one only in being

Fig. 255.—Ground plan of Earth-house at Culsh, parish of Tarland. (From a plan by Mr. Jervise.)

curved to the right instead of to the left. It is 47 feet in length and 2 feet wide at the entrance, the width increasing gradually to about 6 feet at the farther end. The walls are partially formed of large boulders set on end or on edge to form the lower course, with rudely-built masonry over them. They converge but slightly, and the roof is formed in the usual manner by large heavy slabs laid across from wall to wall. The floor is formed of the natural underlying rock, and the height from floor to roof increases from 5 feet near the entrance to an average of about 6 feet farther in. When cleared out in 1853, the earth which filled the chamber was found largely mixed with ashes on the floor, and the only relics obtained from its excavation were fragments of coarse unglazed pottery, a large bead, the bones of cattle, and two querns.

Another (Fig. 256) excavated a few years ago at Clova, near Kildrummy, also in Aberdeenshire,[1] differs from these in being so slightly curved to the left as to be almost straight. It measures 57 feet in length, 2½ feet wide at the entrance, suddenly widening to about 8 feet at about 20 feet within

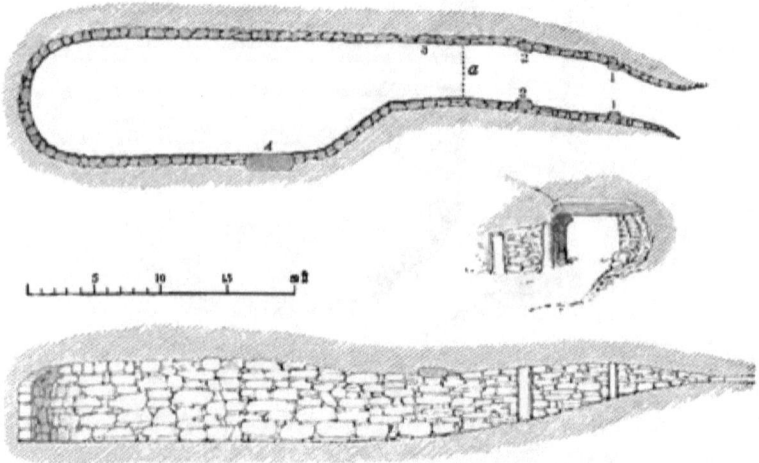

Fig. 256.—Ground plan and sections of Earth-house at Kildrummy, Aberdeenshire.   (From a Plan by Mr. Lumsden of Clova.)

the entrance. At a short distance from the entrance there were checks for two doors about 8 feet apart. The covering stones had been removed from the first 15 feet of the narrow part, but the roof remained entire over the whole of the wider part of the structure, at an average height of about 6 feet from the floor. The earth with which the chamber was filled was largely mixed with charcoal and bones of animals,

[1] *Proc. Soc. Antiq. Scot.*, vol. xii. p. 356.

among which those of the horse and dog were recognised.
No manufactured relics were found, but two of the stones
in the walls, one being a large boulder, were covered with
the small hemispherical pits known as cup-markings.

An Earth-house at Eriboll, in Sutherlandshire[1] (Fig. 257),
resembles that at Clova in presenting so little curvature as
to be almost straight. The curvature which it has is to the
left, and only extends for a few feet within the entrance. It
is said, however, to have been 10 or 12 feet longer than it
was when examined in 1865. It was then 33 feet in length.

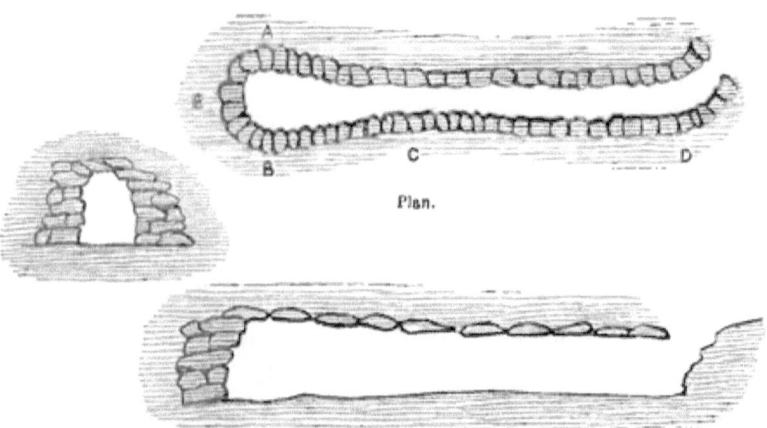

Fig. 257.—Ground plan and section of Earth-house at Eriboll, Sutherlandshire.
(From a Plan by Dr. Arthur Mitchell.)

It is peculiar for the smallness of its size, being nowhere
more than $4\frac{1}{2}$ feet in height, and for the greater part of its
length only 2 feet wide, expanding to $3\frac{1}{2}$ for about 3 feet
only from the inner end. In view of this feature of its
character, Dr Mitchell remarks that it is exceedingly difficult
to see what purpose such a structure could have served ; but
he adds that it is worthy of note that in this district similar
underground constructions are not rare, and that they are

[1] Described by Dr. Arthur Mitchell, *Proc. Soc. Antiq. Scot.*, vol. vi. p. 249.

called by a Gaelic name which signifies Hiding-beds. The use of such underground places of concealment is referred to in the *Saga of Gisli the Soursop*, which relates to events occurring between the years 930 and 980, and was written in Iceland about the beginning of the twelfth century. It states that when Gisli was outlawed and every man's hand was against him, he went to Thorgerda in Vadil. "She was often wont to harbour outlaws, and she had an underground room. One end of it opened on the river-bank and the other below her hall." Again it states that "Gisli was always in his earth-house when strangers came to the isle."[1] The form of Earth-house thus described as then in use for concealment in Iceland is not the form of the Earth-houses found in Scotland, which have rarely two openings, but the passage is interesting because it shows that the traditional use ascribed to the Scottish examples is a use which was practised among a people who had close relations with the district in which the tradition still remains attached to these structures.

But whatever may have been the actual purpose or purposes to which they were applied, the fact which is of importance in our investigation is that these Earth-houses, though ranging in area from Berwickshire to the north coast of Sutherland, are all of one special character, long, low, narrow galleries, always possessing a certain amount of curvature, sometimes greatly, and at other times doubly curved, always widening and increasing in height from the low and narrow entrance inwards, usually built with convergent walls and roofed with heavy lintels, which are always lower than the surrounding level of the ground, so that the whole structure is subterranean. Occasionally they present variations in structure as in the case of one at Murroes, in Forfarshire, which, instead of being built, has its walls con-

---

[1] *The Saga of Gisli the Outlaw*, Dasent's Translation, p. 72.

structed entirely of flagstones set on edge. Similarly, the

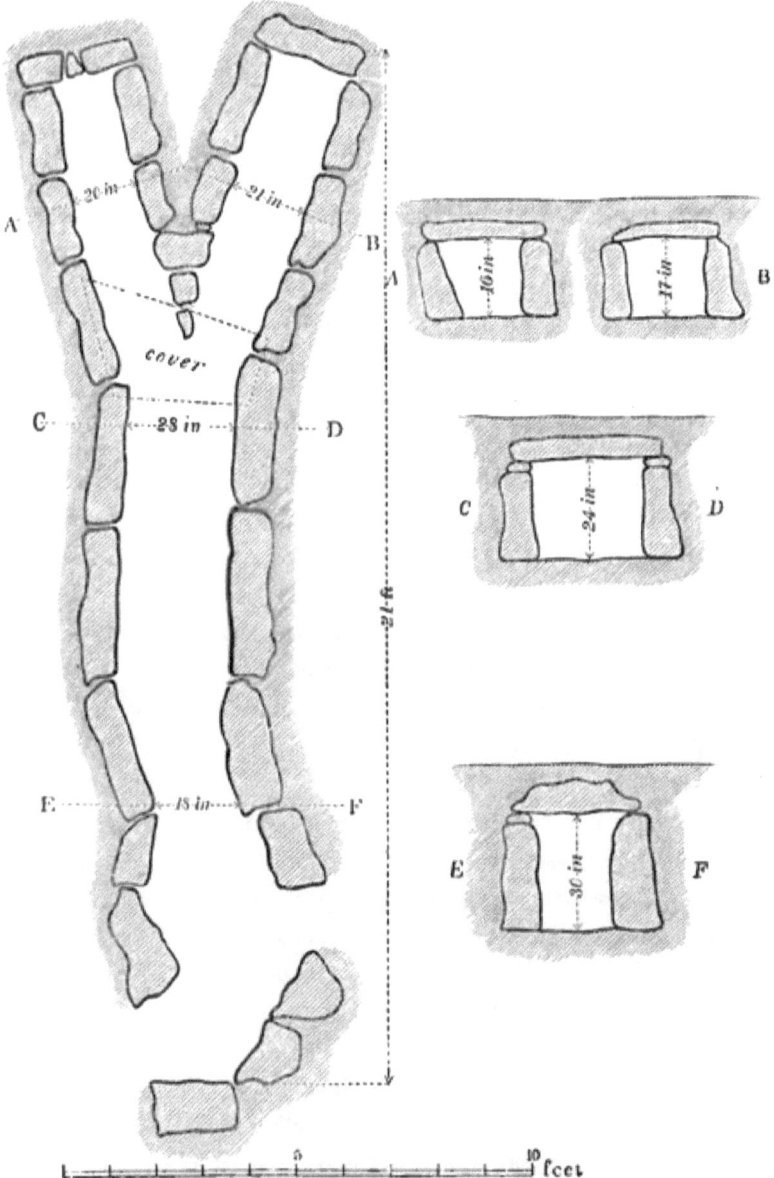

Fig. 258.—Ground plan and sections of Earth-house at Kinord, Aberdeenshire.

example at Kinord, in Aberdeenshire (Fig. 258), has its walls constructed of single boulders set on edge or on end, and it presents the further peculiarity of the chamber being divided into two branches at the farther end.   One at Pirnie, in the parish of Wemyss, in Fife, and another at Elie, had steps leading down to the entrance.

Occasionally they occur in considerable groups, as at Airlie, in Forfarshire, where there is a group of five.   One of these is of great size, its length being 67 feet, and its average breadth, from the farther end to within about 12 feet of the entrance, $7\frac{1}{2}$ feet.   The height at the entrance is only about 22 inches, and the floor slopes down for about 20 feet till a height of about 6 feet is obtained.   The walls are built of rough undressed boulders laid in pretty regular courses, and they converge from a width on the floor of a little over 7 feet to about 4 feet at the roof.   The covering stones are of great size, many of them 7 or 8 feet in length and 4 feet wide.   It contained the usual traces of cookery in the accumulation of ashes and bones of animals upon the floor. The only other relics found in it were a brass pin, a stone mortar-like vessel, and fragments of querns.   The other four examples in the same neighbourhood are known to have existed, but have neither been measured nor described.

A still more remarkable group was brought under the notice of the Society in 1816 by Professor Stuart of Aberdeen.   They are spread over a space of a mile or two in diameter on what was then a dry moor in the parishes of Auchindoir and Kildrummy, in Aberdeenshire.   These excavated houses, he says, are most frequently discovered by the plough striking against some of the large stones which form the roof.   The only opening to them appears to have been between two large stones placed in a sloping direction at one end, and about 18 inches asunder.   Through this narrow opening one must slide down to the depth of 5 or 6 feet, when he comes to a vault generally about 6 feet high, upwards of 30 feet long, and 8 or 9 feet wide. The floor is smooth, as if of clay, and the sides are built of rude undressed stones without cement. The walls bend inwards to form a rude arch, and the roof is covered with large stones 5 or 6 feet long, some of them being over a ton in weight. The whole structure is beneath the level of the ground and quite invisible, but many of them were detected by the existence close to them of a square space about 10 to 15 paces each way dug a foot or two deep with the earth thrown outwards. These he conjectures to have been the sites of the summer huts of the people, who retreated to these underground places in winter, and stored their provisions and concealed their valuables in them all the year round. But he adds that no article of furniture, and no utensils or instruments either of stone or metal have been found in them so far as can be learned, but only a quantity of wood-ashes and charcoal, chiefly at the farther end, where there sometimes appears a small aperture at the top as an outlet for the smoke. The whole number discovered in this locality he estimates at between forty and fifty. They are found, he says, in other localities, but so great a number collected in one place has probably never before occurred. The number is certainly very large, and may probably be over estimated, but it would not be difficult to find in other parts of Scotland, and specially in Aberdeenshire, a series of groups of similar structures which, though not so numerous or so closely aggregated, are so distributed over wide districts as to show that the custom of constructing these underground edifices was general and prevalent. Wherever they occur they present the same individuality of character and the same strongly marked typical features. Their range in area extends from Berwickshire to Shetland. They occur in greater or less abundance in most of the counties bordering on the east

coast. A few doubtful examples only are recorded in those
bordering on the west coast. But it is only of late years
that the importance of securing a permanent and exhaustive
record of such casual discoveries has begun to be recognised,
and in this direction of defining the areas of the respective
types of structural antiquities, we are still groping in dark-
ness on the threshold of a great investigation.

I now proceed to notice a few examples which, by their

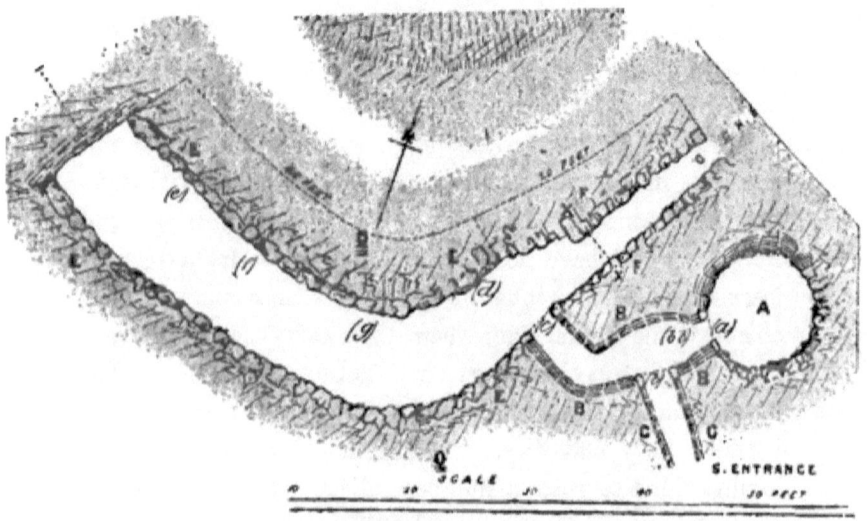

Fig. 259.—Ground plan of Earth-house at Cairn Conan, near Arbroath,
Forfarshire. (From a Plan by Andrew Jervise.)

associations or their contents, disclose indications of the
period of the type.

In the spring of 1859 an underground structure of this
type (Fig. 259) was discovered on the farm of West Grange
of Conan, near Arbroath, Forfarshire. It occupies an elevated situation on the south-east slope of an eminence
commanding an extensive view. The structure differs from
all those that have been described, inasmuch as in addition
to the long, low, narrow, and curved gallery widening and

increasing in height from the entrance inwards, which is the typical form, it presents the additional feature of a circular chamber (A) attached to the long curved chamber near the narrow end, and also communicating with the surface by a passage (C C), thus giving to the composite structure a second entrance. The main chamber or gallery is 65 feet in length along the curvature of the central line of the floor. Its entrance is 2½ feet wide, and apparently little more than 18 inches high. It widens but slightly, till at a distance of 20 feet from the entrance there is an offset formed by a large stone set at right angles to the passage, beyond which it widens more rapidly to about 8½ feet across at the farther end. The walls are built of undressed stones, but in some places they are partially cut out of the soft rock, which, for a considerable portion of its length, also forms the floor of the chamber. The circular chamber (A) is about 10 feet in diameter and 7½ feet high. The floor is partly excavated in the underlying rock. The walls are rudely built of undressed boulders. They converge almost from the floor, and the covering stone was a large boulder resting on the circular apex of the vaulted roof which impeded the plough and thus led to the discovery of the structure.

About 20 feet to the north of the underground chamber there was a circular space from which the soil had been removed. It was rudely laid with a pavement of undressed flags forming a circular floor a few inches below the level of the surrounding soil, and about 20 feet in diameter. Among the flags of this paved space there were found a portion of a plain bronze ring about 3 inches diameter, the upper stone of a quern or hand-millstone, two whorls of lead, a number of rudely-hollowed stone vessels of various sizes, and fragments of implements in iron so greatly corroded as to be unrecognisable except as fragments of implements with cutting edges.

The articles found in the underground chambers were

few in number. They consisted of some fragments of pottery, coarse, but wheel-made, pale yellow in colour, and differing in texture and manufacture from the usual hand-made pottery of native origin found in many of the other structures of the same class. It closely resembles some varieties of pottery that are constantly found in the vicinity of Roman stations in Scotland. A bronze needle and a portion of a quern were the only other objects found. But that the place had been long occupied was sufficiently apparent from the quantity of ashes mixed with calcined and broken bones of the common domestic animals which it contained.

In this case we have distinct evidence of an underground chamber associated with an overground habitation of less permanent structure, of which time and cultivation had removed all traces except the circular paved floor and the casual relics which it contained. There can be no doubt that the people who occupied this overground habitation also possessed the underground structure, and used it for purposes connected with their daily life. There is little now left to disclose what the manner of that life was, but that little is highly significant. It discloses that they were a people cultivating grain and rearing cattle and sheep. They had utensils of stone it is true, and these of the very rudest form and fabrication, but they also possessed wheel-made pottery and weapons or implements of bronze, iron, and lead.

A singular interest attaches to this little settlement, inasmuch as it not only shows us the association of the two forms of underground and overground structure which united to make one habitation, but also gives the associated grave-ground of the family. A few yards distant from the dwelling there was a group of six graves. They were full-length, stone-lined graves, rudely constructed, with three or four flattish slabs forming the sides, and one stone placed for

each end. They lay so near the surface that the covering
stones had mostly been removed by the plough, and the
remains in them were greatly decayed. The only manufactured object found in them was a single ring or child's
bracelet of cannel coal. This is the only instance on record
of the discovery of a cemetery associated with the double
dwelling of the people who constructed these subterranean
galleries.

Among the rubbish thrown out in the course of the
excavation there was found a beautiful spiral bronze bracelet
of the form of a double serpent, decorated in that peculiar
style of art which has been described in the third Lecture of
this course as the precursor or earlier development of the art
of the Celtic Christian time.[1] Here we find the earlier art
associated with this peculiar type of structure, and with a
manner of sepulture which is destitute of all indications of
Christianity. It is associated also with wheel-made pottery
of a type that is only found in situations suggestive of Roman
intercourse, and therefore indicates a period when Christianity
had not yet supplanted the Paganism of the country. It was
also in a precisely similar association with one of these underground structures that the massive bronze armlets (Figs.
115, 116), described in the same Lecture, were discovered at
Castle Newe. They also are decorated in this peculiar style
of art and enriched with enamels. Their workmanship
evinces skill and taste of a very high order, and the occurrence of these works of art in such associations may serve to
remind us how greatly we should have erred if we had estimated the capacity and culture of the inhabitants of these
structures by their architectural character alone, or if we had
measured their condition and acquirements merely by the
fact that they burrowed under ground.

[1] This bracelet is described and figured as Fig. 140, at p. 160 of this
volume in the Lecture on the Celtic Art of the Pagan Period.

Another structure of the same type (Fig. 260), but of larger dimensions, was discovered in 1871 in a field at Tealing. It was 80 feet in length measured along the curve, 3 feet wide at the entrance and widening gradually to 8½ feet at the inner end, where it is a little more than 6 feet high. It has checks for a door at a little distance within the entrance, and a second pair about 16 feet from the farther end. The usual evidences of occupation were found in the presence of ashes, charcoal, and animal bones throughout the excavation. The manufactured relics unfortunately have

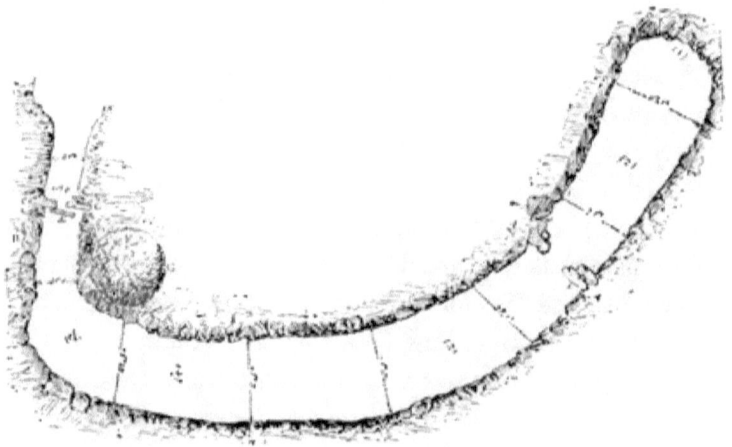

Fig. 260.—Ground plan of Earth-house at Tealing, Forfarshire.
(From a Plan by Andrew Jervise.)

neither been described nor figured, although they constitute the largest and most varied collection of objects ever obtained from such a structure. They are enumerated by Mr. Jervise as follows :—A piece of the red lustrous ware commonly called Samian, a bracelet, bronze rings, and coarse pottery, no fewer than ten querns, a number of whorls and stone cups, and an article made of iron slightly mixed with brass. The occurrence of the red lustrous ware in these Earth-houses, as well as in the Brochs and Crannogs, is an indication of the period of the occupation of these structures which is of great significance. The large size of the gallery, in the present instance, and the occurrence in it of ten querns, indicate that it was frequented by a considerable number of people. It has another feature of interest in the presence, on one of the rude boulders which form the walls, of a number of cup-markings, one of which is surrounded by five concentric circles. Another stone with forty-six cup-markings on it lay on the margin of a circular paved space close to the entrance of the structure. These cup-markings form one of the enigmas of archæology. They are shallow pits, roughly hemispherical in form, hollowed by pointed tools in the surfaces of rocks, boulders, and standing stones. Sometimes they are on vertical surfaces, sometimes on horizontal surfaces, occasionally on the under surfaces of stones placed as the covers of cists. Most frequently the cups are simple rounded hollows, but very frequently they are surrounded by a series of concentric circles of varying number, and often a straight gutter proceeds from the central cup through the circles. They are sometimes hewn in groups upon the solid rock of a hillside, sometimes on earth-fast boulders, occasionally on the stones of stone circles, and often on stones in sepulchral cairns or in connection with cists. They are not confined to Scotland, or even to Britain. They are found in Scandinavia, in France, in Germany, and Switzerland. They appear on the Continent in associations which refer them to the Bronze Age at least, but they also occur in associations which show that the custom survived to the late Iron Age, and even in a modified form to Christian times. Their occurrence here, in connection with this underground structure, has therefore no special significance with respect to the age of the structure, and there is nothing in the association or the circumstances in which they occur in this particular instance which contributes to our knowledge of the purpose or significance of the markings themselves. They may or may not have been sculptured on the stone before it was taken to form part of this underground gallery, and the only thing they tell us for certain is that here, at some time or other, there was a custom of which traces are found scattered over a wide area of Western Europe.

But other indications have been found in connection with the structure and contents of these singular buildings, which carry the period of their construction close up to the time of the Roman occupation of the southern portion of Scotland. An underground structure of this special type (Fig. 261) was

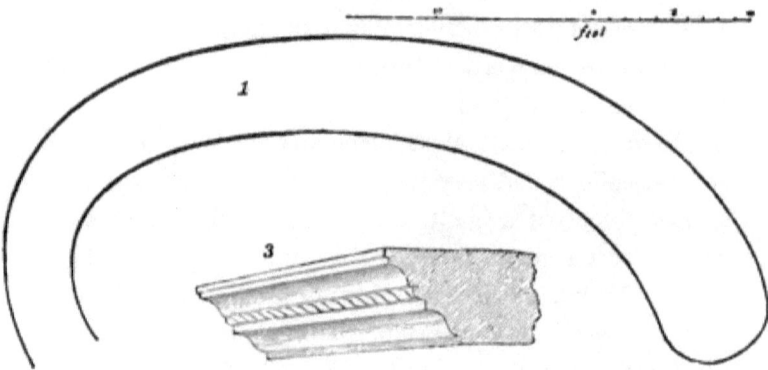

Fig. 261.—Sketch ground plan of Earth-house at Newstead, and stone with Roman moulding found in it.

discovered near the village of Newstead, in Roxburghshire, in 1845.[1] It fortunately came under the observation of Dr. John Alexander Smith, who has given a carefully prepared notice of its peculiarities in the *Proceedings* of the Society. It was of the usual form, a long, low, and narrow gallery turning sharply to the right and widening and gradually increasing in height from the entrance. It measured 54 feet in length along the curve of the central line of the floor, and

[1] Described by Dr. John Alexander Smith in *Proc. Soc. Antiq. Scot.*, vol. i. p. 213.

widened gradually from 4 feet at the narrow end to 7 feet at
the farther end. The height was not ascertainable, as the
roofing stones were gone, and scarcely more than 3 feet of
the height of the side walls remained. But the walls presented the peculiarity of being built with hewn stones, laid
in pretty regular courses, though not jointed with mortar or
any other cement. Among the fallen stones in the interior
of the structure there were many flat slabs bevelled on one
edge, and two measuring about 4 feet in length which pre-

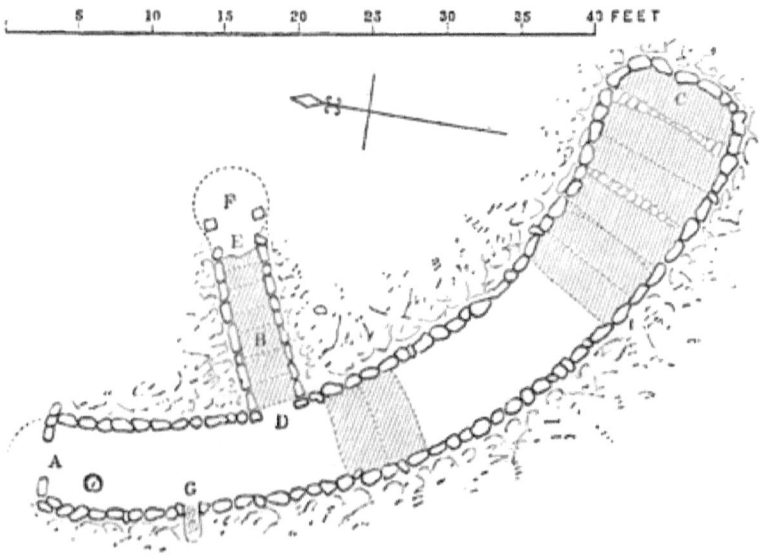

Fig. 262.—Ground plan of Earth-house at Crichton Mains, Midlothian.

sented a rope-moulding (Fig. 261) of distinctively Roman
character. No relics were obtained from the excavation of
the building, but the character of the squared and bevelled
stones and the presence of the Roman moulding indicate
that the construction of the underground structure was subsequent to the period of the Roman occupation of that part of
the country. Another structure of similar character was

found in an adjoining field, but not built with squared stones. In all probability the squared stones of the one structure were due to the presence in its immediate neighbourhood of some Roman construction, the stones of which were utilised by the underground builders.

Another structure of the same type (Fig. 262) was found in 1869 at Crichton Mains, in Midlothian.[1] It was of the usual long, narrow, curved form, 51½ feet in length, and gradually widening from 5 feet 10 inches just within the entrance to 9 feet at the farther end. A number of the roof-stones remained in position, and the floor throughout being

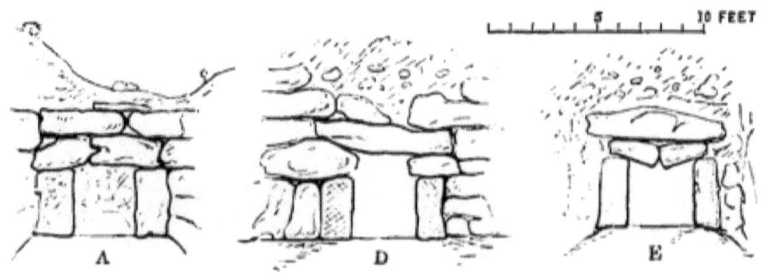

Fig. 263.—Sections of Earth-house at A, D, and E on ground plan.

formed of the natural rock it was seen that the average height was about 6 feet. The walls converge from the floor for about half their height and rise somewhat perpendicularly above that, thus giving to the cross-section the form of an ogee vault. The door (A, in Figs. 262, 263), formed of two upright stones crossed by a lintel, is 3 feet high by 33 inches wide, and the top is about 5 feet under the present surface of the ground. Fourteen feet inwards is a passage at right angles to the gallery, the entrance to which is shown at F in Fig. 262. It is 13 feet long, 3 feet wide, and 3 feet 6 inches high, rising by low sloping steps in the rock to what seems

[1] Described by Lord Rosehill in *Proc. Soc. Antiq. Scot.*, vol. viii. p. 105.

another entrance nearer the surface, also shown in Fig.
262 at E. At G is a small
ambry (Fig. 264). No relics
were found in the excavation;
but here and there in the
interior faces of the walls
there were a number of
squared stones faced with the
diagonal broaching and stug-
ging which is so common in
late Roman work.[1] About
thirty of these are visible.
Two are shown in Fig. 265.

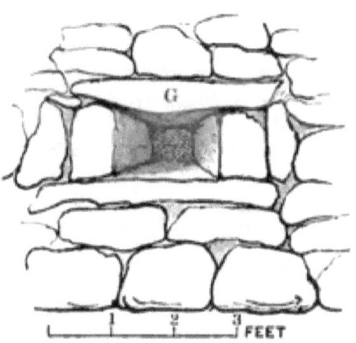

Fig. 264.—Ambry in Earth-house at
Crichton Mains.

There were also other hewn stones, some of which had apparently formed portions of water conduits (H, Fig. 265), and

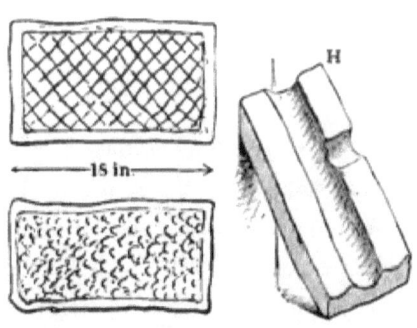

Fig. 265.—Stones in Earth-house at
Crichton Mains.

others adapted to differ-
ent purposes. The
lintel-stone of the door
of the side passage is
moulded and bevelled on
the edge in a similar way
to the bevelled stones
found in the structure
at Newstead. It seems
evident that this under-
ground building, like

that at Newstead, has been partially constructed with
stones taken from a ruined building of late Roman workmanship, and that both are consequently later than the commencement of the Roman occupation of the country. Similar

[1] This "diamond broaching" is very common in the reparations of the
Roman wall and its stations between the Solway and the Tyne, while the
stones used in Hadrian's original erections are severely plain.—Dr. Bruce, in
Lapidarium Septentrionale, p. 39.

indications are given by the discovery of wheel-made pottery of Roman type in the Earth-house at Cairn Conan, and of fragments of the red lustrous ware commonly called Samian in the Earth-houses at Tealing, Pitcur, and Fithie. The presence in most of them of querns and implements of iron, and the entire absence of such implements as are characteristic of the ages of stone and bronze, are indications pointing to the same conclusion. On the other hand there is a complete absence of indications of Christianity, and the characteristics of the ornamentation of the bronze armlets found in association with them are those which belong only to the earlier and partial development of Celtic art, which preceded its subsequent and complete development under the new impulses and opportunities afforded by Christianity. It seems therefore that, so far as our present knowledge will carry us towards a definite conclusion, the period of this peculiar type of structure will lie between the time of the general establishment of Christianity and the departure of the Romans from Scotland.

The range of the type includes the whole eastern area of Scotland, stretching from Berwickshire on the south to the Shetland Isles. Its special form is so peculiar that it must be held to constitute a distinction sufficiently characteristic to separate the Scottish group from all other varieties of underground structures, and sufficiently constant to warrant us in assigning to it a specific value. There is an Irish group and a Cornish group of underground structures, but they do not generally present the special features of form which characterise the Scottish group. The Irish examples are usually associated with raths, thus resembling the specimen in the rath of Dunsinnane, which is the only one known of that special variety in Scotland. They are excavated in the area enclosed by the interior rampart of the rath, and consist of one or more chambers, sometimes circular or oval in plan but often rectangular, and connected together by low narrow passages. Sometimes the chambers are lined with masonry, and roofed by overlapping courses forming a rude dome-shaped vault; at other times they are simply excavated in the hard earth, while the passages and doorways are lined with stones. They thus differ considerably in form from the Scottish variety, and they differ also in being usually associated with raths or earthworks, while the Scottish structures are usually contiguous to the sites of overground habitations.

The general features of the Cornish group, on the other hand, are more allied to those of the Scottish area, inasmuch as they are often associated with clusters of overground habitations. One at Chapel Euny, in the parish of Saucreed, near Penzance, contiguous to the sites of four circular huts, is an underground gallery presenting features of remarkable similarity to that at Cairn Conan, in Forfarshire. The gallery, which is slightly curved, is about 60 feet in length, 6 feet wide, and from 6 to 7 feet high. A circular chamber, 16 feet in diameter, constructed of large granite blocks, each overlapping the one below it and thus forming a domed roof which must have been 10 or 12 feet high, was connected with the wider end of the gallery by a passage 10 feet long, opening off one side. Another small offset near the narrower end of the gallery, also about 10 feet long, slopes up to the surface, presenting an entrance doorway 2 feet 8 inches in height, with recesses on either side as if to retain a slab to close the doorway. The floors of the gallery and chamber were paved with flat stones, and provided with drains underneath the pavement. The relics found in the structure were whetstones; hammer-stones; spindle-whorls; several varieties of domestic pottery, red and black, mostly plain, but occasionally ornamented with markings made by a pointed instrument; an iron spear-head; and a fragment of the

red lustrous ware commonly called Samian.[1] Another at
Halligey, near Trelowarren, consists of a slightly-curved
gallery 90 feet in length, from 3 to 5 feet in width, and about
6 feet high in the middle, becoming lower towards the
extremities. It has a small rectangular chamber off one
side at the farther end of the main gallery. The main
gallery opens off the middle of the side of a shorter and
wider gallery 28 feet in length, 5½ feet wide, and 6 feet high.
At one end of this shorter gallery a narrow passage rises to
the surface. The entrance passage is provided with checks
for two doors, and the whole structure is strongly and substantially built and lintelled with large flags. On the
surface there are traces of two embankments with an intervening ditch surrounding a large area within which there
may have been a cluster of overground structures.[2]

Like the Scottish examples the Earth-houses of Cornwall
are long narrow galleries of dry-built masonry, but they are
not so strongly marked by the peculiar feature of single or
double curvature which distinguishes the Scottish group.
They are comparatively few in number, and any indications
of the period of their occupation that have been observed
point also to a time not far distant from the close of the
Roman occupation of the country. No other group of such
underground structures is known in any other part of Europe,
or indeed anywhere else in the world. These excavated
chambers, possessing the characteristics which have been
described, are peculiar to the Celtic area, and the specially

---

[1] These details are taken from a paper by William Borlase, Esq., in the
Proceedings of the Society of Antiquaries of London, 1868 (Second Series,
vol. iv. p. 161), where a ground plan and sections, with woodcuts of the
structural appearance of the building are given. Mr. Borlase mentions
other structures of the same class at Pendeen, Bolleit, Chysoster, and
Bodinar.

[2] Paper by J. T. Blight, Esq., in *Archæologia*, vol. xl. p. 113, with ground
plan and woodcuts.

typical form with the strongly marked curvature is found only in Scotland.

Of the culture and civilisation of the people who constructed these strange subterranean cells, it may be impossible in the present condition of our knowledge to form an adequate estimate. But we can say this of them with certainty, that whatever may have been the special motives and circumstances that induced them to give this peculiar expression to their architectural efforts, they exhibit in other respects evidences of culture which, though it may be held to be inferior in range and quality to the culture of the Christian time, compares not unfavourably (so far as it goes) with that which is exhibited in connection with the superior architecture of the Brochs.

And while on all these lines of investigation we have traced the manifestations of these early forms of culture and civilisation up to points at which they seem to touch the culture and civilisation of the Roman Empire, it is to be observed that they do no more than touch it—they are not merged in it. In all their distinctive features they are still Celtic, and Celtic exclusively. There is nothing Roman in the forms of the prevailing types; there is nothing Roman in the art that decorates these forms; there is nothing Roman in the typical character of the structures in which they are found. The forms, the art, and the architecture are those of Scotland's Iron Age—the Pagan Period of her Celtic people.

INDEX.

THE END.

Printed by R. & R. CLARK, *Edinburgh.*

ARCHÆOLOGICAL AND HISTORICAL WORKS
RECENTLY PUBLISHED.

*Now ready, in One handsome Vol., 8vo, pp. xx., 326, with 270 Illustrations,
price 21s.*

ANCIENT SCOTTISH LAKE-DWELLINGS
OR CRANNOGS

WITH A

SUPPLEMENTARY CHAPTER ON REMAINS OF
LAKE-DWELLINGS IN ENGLAND

BY

ROBERT MUNRO, M.A., M.D.

F.S.A. Scot.

EXTRACTS FROM REVIEWS.

Times, October 4, 1882.

" It is a most valuable and methodical statement of all the facts connected with his own excavations in Ayrshire, supplemented by a summary
of what is known of Crannogs and Lake-Dwellings elsewhere. The work is
profusely illustrated with charts, plans, and engravings of many of the
objects discovered during the excavations : it will doubtless become a
standard authority on the subject of which it treats."

EDINBURGH : DAVID DOUGLAS.

Sir John Lubbock, in Nature, December 14, 1882.

" Whilst thanking him for what he has already accomplished, we may express a hope that he will continue his researches."

Glasgow Herald, October 27, 1882.

" As we have pointed out, the explorations of the last two years have, so to speak, resurrected an ancient people, and we may hope that further explorations will enable us better to fix their position in prehistoric times, and better to understand their modes and habits of life and their surroundings. In the meantime we heartily welcome Dr. Munro's admirable study, and recommend it to the perusal of all interested in the important subject of which it treats. . . . The volume is a most interesting one, and will remain for many years to come *the* authority on the subject."

Scotsman, November 22, 1882.

" In this handsome and copiously illustrated volume, the results of the investigations of the Scottish Lake-Dwellings (in which Dr. Munro has himself taken the chief part) are systematised ; and the story of this forgotten phase of life in Scotland is presented with all the freshness of a new interpretation of a large and interesting portion of the early history of the country. . . . And his work has now done for Britain what the well-known work of Keller had previously done for the Lake-Dwellings of Central Europe."

Aberdeen Free Press, October 23, 1882.

" A most valuable contribution to Scottish Archæology—a volume that ought to find a place on the shelves of every district library in the country."

Inverness Courier, August 24, 1882.

" It will serve at once as a record of what has been achieved, as an incentive to further research, and as a guide to the direction in which that research should be made."

North British Daily Mail, August 14, 1882.

" The plan of the work is admirable, and it has been wrought out in masterly fashion, so much so indeed that it may be placed on the same shelf with the historical volumes of Anderson, Skene, and Robertson, without

EDINBURGH : DAVID DOUGLAS.

any danger of their falling out. . . . As a scholarly conspectus of
everything of real significance that has been published relating to Crannogs
since Dr. Joseph Robertson first directed attention to their prevalence in
Scotland, it will be welcomed as a serviceable index even by the most
learned archæologists ; while to the general reader, desirous of becoming
acquainted with the hitherto widely-scattered results of inquiry on this
subject, it will be a boon, the value of which cannot be exaggerated."

Dundee Advertiser, August 22, 1882.

" Dr. Munro had a voluminous but confused literature before him when
he began his explorations, and he has succeeded in bringing together in
this volume such a mass of original matter and of detailed discovery as
should enable the least imaginative student to frame a theory. . . . We
have much pleasure in recommending this book as one of the most exhaustive works upon the subject yet published. The illustrations are profuse
and well executed."

The Antiquary, Vol. vii. p. 67.

" Dr. Munro has come forward in a very acceptable volume, which is
now before us, and has undertaken to give a history of the excavations into
ancient Scottish Lake-Dwellings, together with some very valuable suggestions as to the age and general characteristics of these prehistoric remains.
We cannot, of course, follow Dr. Munro into all the details he treats of, but
our readers will, we are sure, thank us for a summary of what Dr. Munro
so ably tells us, and for the rest we most warmly recommend all antiquaries
to make themselves possessors of this really remarkable book—remarkable in
many ways, in closeness of detail, in extent of learning, in breadth of philo-
sophical treatment, in the wealth of admirably executed and thoroughly
appropriate illustrations.[1]

[1] " We cannot pass over one other important accessory to the characteristics of this
book. The publisher has certainly spared nothing to make his part of the work equal
to the importance of the subject, and in paper, print, and tasteful appearance, there
is nothing to be desired. We cannot always say this much of the publications which
come before us ; but it is a pleasure to do so in a case like this."

Westminster Review.

" The book is throughout a model of the careful record of facts, which
require the most intelligent and patient observation to make the record of
any value."

EDINBURGH : DAVID DOUGLAS.

RHIND LECTURES.

Now ready, in One Vol. 8vo,

276 pp., with 84 Woodcuts and three 4to Plates, price 12s.

SCOTLAND

IN

EARLY CHRISTIAN TIMES

THE RHIND LECTURES IN ARCHÆOLOGY—1879

By JOSEPH ANDERSON, LL.D.

KEEPER OF THE NATIONAL MUSEUM OF THE ANTIQUARIES OF SCOTLAND

IN THE BURYING-GROUND, EILEAN NA NAOIMH

EDINBURGH: DAVID DOUGLAS

1881

CONTENTS.

Illustrated with 5 plates on separate pages and 82 in the text.

From the British Architect and Engineer.

" We know of no work within the reach of all students so completely realising its professions, and we can confidently recommend to the architect, artist, and antiquary, young and old, this volume on Celtic art in Scotland."

EDINBURGH: DAVID DOUGLAS.

RHIND LECTURES.

In One Vol. 8vo, price 12s.,
with 143 Illustrations in the text, and 3 Full-page Photographs in carbon.

SCOTLAND

IN

EARLY CHRISTIAN TIMES

(SECOND SERIES)

THE RHIND LECTURES IN ARCHÆOLOGY FOR 1880

By JOSEPH ANDERSON, LL.D.

KEEPER OF THE NATIONAL MUSEUM OF THE ANTIQUARIES OF SCOTLAND

EDINBURGH: DAVID DOUGLAS

1881

CONTENTS.

Journal of the British Archæological Association.

Scotland in Early Christian Times.—"*The Past in the Present* has been rapidly followed by the issue of the book, the title of which stands at the head of this paragraph. It would be difficult, perhaps, to find two books on archæological subjects, published in England during the past year, which can compete with these in the excellence of their production, and the logical and argumental value of their teaching."

DANIEL IN THE DEN OF LIONS—JONAH (1) CAST INTO THE SEA; (2) DISGORGED BY THE WHALE; (3) REPOSING UNDER THE GOURD.

EDINBURGH: DAVID DOUGLAS.

RHIND LECTURES.

Now ready, in One Vol. 8vo, 372 pp., with 148 Woodcuts, price 15s.

THE

PAST IN THE PRESENT:

WHAT IS CIVILISATION?

BY ARTHUR MITCHELL, M.D., LL.D.

Page 10.

EDINBURGH: DAVID DOUGLAS

1880

CONTENTS.

CART WITHOUT WHEELS.

The Nation, New York.

"The early portion of the work, devoted to an account of the primitive manners and customs of the Scotch islanders, their implements, houses, and superstitions, is an attempt made, on historical grounds, to prove the futility of the reasoning which attaches to archæological finds an immense antiquity, and to demonstrate the existence already in the Stone Age of an intellectual culture perhaps equal to that of the present day."

Saturday Review.

"Few more interesting Archæological works have lately been published than the ten 'Rhind Lectures' which make up Dr. Mitchell's Volume, 'The Past in the Present.' We must thank him heartily for the manner and the method of his book, for the curious and valuable facts which he has collected from personal observation, and for the admirable woodcuts which adorn as well as illustrate his volume."

EDINBURGH: DAVID DOUGLAS.

*In One Vol. Royal 8vo, with Maps, Plans, and numerous Illustrations
in Wood-Engraving and Chromolithography.*

RESEARCHES

AND

EXCAVATIONS AT CARNAC

(MORBIHAN)

THE BOSSENNO AND MONT ST. MICHEL

By JAMES MILN

EDINBURGH DAVID DOUGLAS

1877

In One Vol. Royal 8vo, with Maps, Plans, and numerous Illustrations in Wood-Engraving.

EXCAVATIONS AT CARNAC
(BRITTANY)

A RECORD OF ARCHÆOLOGICAL RESEARCHES IN

THE ALIGNMENTS OF KERMARIO

By JAMES MILN

EDINBURGH: DAVID DOUGLAS

1881

Mr. JAMES MILN'S ARCHÆOLOGICAL WORKS.

EXTRACTS FROM REVIEWS.

"Mr. Miln has made some interesting discoveries, and his record of them is simply and modestly written. He seems to have spared no pains either in making his excavations or in writing and illustrating an account of them. The Bossenno at Carnac in Brittany was a heap of ruins of Roman buildings, and though some attention had been already bestowed on the Roman remains of the neighbourhood, it had not been previously explored. Mr. Miln had thus an opportunity worthy of an ambitious archæologist, and he succeeded in using it well. He is careful to commit himself to few theories, and shows coolness and judgment in the presence of the most attractive fields for speculation. He has brightened his pages, however, by one or two interesting passages on modern customs among the Breton peasantry which he can trace, as he seems to show, to remains of the Pagan worship of their half-Romanised ancestors. The nocturnal procession and fête of St. Cornely are very picturesquely described; and the whole book, considering its subject, is wonderfully devoid of the dryness we might expect in it."—*The Saturday Review.*

"We have no space for remarks upon the glass, coins, fragments of iron sword-blades, bronze statuette of an ox, spurious Samian ware, etc., or upon the excavations at Mont St. Michel of foundations of a much later date than the preceding. We must refer our readers to the work itself, from which they will derive much interesting and useful information."—*Academy.*

The remaining Copies of these two valuable Books are to be sold together at 31s. 6d.

ICELANDIC SAGAS, Translated by Sir GEORGE DASENT.

Two Vols. Demy 8vo, with Maps and Plans, 28s.

THE NJALA SAGA

BURNT NJAL

FROM THE ICELANDIC OF THE NJAL'S SAGA

BY

SIR GEORGE WEBBE DASENT, D.C.L.

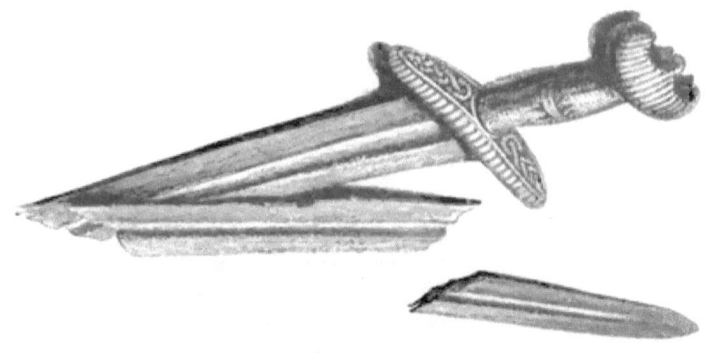

Graysteel.

Small 4to, with Illustrations, 7s. 6d.

THE GISLI SAGA

GISLI THE OUTLAW

FROM THE ICELANDIC

BY

SIR GEORGE WEBBE DASENT, D.C.L.

EDINBURGH: DAVID DOUGLAS.

𝔇𝔢𝔡𝔦𝔠𝔞𝔱𝔢𝔡 𝔟𝔶 𝔰𝔭𝔢𝔠𝔦𝔞𝔩 𝔭𝔢𝔯𝔪𝔦𝔰𝔰𝔦𝔬𝔫 𝔱𝔬 𝔥𝔢𝔯 𝔐𝔞𝔧𝔢𝔰𝔱𝔶 𝔱𝔥𝔢 𝔔𝔲𝔢𝔢𝔫.

Will shortly be issued in One Vol. Quarto, Half Citron Morocco.

A DESCRIPTIVE CATALOGUE

OF THE

MEDALS OF SCOTLAND

𝔉𝔯𝔬𝔪 𝔱𝔥𝔢 𝔈𝔞𝔯𝔩𝔦𝔢𝔰𝔱 𝔓𝔢𝔯𝔦𝔬𝔡 𝔱𝔬 𝔱𝔥𝔢 𝔓𝔯𝔢𝔰𝔢𝔫𝔱 𝔗𝔦𝔪𝔢

BY R. W. COCHRAN-PATRICK, M.P.

LL.D. GLAS., LL.B. CANTAB., B.A. EDIN., V.P.S.A. SCOT., F.S.A., MEMBER OF THE
NUMISMATIC SOCIETY OF LONDON, ETC. ETC.

THE object of this Work is to give, as far as possible, a complete series of the Medals relating to Scotland. It will contain descriptions of all now known to exist of the Sovereigns of Scotland, and those of the Sovereigns of Great Britain specially relating to Scottish events. The series of Medals of the Stuart Family, both before and after the Revolution, will be fully described ; as well as those relating to National events and to private persons. A selection of the more modern local Medals will also be given. The Work will be illustrated in facsimile by plates of all the important pieces.

Price to Subscribers, 2 : 10s. (price to be raised after Publication).

EDINBURGH : DAVID DOUGLAS.

In Two Vols. 4to, Half Bound in Citron Morocco.
A few Copies may still be had at Five Guineas.

RECORDS

OF THE

COINAGE OF SCOTLAND

From the Earliest Period to the Union

COLLECTED BY

R. W. COCHRAN-PATRICK, M.P.

ONLY TWO HUNDRED AND FIFTY COPIES PRINTED.

With Sixteen Full-page Illustrations printed in permanent Ink by the Autotype Company.

EDINBURGH: DAVID DOUGLAS

Uniform with the foregoing, in One Vol. 4to, price 31s. 6d.

EARLY RECORDS

RELATING TO

MINING IN SCOTLAND

COLLECTED BY

R. W. COCHRAN-PATRICK, M.P.

EDINBURGH: DAVID DOUGLAS

RECORDS OF THE COINAGE OF SCOTLAND.

EXTRACTS FROM REVIEWS.

" The future Historians of Scotland will be very fortunate if many parts of their materials are so carefully worked up for them and set before them in so complete and taking a form."—*Athenæum*.

" When we say that these two volumes contain more than 770 records, of which more than 550 have never been printed before, and that they are illustrated by a series of Plates, by the autotype process, of the coins themselves, the reader may judge for himself of the learning, as well as the pains, bestowed on them both by the Author and the Publisher."—*Times*.

" The most handsome and complete Work of the kind which has ever been published in this country."—*Numismatic Chronicle*, Pt. IV., 1875.

" We have in these Records of the Coinage of Scotland, not the production of a *dilettante*, but of a real student, who, with rare pains and the most scholarly diligence, has set to work and collected into two massive volumes a complete history of the coinage of Scotland, so far as it can be gathered from the ancient records."—*Academy*.

EARLY RECORDS RELATING TO MINING IN SCOTLAND.

EXTRACTS FROM REVIEWS.

" The documents contained in the body of the work are given without alteration or abridgment, and the introduction is written with ability and judgment, presenting a clear and concise outline of the earlier history of the Mining Industries of Scotland."—*Scotsman*.

" The documents . . . comprise a great deal that is very curious, and no less that will be important to the historian in treating of the origin of one of the most important branches of the national industry."—*Daily News*.

" Such a book . . . revealing as it does the first developments of an industry which has become the mainspring of the national prosperity, ought to be specially interesting to all patriotic Scotchmen."—*Saturday Review*.

EDINBURGH: DAVID DOUGLAS.

ARCHÆOLOGICAL ESSAYS

BY THE LATE

SIR JAMES Y. SIMPSON, Bart.

EDITED BY THE LATE

JOHN STUART, LL.D.
AUTHOR OF THE "SCULPTURED STONES OF SCOTLAND."

Two Vols. 4to. 21s.

ANCIENT ORATORY IN THE ISLAND OF INCHCOLM.

EDINBURGH : DAVID DOUGLAS.

"The (then) chief, journeying with his clan to join Bruce's army before Bannockburn, observed, on his standard being lifted one morning, a glittering something in a clod of earth hanging to the flagstaff. It was this stone. He showed it to his followers, and told them he felt sure its brilliant lights were a good omen and foretold a victory—and victory was won on the hard-fought field of Bannockburn.

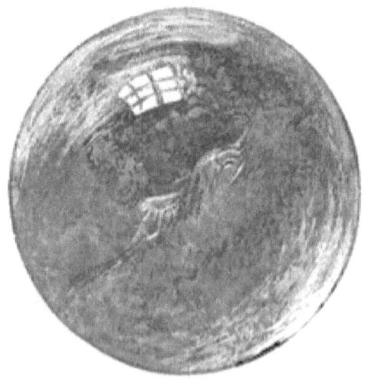

Fig. 17.   Clach-na-Bratach.

"From this time, whenever the clan was 'out,' the Clach-na-Bratach accompanied it, carried on the person of the chief, and its varying hues were consulted by him as to the fate of battle. On the eve of Sheriffmuir (13th November 1715), of sad memory, on Struan consulting the stone as to the fate of the morrow, the large internal flaw was first observed. The Stuarts were lost—and Clan Donnachaidh has been declining in influence ever since.

"The virtues of the Clach-na-Bratach are not altogether of a martial nature, for it cures all manner of diseases in cattle and horses, and formerly in human beings also, if they drink the water in which this charmed stone has been thrice dipped by the hands of Struan."

The Clach-na-Bratach is a transparent, globular mass of rock-crystal, of the size of a small apple. (See accompanying woodcut, Fig. 17.) Its surface has been artificially polished. Several specimens of round rock-crystal, of the same description and size, and similarly

ANCIENT CELTIC SCOTLAND.

WORKS BY WILLIAM F. SKENE

HISTORIOGRAPHER-ROYAL FOR SCOTLAND.

I.

THE FOUR ANCIENT BOOKS OF WALES

CONTAINING THE CYMRIC POEMS ATTRIBUTED TO THE BARDS OF
THE SIXTH CENTURY, BY WILLIAM F. SKENE.

With Maps and Facsimiles, Two Vols. 8vo, 36s.

II.

CELTIC SCOTLAND
A HISTORY OF ANCIENT ALBAN.

In Three Vols. 45s, Illustrated with Maps.

I.—HISTORY AND ETHNOLOGY.   II.—CHURCH AND CULTURE.
III.—LAND AND PEOPLE.

" Forty years ago Mr. Skene published a small historical work on the Scottish Highlands,
which has ever since been appealed to as an authority, but which has long been out of print. The
promise of this youthful effort is amply fulfilled in the three weighty volumes of his maturer years.
As a work of historical research it ought in our opinion to take a very high rank."—*Times.*

III.

CHRONICLES OF THE PICTS
CHRONICLES OF THE SCOTS

AND OTHER EARLY MEMORIALS OF SCOTTISH HISTORY.

In One Vol., Royal 8vo.

EDINBURGH : DAVID DOUGLAS.

Two Vols. Demy 8vo, 19s. 6d.

SOCIAL LIFE IN FORMER DAYS

CHIEFLY IN THE PROVINCE OF MORAY

Illustrated by Letters and Family Papers

By E. DUNBAR DUNBAR

LATE CAPTAIN 21ST FUSILIERS

THUNDERTON HOUSE.

In One Vol. Demy 8vo, 12s.

STUDIES IN ENGLISH HISTORY

By JAMES GAIRDNER AND JAMES SPEDDING

1. THE LOLLARDS.
2. SIR JOHN FALSTAFF.
3. KATHERINE OF ARRAGON'S FIRST AND SECOND MARRIAGES.
4. CASE OF SIR THOMAS OVERBURY.
5. DIVINE RIGHT OF KINGS.
6. SUNDAY, ANCIENT AND MODERN.

"The authors' names alone are a sufficient guarantee that the Essays in this beautifully printed volume were worth reprinting."—*St. James's Gazette.*

EDINBURGH: DAVID DOUGLAS.

Mr. G. W. T. OMOND.

In Two Vols. Demy 8vo.

THE

LORD ADVOCATES OF SCOTLAND

From the Close of the 15th Century to the Passing of the
Reform Bill

By GEO. W. T. OMOND, Advocate.

Prof. PIAZZI SMYTH.

Three Vols. Demy 8vo, 56s.

LIFE AND WORK AT THE GREAT PYRAMID

With a Discussion of the Facts Ascertained

BY

C. PIAZZI SMYTH, F.R.SS.L. AND E.
ASTRONOMER-ROYAL FOR SCOTLAND

Prof. SCHIERN.

Demy 8vo, 16s.

LIFE OF JAMES HEPBURN

EARL OF BOTHWELL

By Professor SCHIERN
COPENHAGEN

Translated from the Danish by the Rev. David Berry, F.S.A. Scot.

Prof. WILSON.

Two Vols. Post 8vo, 15s.

REMINISCENCES OF OLD EDINBURGH

By DANIEL WILSON, LL.D., F.R.S.E.
PROFESSOR OF HISTORY AND ENGLISH LITERATURE IN UNIVERSITY COLLEGE, TORONTO
AUTHOR OF "PREHISTORIC ANNALS OF SCOTLAND," ETC. ETC.

EDINBURGH : DAVID DOUGLAS.

To be completed in Three Vols. Demy 8vo.

THE

USES AND MANUFACTURE

OF

IRON AND STEEL

From Prehistoric Ages to the Present Time

BY

St. JOHN V. DAY

C.E., F.R.S.E., F.S.A. (SCOT.); MEMBER OF THE IRON AND STEEL
INSTITUTE; MEMBER OF THE INSTITUTION OF MECHANICAL ENGINEERS;
ASSOCIATE OF THE INSTITUTION OF CIVIL ENGINEERS; MEMBER
OF COUNCIL OF THE INSTITUTE OF PATENT AGENTS, ETC.

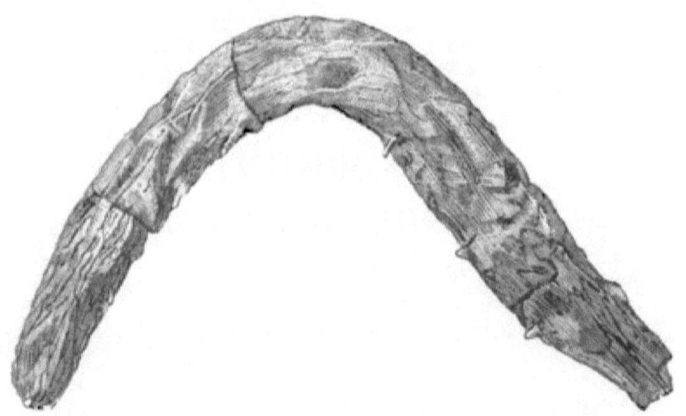

EGYPTIAN SICKLE FOUND AT KARNAK.

Vol. I. in October.

EDINBURGH: DAVID DOUGLAS.

One Vol. Small 4to,

With Index, and thirteen Full-page and ten Woodcut Illustrations, 21s.

LINDORES ABBEY

AND

THE BURGH OF NEWBURGH

Their History and Annals

BY

ALEXANDER LAING, LL.D.

F.S.A. Scot.

"This is a charming volume in every respect."—*Notes and Queries.*
"The prominent characteristics of the work are its exhaustiveness and the thoroughly philosophic spirit in which it is written."—*Scotsman.*

EDINBURGH: DAVID DOUGLAS.

In One Vol., 4to, price £3 : 3s.
A few Copies for sale on large Paper, price £5 : 15 : 6.

KALENDARS

OF

SCOTTISH SAINTS

WITH

𝔓ersonal 𝔓otices of those of 𝔄lba, etc.

BY THE LATE

ALEXANDER PENROSE FORBES, D.C.L.

BISHOP OF BRECHIN

" A truly valuable contribution to the archæology of Scotland."—*Guardian.*
" We must not forget to thank the author for the great amount of information he has put together, and for the labour he has bestowed on a work which can never be remunerative."—*Saturday Review.*
" His laborious and very interesting work on the early Saints of Alba, Londonia, and Strathclyde."—*Quarterly Review.*

In One Vol., 8vo, Half Morocco, price 12s.

MISSALE DRUMMONDIENSE

THE ANCIENT IRISH MISSAL IN THE

POSSESSION OF BARONESS WILLOUGHBY D'ERESBY

DRUMMOND CASTLE, PERTHSHIRE

EDITED BY THE LATE REV. G. H. FORBES
SCOTCH EPISCOPAL CLERGYMAN AT BURNTISLAND, ETC. ETC.

EDINBURGH : DAVID DOUGLAS.

In Preparation, in One Vol. Demy 8vo, with numerous Illustrations.

ECCLESIOLOGICAL NOTES

ON

SOME OF THE ISLANDS OF SCOTLAND

With other Papers relating to Ecclesiological Remains on the Scottish Mainland and Islands

BY

THOMAS S. MUIR

AUTHOR OF "CHARACTERISTICS OF CHURCH ARCHITECTURE," ETC.

––––––––––

CRAIG'S CATECHISM.

In Fcap. 8vo, Half Morocco, price 12s. 6d.

A SHORTE SUMME

OF THE

WHOLE CATECHISME

BY JOHN CRAIG

REPRINTED IN FACSIMILE FROM THE ORIGINAL EDITION OF 1581

With an Introductory Memoir of the Author

By THOMAS GRAVES LAW

ONLY ONE HUNDRED COPIES PRINTED FOR SALE

EDINBURGH: DAVID DOUGLAS

MDCCCLXXXIII

In the Press, to be ready in November.

THE

HISTORY OF LIDDESDALE

ESKDALE, EWESDALE, WAUCHOPEDALE

AND THE

DEBATEABLE LAND

Part I. from the Twelfth Century to 1530

BY

ROBERT BRUCE ARMSTRONG

The Edition will be limited to 275 Copies, demy quarto, and 105 Copies on large paper (10 inches by 13).

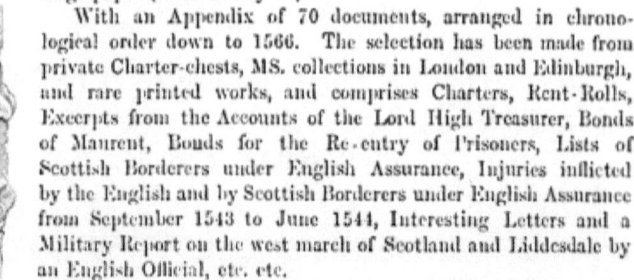

With an Appendix of 70 documents, arranged in chronological order down to 1566. The selection has been made from private Charter-chests, MS. collections in London and Edinburgh, and rare printed works, and comprises Charters, Rent-Rolls, Excerpts from the Accounts of the Lord High Treasurer, Bonds of Maurent, Bonds for the Re-entry of Prisoners, Lists of Scottish Borderers under English Assurance, Injuries inflicted by the English and by Scottish Borderers under English Assurance from September 1543 to June 1544, Interesting Letters and a Military Report on the west march of Scotland and Liddesdale by an English Official, etc. etc.

The Volume will be illustrated by Maps, Etchings, Lithographs, and Woodcuts, all of which, with the exception of Blaeu's Maps of Liddesdale and Eskdale, and the Etchings of James IV., James V., and the Earl of Angus, by C. Lawrie, will either be from the author's drawings or wholly executed by himself.

The Lithographs in colour will include facsimiles of four interesting representations of Scottish Border Castles and Towns drawn between the years 1563 and 1566, Plates of Arms of the Lords of Liddesdale, of the Clans of the District, of Lindsay of Wauchope, also of the Seals of John Armstrong and William Elliot, etc. etc.

EDINBURGH : DAVID DOUGLAS.

www.ingramcontent.com/pod-product-compliance
Lightning Source LLC
Chambersburg PA
CBHW051114120726
47905CB00005B/1275